Performing History

FOR STATE AND LOCAL HISTORY
BOOK SERIES

ABOUT THE SERIES
The American Association for State and Local History Book Series addresses issues critical to the field of state and local history through interpretive, intellectual, scholarly, and educational texts. To submit a proposal or manuscript to the series, please request proposal guidelines from AASLH headquarters: AASLH Editorial Board, 2021 21st Ave. South, Suite 320, Nashville, Tennessee 37212. Telephone: (615) 320-3203. Website: www.aaslh.org.

ABOUT THE ORGANIZATION
The American Association for State and Local History (AASLH) is a national history membership association headquartered in Nashville, Tennessee. AASLH provides leadership and support for its members who preserve and interpret state and local history in order to make the past more meaningful to all Americans. AASLH members are leaders in preserving, researching, and interpreting traces of the American past to connect the people, thoughts, and events of yesterday with the creative memories and abiding concerns of people, communities, and our nation today. In addition to sponsorship of this book series, AASLH publishes *History News* magazine, a newsletter, technical leaflets and reports, and other materials; confers prizes and awards in recognition of outstanding achievement in the field; supports a broad education program and other activities designed to help members work more effectively; and advocates on behalf of the discipline of history. To join AASLH, go to www.aaslh.org or contact Membership Services, AASLH, 2021 21st Ave. South, Suite 320, Nashville, TN 37212.

Performing History

How to Research, Write, Act, and Coach Historical Performances

ANN E. BIRNEY AND JOYCE M. THIERER

ROWMAN & LITTLEFIELD
Lanham • Boulder • New York • London

Front cover photos: TOP: Youth Chautauquans at Prairie Museum of Art and History, Colby, Kansas. Photograph by the authors. BOTTOM: Junction City Sesquicentennial Youth Chautauqua at Dorothy Bramlage Public Library, Junction City, Kansas. Photograph by authors.

Published by Rowman & Littlefield
A wholly owned subsidiary of The Rowman & Littlefield Publishing Group, Inc.
4501 Forbes Boulevard, Suite 200, Lanham, Maryland 20706
www.rowman.com

Unit A, Whitacre Mews, 26-34 Stannary Street, London SE11 4AB

British Library Cataloguing in Publication Information Available

Library of Congress Cataloging-in-Publication Data

Names: Birney, Ann E., author. | Thierer, Joyce M., 1949– author.
Title: Performing history : how to research, write, act, and coach historical performances / Ann E. Birney and Joyce M. Thierer.
Description: Lanham : Rowman & Littlefield, 2018. | Series: American Association for State and Local History book series | Includes bibliographical references and index.
Identifiers: LCCN 2017051882 (print) | LCCN 2017053941 (ebook) | ISBN 9781442278912 (Electronic) | ISBN 9781442278899 (cloth : alk. paper) | ISBN 9781442278905 (pbk. : alk. paper)
Subjects: LCSH: Historical reenactments—United States—Handbooks, manuals, etc. | Historical reenactments—Handbooks, manuals, etc. | First person narrative—Handbooks, manuals, etc. | Historical museums—Educational aspects—Handbooks, manuals, etc. | United States—History—Methodology—Miscellanea. | United States—History, Local—Miscellanea. | History—Methodology—Miscellanea.
Classification: LCC E175.7 (ebook) | LCC E175.7 .B57 2018 (print) | DDC 973—dc23
LC record available at https://lccn.loc.gov/2017051882

Printed in the United States of America

Contents

List of Illustrations

List of Tables

Preface

Power, Love, and the Willing Suspension of Disbelief

This preface focuses first on the "why" of historical performance: the source of our power and the responsibility that comes with that power. We then provide an overview of this book.

Historical performance is a first-person, direct-address portrayal of a historic figure or composite character. It is usually performed as a monologue followed by taking questions in character and then taking questions as the scholar/performer. Because it is direct address, the audience inherently participates. The performer tells the audience the direction of their shared travel through time and, often, space. Ann Birney as Amelia Earhart: "It's April fourteenth, 1937, and according to my itinerary, on April fourteenth, 1937 I am in India, not in [wherever the audience is in "real" time]. When the performer is really good, audience members follow that performer wherever she or he takes them, demonstrating what Samuel Taylor Coleridge called the "willing suspension of disbelief."[1]

Ann remembers clearly the first time she really, truly realized that she really, truly had power over an audience. She was portraying Amelia Earhart. "Amelia" told the audience stories about her childhood and how she became a pilot and about her first transatlantic flight when she was just a passenger. All was going well—lots of smiles and nods. Then she told the story of flying across the Atlantic solo in her little red Lockheed Vega with the gold stripes. One problem after another arises: her altimeter fails just as she enters a massive cloud bank, her plane ices over and plummets toward the ocean, her single engine shakes and flames ensue, and gas begins leaking from the overhead fuel gauge. The audience is no longer smiling and nodding. They look stricken. That part of a performer—that part of the brain that watches and critiques and that monitors the performance while the other part of the brain continues with the job at hand—is worried. What on earth is causing her audience such distress? Ann fights the urge to turn around and look behind her to see what tragedy has occurred that they can see and she cannot. Amelia finally lands safely in Ireland. The audience looks relieved. It took a few moments more, but Ann finally got it: at some point, even those who knew her personally had come to accept her as Amelia, and they had gone back in time with her twice: first to 1937 (the frame of the story) and then to 1932 (the solo flight). By the time of that perilous ocean crossing, about forty minutes into the performance, audience members were fully engaged and had suspended disbelief.

The "we" in this book's narrative is Ride into History, the historical performance touring troupe of Joyce Thierer and Ann Birney, begun in 1989. One reason we do historical performance is that there are few pleasures in life as great as that of having an audience trust you to transport them to another place and time. But we did not know about these pleasures when we began. Other motivators were operating.

Actually, Ride into History's very first performance, even before Joyce founded Ride, was created not from some grand philosophical or emotional imperative but from an attempt to overcome Joyce's fear of teachers. We have told before how Ride into History began with Joyce's commitment to deliver lectures for a National Endowment for the Humanities / Kansas Humanities Council / Emporia State University secondary school teacher seminar.[2] When she was making her way through elementary and high school, Joyce was frequently sent to the principal's office for being overly willing to share historical and scientific knowledge that she could not possibly have because she was not a good reader, so she must therefore be a frequent liar. Several decades later, teaching college history following two master's degrees and almost finished with her doctorate, Joyce had learned to cope with her dyslexia even before it was officially diagnosed. She was now teaching future teachers. But she was still convinced that a classroom of teachers would judge her no more credible than had teachers when she was a youngster. So she chose to first meet the teachers as Calamity Jane: on horseback, galloping up to them. It was empowering.

But a funny thing happened on the way to empowerment. The audience responded to Calamity Jane with far more love than Joyce had ever imagined could be shown her by teachers, even teachers outdoors around a fire ring who had begun the evening with wine and cheese. They loved her, and she gave them love in return, first as Calamity and then as Joyce. It was a mutual admiration society. Joyce's audience and her newborn Calamity Jane were swimming in oxytocin.[3]

"What is needed is a realization that power without love is reckless and abusive, and that love without power is sentimental and anemic."[4] In his speech to the 1967 Southern Christian Leadership Conference convention, Martin Luther King Jr. was addressing strategies for obtaining justice, but what he says about power and love speaks also to historical performance. Good performers have great power. Our performance is powerful because it moves people. That power gives us responsibility. People entrust themselves to us; they trust us to make our flight together intellectually and emotionally honest. We are responsible for caring about both our subject and our audience.

Early in our historical performance careers, we recognized the immense responsibility that comes with the expectation of a suspension of disbelief. We have a responsibility to respect and honor the person being portrayed, the stories being told, and the audience—and, of course, to honestly appreciate the people who are sponsoring our performance. Self-respect is also required of us. People trust us to give an honest performance as well as one that is entertaining. In return, they are letting themselves travel through time with us.

As historical performers, we think of our audiences as we work to increase our skills and knowledge, improving our storytelling technique, and always expanding our knowledge so that our content is both compelling and accurate. We use our power for "good"—we know that what we are doing is important and why. We respect our subject and our audience, and we acknowledge our responsibility to both.

The process of developing a first-person narrative can, we acknowledge, be intimidating. And the performance itself might be the most intimidating aspect. However, when we are respectful of the historic figure we are representing and respectful of the audience, when we not only "become" the historic figure but also, as street performer Ann-Elizabeth Shapera says, "love the audience,"[5] we choose to continually prepare well and perform with confidence and respect. When you hear that you have taken someone to another place, to another time, you know that you have accomplished at least part of your goal. You have been convincing.

While we worked on sharpening our skills and increasing our content knowledge, we also tried to tease out which factors made even those early performances as Amelia, Calamity Jane, and the composite suffragist as rich as they were. Some of those factors involved what might be considered the philosophy of historical performance:

Why is costumed first-person interpretation significant?

Why do I want to put myself in front of an audience when I am a shy person?

What makes it worth the continual research?

What makes it worth the cost and hassle of travel?

Why do historical performance?

Admittedly, one of our motivators was financial. We, like Amelia Earhart, Calamity Jane, and the suffragist, could make a living from giving talks. As one youngster observed, "You made your own job!" We are entrepreneurs with low overhead. We decide who and what we want to research, which stories to tell, where and how to market our product, and how to share our skills with others—and earn money for our desired lifestyle. Initially, we even involved the horses in earning their "hay checks."

But eventually, as work and lifestyle choices arose and we began to ask ourselves why historical performance was and would continue to be central to our lives, the answer became, "The stories must be told." That, of course, led us to ask, "*Why* must the stories be told?" Must all stories be told? If not all stories, then which stories?

Early on, we observed that women's stories were not being told. School assemblies about history were not done by or about women. There were a few female skill demonstrators (fiber, cooking, candles) but nothing more sustained. The lesson seemed to be that the only historical event was the Civil War, and only men were involved. Girls and boys could very well think that only men made the decisions that became the history in their textbooks. So, very simply, we wanted women onstage. Women's stories must be told, and if we did not tell those stories, then who would? It became a mission that became a responsibility. Not only were we to tell women's stories, but we were responsible for learning as much as we could and for recruiting others to do so. We also had the responsibility of knowing why, other than just increasing the numbers of women being represented, we were telling a given story. For each historic figure or composite character, we had to know, "Why this person?"

We had to be entertaining and interesting, but the entertainment factor, in our case, was to bring audience members' sustained attention to the story. Joyce decided early in her relationship with Calamity Jane that she wanted people to understand Martha Jane Cannary as a survivor, not a victim. Jane not only lived large, switching gender to earn more money, but also shaped her story, so she had double agency. She made herself larger than life by telling her story to reporters in exchange for food or money.

Why is what you are doing important? Because history's stories need to be told to the fullest. Both of us are on the introvert side of the introvert/extrovert scale.[6] We get energy from taking time for ourselves instead of going to social gatherings (partying with others being the preferred means of recharging for extroverts, which includes most people). But when we found out that the only living history available to children in our geographical area was Civil War reenactors, we were motivated. We would put ourselves in front of audiences to tell what was not being told. Women are historical decision makers. But our children did not know this.

It is not just a Kansas problem. Emily Curran, director of the Old South Meeting House in Boston, tells about one of the public school groups that visited to learn about the debate held in that historic building in 1773. She staged a reenactment with the students taking parts. "Once I asked the kids, 'Why do you think all the roles you're playing today are men?' One girl raised her hand and said, confidently, 'Because there were no women back then.'"[7]

"There were no women back then." This child was not stupid, nor were the others who did not raise their hands but presumed the same thing. She was just limited in her experience. She was dependent on adults to tell her what it was like back then, and what she had learned was that "there were no women."

We need more women—and people of color for that matter—providing historical performances, showing children that women not only existed "back then" but were decision makers and, hence, history makers. But we also need more people who are portraying male historic figures to include women in their stories. It is only ethical to do so. As Abigail Adams cautioned her husband, "Remember the Ladies." Men, you need to include women in your stories not only out of respect for the women and girls in your audiences and out of respect for the women who have been largely written out of history but also out of self-respect. You do not want to be one of those who perpetuate the myth that "there were no women back then" or that women were not important. It is not true now, and it was not true then.

Neither men nor women were born with this knowledge. We all had to learn it, and most men—and the majority of history teachers are men—have not thought to ask why it appears that "there were no women back then." If you don't know what women were doing at the time you are interpreting, find out. There is, at long last, a plethora of sources, both secondary and primary. A good starting point for U.S. history would be *Women's America: Refocusing*

PHOTO 0.1
Kitty Frank as Kittie Hays on the Santa Fe Trail. Photo by Betty Anderson, Emporia, Kansas.

the Past, edited by Linda K. Kerber and three other respected historians, now in its eighth edition.[8] A new overview by another very highly respected author is Susan Ware's *American Women's History: A Very Short Introduction*.[9] Both have lists of other sources so that you can be endlessly entertained as you learn—just follow those bread crumbs that lead you from one source to that source's sources to those sources' sources. But more on that in chapter 2.

This book is crafted for people who want to develop a first-person narrative, those who have created a first-person narrative but want to make it better, and those who want to help others develop first-person narratives— museum and historic site volunteer coordinators, program and education curators, and, of course, those who wear many hats in small staffs. It is also for teachers, parents, friends, volunteers, and partners who are providing support for historical performers. A special audience is those individuals who have read *Telling History: A Manual for Performers and Presenters of First Person Narrative*s and are still not convinced that they know enough or are engaging enough to represent a historic figure in front of an audience.

What You Won't Find in This Book

What you will find in *Telling History* that you will *not* find in this book:

- A differentiation between historical performance and other traditions of costumed interpretations of history (i.e., reenacting, look-alikes, skills demonstrators)
- The business of doing historical performance
- How much you are likely to pay (presenting organizations) / how much you might charge (performers)
- How to put together your look/costume
- Joyce's story

As for the hesitation that many people feel about speaking or performing in public, this book will help new performers focus on their historic figure's story and on the people who come to hear that story, setting their own ego aside. Some people who tell us that they really want to do historical performance have a really difficult time getting their project off the ground. This makes us very sad because their stories are not being told and they are not experiencing the "high" of hearing "I really thought you were her" and "How do you remember so much?" More people should have access to more of history's stories, so more people should be providing this time travel opportunity for eager audiences. The most common block seems to be fear—fear of failing to find enough information or the right information and/or fear of failing in front of an audience. Fear of something is overcome by knowing how to do small increments instead of jumping in over one's head. How do you eat an elephant? One bite at a time. But there will be more on these fears in the respective chapters.

TRAIL STORY

THOSE TERRIFYING YOUNGSTERS

Ann's first performance was for an outdoor festival, and her next several were for adults. Then an elementary school asked for Ann's suffragist and Joyce's Calamity Jane. Ann was terrified—the average age of her library school students had been thirty-six. No problem with Calamity. Everyone understood a "cowgirl." But how would children relate to a campaign to get the vote for women? And she would have to expunge the really entertaining story about the medical establishment's concern that women would lose their virginity by riding astride. The saving grace was that if Ann went first, she could end quickly, Joyce could bat "cleanup," and hopefully no one would remember Ann's failure. So Ann walked out into the gymnasium, looked into a sea of eager upturned faces, and fell in love with about 300 kindergarten through fourth graders, all at once—especially one of the youngest who, when Ann's suffragist character said that as a child she had helped her father with the farming and so was her father's son, loudly protested, "No!" at this thoughtless attempt to shift his carefully constructed sexual dichotomy. You do not protest if you are not engaged. These children were engaged. Ann knew that she had faced her most difficult audience and wanted to do this again. And again. And again. But she would not have known this about herself had she not tried.

You will find in this book really good stuff for both presenting organizations and performers. To summarize (and to save time for presenting organizations), if you are a presenter (the person or organization that hires the performer), read chapters 1, 5, and 7. If you are a performer or a prospective performer, chapters 1 through 4 and 6 are most important for you. Whether you are a presenter or a performer, we will, however, attempt to tantalize you to read the entire book by 1) summarizing the chapters below and 2) sprinkling Trail Stories (sidebars) throughout the book, as we did in *Telling History*.

Chapter 1 is important to both those sponsoring performances and those whose bodies will be in front of the audiences. If you are at a library, museum, or school, do not bring in someone who is second-rate. You want someone who can entertain with an engaging monologue, who can also step out of character after the monologue and discuss the subject matter intelligently, and who can confidently and competently take questions in front of the audience. Do not hire a humorist when you want good history—unless the humorist is, indeed, well versed in her or his subject (Doug Watson as Will Rogers comes to mind or Warren Brown as Samuel Clemens). Likewise, we ask that performers not do professional historical performances unless they respect themselves, the audience, and their subject matter enough to invest the time to do a really good job. This includes finding coaches who respect them, their audiences, and their subject matter enough to be honest in their assessment. Everyone needs at least one partner—maybe even a village—in their process.

Chapter 2 is about the research process and goes into more detail than in the first book. Performers, we counsel you to not research until you have questions written out. And we counsel you, that after you have done your online research and written out your questions, you make an appointment with a librarian or archivist in the collections you visit. These people are your friends, your allies, and your mates. They know where the good stuff is hidden. They don't want to do what you are doing (performing your character), but they live to be helpful. They are your best weapon against research stress. Also in chapter 2, we discuss some online sources that are generally available to academic (college or university) researchers and how to gain access to them.

Chapter 3 is about designing a performance for a given audience, which also works vice versa: finding an audience and creating a script that will work well for you and the stories you want to share. This includes tapping into "hot topics" and anniversaries. For example, in 2017, U.S. history programmers focused on World War I; 2017 being the centennial year for the U.S. entry into the war. You will also want to know what is being taught in schools so that you can link your performance to their curriculum. You don't think you can be engaging and relevant to both children and adults? We have been there, and we can help.

The fear of public speaking is the most common among many people.[10] Chapter 4 is about overcoming that anxiety because you have something really important to tell people, something they want to know and will enjoy finding out about. It is not about you: historical performance is about the audience and about the message. You are only the means of getting the message to the people. This makes you important, but from the perspective of the audience, you are not the most important of the three factors in the room. This should remove a bit of the burden. Besides, you are in control of the script, and you get to tell audience members who they are watching during this bit of time travel (more on that later).

Chapter 5 is about tapping an underutilized resource: youngsters. We have had good fortune in conducting Youth Chautauqua camps for humanities council Chautauquas for more than fifteen years. We are firmly committed to coaching young people to become historians/researchers/scriptwriters/actors. Young people have traditionally been overlooked as contributors to the telling of stories at museums and historic sites. Just think: we are bringing along not just the next generation of Chautauquans, historians, and museum curators, but also the next generation of museum supporters and volunteers. They are the next generation that understands why civic engagement is important, and that involvement, although challenging, is also rewarding. Involving young people as first-person interpreters also involves that child's siblings, parents, grandparents, and even teachers and friends. A stand-alone program to which the public is invited can be spun into an ongoing program in which the young people's presentation is part of museum outreach, going to civic organization meetings and libraries, and recruiting other youngsters. To be even more radical, we encourage communities to conduct a "camp" for *all* ages (fourth grade through adult). When children and adults are colleagues, learning together and practicing together, the adults are braver. In fact, in a group or a workshop, everyone is braver as long as we recognize that some people will need quiet time to themselves to fine-tune their performance, which will likely happen away from the workshop setting.

Sometimes people say that they "only" want to dress up and demonstrate skills at their museum or "only" want to learn a few lines for a cemetery tour. In chapter 6 we hope to convince program staff and costumed interpreters that learning the process of historical performance for one or more historic figures will enhance all of the other types of costumed work that you do. Historical performance skills provide you with flexibility and make any and all of your other presentations more dynamic. Historical performance adds another major skill to costumed interpreters' skill sets. An individual who has researched a historic figure or composite character and that person's historic context so well that she or he can take questions graciously as the historic figure or, if more appropriate, as the scholar behind the performance can adapt to a wide range of programs and settings, whether repeating a single ten-minute story to children rotating between stations at a school, standing next to Amelia Earhart's Lockheed Vega and discussing her solo flight across the Atlantic, or providing an after-dinner program to medical professionals (Earhart volunteered at a military hospital during World War I, inspiring her first to plan a medical career, then to switch to medical research, and finally to allow herself to be seduced by aviation). Because it is the most challenging tradition in costumed interpretation, when an individual has developed a three-part historical performance (a monologue followed by discussion in character and then discussion as the scholar), they can adapt their knowledge to any of the other traditions in costumed interpretation.

People passionate about neglected slices or perspectives of history might want to develop a first-person narrative to make their interests more accessible to others. They like the idea of sharing the story of a person, a time, an idea, an event, or maybe a sport, a place, or a landscape. They (you?) have a story that has been overlooked—maybe a group of people whose story is not being told and should be. And there are historic sites and museums crying out for staff or volunteers who would be excellent first-person interpreters, who would bring life to static objects in their collection. They wish they had people who knew their stuff and could be counted on to interact with the public without a script.

Our final chapter is on dreams and plans. This chapter was not in our original proposal to the American Association for State and Local History, but no sooner was the proposal accepted, several great ideas about the future of historical performance developed, which we shared in this final chapter. And maybe some of them will resonate with you and you will contact us and say, "Include me!"

Now, on with the show—or at least with a description of what makes a good show, beyond power, love, and the willing suspension of disbelief.

NOTES

1. Samuel Taylor Coleridge, *Biographia Literaria* (1817), chapter 14, http://www.english.upenn.edu/~mgamer/Etexts/biographia.html (accessed December 23, 2015).

2. Joyce Thierer, *Telling History: A Manual for Performers and Presenters of First-Person Narratives* (Lanham, MD: AltaMira Press, 2010), 4–6.

3. We are told that readers are likely to confuse the hormone oxytocin, which influences us to bond with dogs and babies, with the problem drug oxycontin. If this is a new concept, we recommend the very accessible *Smithsonian* article "Oxytocin Affects Bonding between Dogs and Humans," http://www.smithsonianmag.com/science-nature/dog-gazes-hijack-brains-maternal-bonding-system-180955019.

4. Martin Luther King Jr., "Where Do We Go from Here?" (speech delivered at the 11th Annual SCLC Convention, Atlanta, GA, August 16, 1967), https://kinginstitute.stanford.edu/king-papers/documents/where-do-we-go-here-delivered-11th-annual-sclc-convention.

5. Ann-Elizabeth Shapera, *Easy Street: A Guide for Players in Improvised Interactive Environmental Performance, Walkaround Entertainment, and First-Person Historical Interpretation* (Phoole Skoole Press, 2012), http://www.lulu.com/spotlight/phoole.

6. "MBTI Basics," http://www.myersbriggs.org.

7. Jill Lepore, *The Whites of Their Eyes: The Tea Party's Revolution and the Battle over American History* (Princeton, NJ: Princeton University Press, 2010), 78.

8. Linda K. Kerber et al., eds., *Women's America: Refocusing the Past*, 8th ed. (New York: Oxford University Press, 2016).

9. Susan Ware, *American Women's History: A Very Short Introduction* (New York: Oxford University Press, 2015).

10. Glenn Croston, *The Real Story of Risk: Adventures in a Hazardous World* (New York: Prometheus Books, 2012), 234.

What Does It Take to Do a *Good* Historical Performance?

We promised in the preface that this chapter would be for both those who hire or train historical performers and those who do historical performance. Therefore, for both sets of readers, we first discuss how to recognize a good historical performance: What is historical performance, and how do you know "good" when you see it? We describe historical performance in hopes of convincing you, if you are not already convinced (which you probably are, in which case pay attention because we will give you language that you can use when convincing others), that historical performance is the best thing since sliced bread. And we just discovered sliced cranberry walnut bread, so we're talking some bodacious goodness here. The rest of this chapter is dedicated to telling historical performers, and those who are helping them with their process, what it will take to reach the level of "good."

HOW DO I RECOGNIZE A *GOOD* HISTORICAL PERFORMANCE?

What are we talking about when we say "historical performance"? Historical performance, as described in *Telling History: A Manual for Performers and Presenters of First-Person Narratives*, is a direct-address first-person narrative that takes the audience to a particular historic time and place. The performance consists of a monologue, a representative "look," and a conversation with the audience begun by taking questions as both the historic figure and the scholar.

What is a *good* historical performance?: accurate script, accurate look, accurate responses to questions (no prevaricating)—all in an engaging manner. It inspires audience members to suspend their disbelief. The audience feels involved. Unlike what we usually experience as audiences of plays, during a historical performance, the performance directly addresses the audience. Not only is the audience part of the play, but the venue and audience are well-lit so that the performer can see each person (more in chapter 4 about whether a performer will actually *look* at the audience).

A good historical performance will reinforce what the audience knows to be true or challenge what they know. The performance will add new knowledge. And the performance will be so entertaining that all but the most exhausted audience members will be alert and waiting to hear what is going to happen next. The performer will tell stories, not list facts. And the stories will illuminate not only the choices made by the historic figure but also the historic context in which those choices are made. A historical performer has the responsibility to use primary sources (sources created at the time under study), and the responsibility to decide when sources conflict which truth is most likely; present that truth in an engaging way; and be ready and willing to discuss how it compares to other truths (Calamity Jane: "There are five stories about how I got my name, but the one I prefer to tell is . . .").

It might be useful to think of historical performance as adding interactivity to the three components of a basic communications model. That basic model has a sender, a message, and a receiver. If you have played an instrument or attended a concert or recital, you are familiar with this model. Consider a solo performance: the musician (sender) interprets a piece of music (message) that audience members (receiver) hear. Applause is likely the only feedback. A dance recital seems a bit more complex, but it is the same: dancers use their bodies to send a message (the dance created by a choreographer) to the audience.

In our case, the sender is a scholar/performer in period clothing (the "look" is part of the message). Ideally, the message is a compelling monologue delivered by the performer for thirty to fifty minutes, and the receiver is an audience, presumably there specifically to enjoy the message. Often, overt interactivity occurs during the monologue. The sender may request a response from the audience. Here's an example from Joyce's Calamity Jane script: "I shot twenty, thirty, forty buffalo. [She points to a group of audience members.] Do you three believe me?" In this case, the solicited feedback is never a simple, unified "yes" or "no." Calamity strives to create some repartee and to do so without losing control.

However, even if the sender does not request an audience response, she or he does, of course, expect laughter, tears, leaning forward, or changes in facial expression and body language. So a message with live performers is seldom without feedback, although that feedback might be misinterpreted. An example (in the preface) is Ann misreading her audience during the story about Earhart's transatlantic crossing—the feedback was there. She did not, however, interpret it correctly as audience concern for Amelia.

The monologue is just the first act in a historical performance. There are two more acts, and these are where "good" becomes manifest.

In the second act, the historic figure invites questions from the audience that encourage discussion. Messages originate with the audience instead of the historical performer—"Do you have any children?" "Why did your father move to California?" "Were you ever afraid?"—making those who were receivers into senders and the original sender into a receiver, only to become a sender again.

In the third act, this process is repeated but with one difference: the scholar/performer steps out of character and invites discussion *about* the historic figure, the figure's historic context, and maybe also the scholar/performer's personal and professional experiences ("Are you related to Amelia Earhart?" "What happened to her?"). The sender/scholar/performer might also move in and out of character when a question is asked that would be ideal for an answer from Amelia, for example, instead of Ann. The skilled historical performer carefully signals transitions to and from the scholar by changing look and voice. Calamity Jane takes off her hat to become Joyce. Amelia Earhart sheds her jacket to let Ann answer a question. Audiences love this display of skill, and the change (putting Amelia's jacket back on) has the second advantage of buying a bit of time to ponder the answer.

To repeat, a monologue of at least thirty minutes is followed by inviting questions in character ("How are you getting the money for this flight around the world?") and then inviting audience discussion with the scholar ("What happened to Amelia Earhart?"). The key to "good" is the discussion. The scholar must not only anticipate audience questions ("How did Calamity Jane die?") but also steep herself so well into the story that a new question ("Did you marry for convenience?") does not fluster her but instead may become the opportunity to tell another story.

Can a historical performance be good without a question-and-answer section? Of course it can. It is just incomplete. Sometimes a schedule—say, at a conference—does not allow for an extended discussion. Ride into History will either cut the length of the monologue to accommodate discussion or invite audience members to discuss later ("I will be around for the rest of the day. Please visit with me when you have time.") We have also been contracted to do what we call "schmoozing" in character. An example is the opening of a university art gallery exhibit featuring photographs of jets. "Amelia" offered to tell a story to small groups of people, often children, who had seen the exhibit and were a bit at odds. Sometimes, the story never got told, but questions were asked and answered.

Tessa Bridal, museum educator and museum theater advocate, says that "what happens after a presentation in a museum is as important as the presentation itself. We offer a special opportunity at such times for our visitors to speak to the presenter and to one another."[1] It is this discussion that is lost when museums use actors who memorize scripts instead of scholar/performers who are experts on their subject (more in chapter 7). Although it begins as monologue, historical performance is a form of civic discourse that encourages ongoing dialogue. This irony exists because the monologue provides a text shared by the audience members and the scholar.

Historical performance can, however, disappoint if not done well. Historical performance is more than memorizing and reciting the speeches of a historic figure for forty minutes without looking at notes. While that is an admirable skill, it is likely to put the audience to sleep. The Gettysburg Address was—and is—admired not only because of its style and sentiment but also because it was—and is—brief. Thirty-minute speeches written to be read to nineteenth-century audiences are usually dreary to contemporary audiences. We have sat through "performances" that were readings of text rather than the telling of the stories behind the texts. A good historical performance both entertains and educates. This is why Ride into History has been on both arts and humanities rosters. The entertainment factor keeps the audience awake to hear the message.

The goal is for audience members to be so engrossed in the performance that they lose the sense of the passing of time and forget where they are in time's continuum.

Another word on format: sometimes in a workshop, an aspiring historical performer asks to have a friend onstage to share a dialogue with. We have seen that work well as standard theatrical fare, and it is a way to practice—recruit an audience of one and have that one pretend to be a reporter asking questions. But that is not our goal. A good historical performer welcomes the audience as performers who willingly travel in time with them.

A good living history skill demonstration or good museum theater is not necessarily historical performance. Likewise, you can have an engaging historical performance that teaches no specific skills. However, if you have spent the time to do your research, you will know the skill of which you speak. Anna Smith, for example, learned to shoot a black powder musket before going on the road as Revolutionary War soldier Deborah Samson.

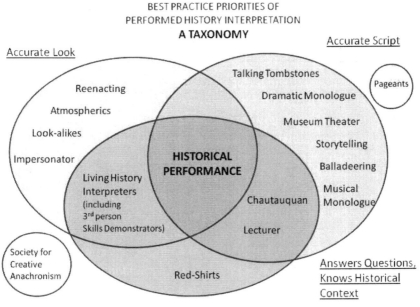

FIGURE 1

HOW DO YOU GET TO "GOOD"?

Now that you know what "good" is (time travel with the audience) and what is not good (reading text and ignoring the needs and wants of the audience), how does one ascend to "goodness"? Short answer: stories and time, passion and partners. That is Ride into History's shorthand for what it takes to create powerful historical performance. Passion about and sharing the stories will lead to a desire to give the time to find, craft, and share them. Sharing should begin early, with colleagues and/or friends (partners) who can serve as research assistants and practice audiences. That, in a nutshell, is what it takes to give a good historical performance—stories, time, passion, and partners.

But let's back up a bit and look first at the qualities of a good historical performer. Chautauquans, the ideological precursors of historical performers, have generally and historically come from the ranks of college faculty. So it might be useful to consider what makes a good college teacher. And realize that many of those qualities are found in a larger population than that made up of people teaching history, literature, and drama.

Rob Jenkins describes four properties of powerful teachers in the *Chronicle of Higher Education: Personality, Presence, Preparation, and Passion*. His prescription for college faculty somewhat parallels ours for historical performers, especially presence, preparation, and passion. And, he reassures, "Even if you weren't born with some of these qualities, you can develop them."[2] We agree.

Jenkins defines "presence" as "the ability to appear completely at ease, even in command, despite being the focal point of dozens (or even hundreds) of people." Note that Jenkins says that a professor should *appear* to be at ease, not necessarily *be* at ease. Historical performers do not themselves need presence if their *historic figure* has presence. If you are going to be true to your historic figure, you are going to bathe the audience in a golden light and tell them what they are there to hear because you are the historic figure, not yourself. This is acting, and in chapter 4 we further address your relationship with the audience while onstage.

Two of Jenkins's other properties of powerful college teachers are preparation and passion: "you must continue your education on a regular basis—by reading extensively in your field, attending conferences and seminars, conducting and presenting your own research." Do you need to be an academic (affiliated with a college or university) scholar to be a good historical performer? Short answer: no. We will deal with that concept more in chapter 2 but know that historical performers whose credentials lie outside academia have not only performed for general public audiences but also brought their knowledge to academics and other specialists. For example, surveyor Steve Brosemer has presented Kansas's first surveyor general, John Calhoun, to the Kansas Association of Historians as well as to his professional organization for which he first prepared his performance. And Norman Joy and Doug McGovern presented their discovery of stereophotographs of Robert E. Lee to that same group of largely academic historians. Blue Hawk of Portal of Time/Shining Mountain Enterprises was the keynote speaker at the Kansas Museums Association annual conference. Be forewarned that at academic conferences, unless you were brought in, like Mike Adams (aka Blue Hawk) was, you will pay—not be paid—for the privilege of adding that credential to your résumé. Your required conference registration will be around $100, and it will cost you time, transportation, food, and lodging—so plan carefully. In general, local or regional conferences will be less expensive—and more likely to welcome your contribution—than will national conferences.

"Passion," according to Jenkins, is "love for students and love for your subject matter."[2] Historical performance, like college history teaching, does not pay well enough to do if you don't care. Again, you have to fully believe that your audience is worthy of that golden light you are casting on them and that your message is worth spending your life revising. Your audiences will appreciate the passion you have for your subject, especially if that passion extends to include a passion for bringing your knowledge to your audience.

If you believe that you can summon from your historic figure the presence to convey your passion, then you will find the time to prepare. You can do this historic performance thing. Let's look again at the four elements of a good historical performance—stories, time, passion, and partners—and discuss how to differentiate between a historical performance and other traditions of costumed interpretation.

Stories

Stories are crucial to society. Stories are how we learn what it means to be human. We learn our family's rules and our culture's rules through stories of

PHOTO 1.1
Preparation never ends. Photo by authors.

transgressions and stories of heroism. Leslie Bedford summarizes storytelling's role: "Something happens in a story—something is wrong in the world—and its resolution serves to help us sort out our basic values and beliefs."[3]

History is nothing more than the stories of how people have made decisions—and how they have explained those decisions. Good stories are ones that resonate with an audience for any of several reasons: they involve conflict and overcoming adversity, they involve animals and an interesting geographic place or historical era, or they involve romance and adventure, suspense and gore, beauty and the beast. Mostly, they are about individuals making decisions, just like audience members make decisions every day of their lives.

One common decision that has been made is that of movement from one place to another. Historians refer to the push–pull theory to understand human migration. Usually, there is both: a push from one place (classic: potato famine in Ireland) and a pull to another (many came to the United States because they believed there were jobs that would allow them to feed themselves and their families). Joyce uses push-pull theory to understand the motivations of her historic figures and composite characters. Her composite Civil War veteran, Jo, remembers her parents' decision to emigrate. The soil in Pennsylvania "grew rocks, rocks, and more rocks" (a push). In Kansas Territory, on the other hand, not only could residents farm, but they could also vote against slavery. Years later, with her father dead and her mother's new husband cornering her in the barn, Jo leaves Kansas to join the military—the push being sexual assault ("How *could* I tell my mother what her husband had done?") and the pull being the opportunity to earn money to send home as well as to become a part of "Father Abraham's army."

Joyce's 1803 mixed heritage (Native American/Scotch-Irish) earth lodge woman, Grower, has been trying to convince the younger women not to use iron trade goods. Her mother's mother had prophesied that when the women used iron hoes instead of buffalo scapula hoes to cultivate the soil, they would lose their culture and their freedoms. But iron kettles and hoes had distinct advantages. Grower is concerned about the land being sold to a man named Jefferson when everyone knows that land can no more be sold than air can be.

Good performances are made of good stories with which audience members can identify. Lake Wobegon creator Garrison Keillor has found that stories are less likely to resonate if they are written too closely so that there is no place in them for the audience/listener/reader. He recommends enough detail to give a sense of place but not so much as to exclude audience members' memories of their own special place:

> I find that if I leave out enough details in my stories, the listener will fill in the blanks with her own hometown. . . . All I do is say the words: cornfield and Mother and algebra and Chevy pickup and cold beer and Sunday morning and rhubarb and loneliness, and other people put pictures to them.[4]

A common concern of new historical performers is having too many stories ("I can't possibly get it all told in forty minutes"). Put it out of your mind. There is no such thing as too many stories. The dilemma is rather like that of a spring garden: too many vegetables planted too closely together. The solution is to "weed." Neither the stories nor the young lettuce and radishes are truly weeds (except in the definition that a weed is a plant that is in the wrong place at a given time). But, like the young plants that can be eaten early when pulled or transplanted to another site, those stories can be tucked away for later use. For example, the fact that Calamity Jane was a midwife does not usually come up in Joyce's monologue, but she might use it if she is performing at a nursing convention. In fact, she met a woman at such a conference who said that her grandmother was delivered by Jane. And if someone asks about Jane's diverse employment during the discussion, Joyce might, either as Jane or as the scholar, tell a nursing story. Likewise, Amelia Earhart planned to become a physician, then a medical researcher, before she fell in love with settlement house work and then earned her living speaking and writing about flying. The first two career aspirations do not usually make the cut *unless* we have knowledge that there are medical personnel in the audience.

Time

It takes time to find stories; time to sculpt the stories for contemporary audiences; time to practice telling the stories; time to learn the skills of finding, sculpting, and presenting the stories; and, yes, time to actually perform the stories (chapters 2–4)—and time to market your storytelling as well as time to travel to your performance venues (more on these in chapter 6). We are often asked, "How long did it take you to learn all that?" Our response is always, "We are still learning."

Nonhistorians presume that history never changes, and maybe it doesn't. After all, what has happened has happened. We cannot go "back" and change history. Someone made a decision, and that decision has affected our lives and the decisions that we make. However, "history" is really not so much what happened as it is our explanation of what happened, the story of what happened. In our workshops, we give the example of a loud, ominous noise coming from a room where young siblings are congregated. A parent throws open the door and says, "What happened in here?" Unless the children have had time to negotiate their stories, there are likely as many stories as there are children.

Crucial to any performance is time to "get into the head" of your historic figure. You want the very best for your audience, so the presenting organization needs to give you time to yourself to morph into that other person. You have already rehearsed walking and talking like that person, but you will need time just before you go on to "find" your friend. Ann's first pair of Amelia Earhart boots had grommets all the way up. It took her ten minutes to lace each boot. The time it took to change her look, plus the twenty minutes to lace her boots, gave her enough time to get into character.

Time to learn should include time to build credentials that will increase your credibility and, hence, the likelihood that a presenting organization will take the risk of hiring you. There should be no gamble on the part of the organization. They want to bring in someone who has experience and who knows her or his stuff. How do they know you have experience? You give them a list of organizations for which you have performed. Haven't performed much? Collect the endorsement of someone who already has a good reputation as a historical performer. Sometimes when a financially challenged venue is seeking a program for less than we charge, we recommend a newer performer with whom we are familiar, usually a new member of the Kansas Alliance of Professional Historical Performers. In that case, our recommendation, our credentials, are augmenting theirs.

Sometimes an academic credential—classes taken or taught—can substitute for performance experience. (I took Women of the West with Dr. Thierer and based my performance of the woman homesteader on the research begun in that class, which I then turned into my master's thesis. Dr. Thierer was on my thesis committee.)

Juried rosters are one of the best sources of credentials. A panel (jury) has judged you against good performers and found you qualified. Membership in the Kansas Alliance of Professional Historical Performers is a juried roster. Your state's art and/or humanities organizations might have such a roster. The Mid-America Arts Alliance, for example, requires that you be on your state's roster to be on theirs. The Kansas Humanities Council no longer has their History Alive! program, but when they did, membership on the roster required an advanced degree in a humanities discipline as well as a juried performance and written curriculum material the council could disseminate to schools.

And, of course, performances are a source of credentials. Give your local library a good deal on a performance, and the librarian will share how wonderful you are (while keeping quiet about the super deal they got) with librarians in other communities. But you are not going to get the credentials unless you take the time to plan your performances and your research.

Humility will help with your concern about time—realize that we cannot know everything; we can only *seek* to know everything. If a question is asked and you do not know the answer, ask if someone in the audience knows the answer. It is a learning opportunity for all, including it being a reminder that none of us knows everything. Besides, audience members like to be acknowledged for their wisdom. Learning from the audience is a valid means of conducting research (just make sure you or a friend have pencil and paper readily available so that you can note the source of your new knowledge).

Passion

You must have passion about your subject, and the public to motivate you, to allocate enough time to find and craft the stories so that you can share them. You can have passion for the stories without feeling the need to share them. You can enjoy learning for your own edification, and that is fine, but the desire to share those stories with the public will inspire you to make the time and do the work. We often have at our workshops individuals who have been members of reenactment troupes. Reenactment exists for reenactors and is not necessarily a public event. Some people, however, want to share their passion and have the flexibility to take a story on the road without the entire brigade.

The task of creating a historical performance may sound huge, but we have recently received advice to share with you. From a fortune cookie: "Listen to what you know instead of what you fear." And from Amelia Earhart: "The most difficult thing is the decision to act, the rest is merely tenacity. The fears are paper tigers. . . . You can act to change and control your life; and the procedure, the process, is its own reward."[5] The process is rewarding (can you imagine a better job than one that lets you spend time with your historic figure?), but audience appreciation for a job well done is also a motivating reward. After she had portrayed environmentalist Rachel Carson for an Audubon Society conference, an audience member pleaded, "Please keep doing this. It is so important, what you are doing." The messages need to be heard. We are keeping the stories alive, reminding today's people of the struggles and successes of those who came before.

What are *your* passions? What do *you* care about? We declared that we wanted to get women's stories to the public. Our colleague and neighbor Kitty Frank loves vintage clothing, has a degree in economics, and lives near the Santa Fe Trail route. Her first character was the daughter of an early trading post operator in Council Grove, Kansas. Kitty described her character's girlhood at the Hays House witnessing hundreds of thousands of dollars being traded for wagons, mules, oxen, blankets, and all manner of trade goods and foods. She also witnessed conflicts between Pawnee and Kanza Indians. Kitty's second character reached out to her in the walnut-paneled Missouri Valley Room of the Kansas City Public Library, where she was researching her first character. Nell Donnelly (aka Nelly Don) was the second self-made woman millionaire in the United States. She made her money in fashion in Kansas City. It turns out that in the early decades of the twentieth century, Kansas City was the largest fashion design and manufacturing center in the country. And she had stories—an abduction, the mob, pistols thrown down an elevator shaft, repeated neighborly rendezvous that resulted in an "adopted" son sired by a presidential candidate, and a country club created to keep the staff from going union. And did we mention money? And stylish clothes? This was a natural for Kitty with her economic background. She can actually explain the economic historical context of her two historic figures because she understands it.

Doug McGovern, also known as Civil War photographer Alexander Gardner, tells us to warn anyone who wants to do historical performance that you do not really have much of a choice in who you "do." *They* choose *you*, he says, so be open and make them glad they chose who they did. Plan, execute, and be open to serendipity. (There is, however, a chapter in *Telling History* that is dedicated to helping you determine which historic figures and/or composite characters you want to portray, including marketing concerns.)

Inventory your interests and your skill set. What are you passionate about, and what do you know how to do? What do you need to learn? Seriously. Make a list. Give yourself a deadline—say, a week of showers or dreams or long walks or however you prefer to allow ideas to filter into your consciousness. At the end of the week, spend several hours planning how you will use your passions and your knowledge. Maybe your first historic figure will not involve all of your passions, but are there patterns in your list? Then start talking to people, especially librarians. Post it on social media: "I'm looking for a historic figure who is passionate about social justice and antique cars."

Making a good match is especially important because if you spend enough time with stories about something or someone, you start seeing the world through their eyes. It's like being in love. Every conversation, everything you hear or read, leads you to your obsession: "Oh, that's like when Amelia. . . ."

If you have ever studied a language to the point where you dream in that language, it is similar. In fact, Kitty Frank reported that she knew she was ready for an audience the morning she awakened as fashion entrepreneur Nell Donnelly, having dreamed not *about* her but *as* her. Joyce's brother is passionate about railroad history. He has his steam engineer certification and volunteers with a group that runs a train out of Abilene, Kansas. Brother and sister grew up with a double track going through the family farm, a long stone's throw from their bedrooms. When we are on the road, we have to brake for train car restaurants, and every museum shop is shaken down for a nifty train gift for Larry. Without Larry, we would not be doing that. If Larry did a historical performance, he would no doubt choose to be a railroader. As it is, he is a skilled skill demonstrator.

Partners

We asked students in Heidi Vaughn's costumed historical interpretation course at the University of Central Oklahoma to evaluate *Telling History*, their textbook. Each had performed for the class. One question we asked was what more they felt they would need before taking a historical performance to the public. A student said, "This all seems so overwhelming." She described it as "scary." While the book was "wonderful" and "provides a great guideline," what she wanted was "a mentor who can provide help," someone who would be there every step of the way. She felt that with such a mentor, she would not have been "very fearful and anxious" as she was when she performed for the class.

A skilled buddy would also have been useful to the university student who believed that "when a performer enjoys his work his performance is flawless—granted his or her history is correct." It is true that we take pleasure in an excellent performance, but very often we are our harshest critics, and we need someone who can evaluate our performance from the perspective of a knowledgeable audience member. Very seldom do we give ourselves a "ten," which is another reason to have a partner along, someone who can remind us that the audience had no idea what was happening and that the performance that we thought rated a "seven" on a scale of one to ten was probably closer to a "nine." *We* know what we left out or where we forgot a name or date, but usually our audience will not.

A reality check is especially needed for that first performance when you felt terrified. Your audience, on the other hand, probably did not notice your

PHOTO 1.2
Sometimes a village is useful. Photo by authors.

terror. A partner can give that feedback and assure you that no one noticed your knees knocking.

As we said in the preface, identify friends, colleagues, and relatives who respect you, your audiences, and your subject matter enough to be honest coaches. We all need help from stand-ins for the audience-to-be. A partner will do the following:

- Make sure you commit to a time line while working toward your first performance.
- Be a research assistant—making copies, downloading to thumb drives, and celebrating "finds."
- Listen to informal story sharing as well as rehearsals.
- Proofread documents, including contracts, news releases, bibliographies, and marketing materials.
- Share ideas about all of the above.

If you were a Girl Scout, chances are you learned about the buddy system. Many activities required a buddy—someone who was nearby and could come to your rescue or call for help if need be. When we think of people who have had some financial success at historical performance, we think of people who are or have been affiliated with another historical performer or with a group. An example of an informal affiliation is that of Norman Joy (NJoy History) and Doug McGovern (Alive with History). They met at a Ride into History workshop. Norman interprets Robert E. Lee, among others, and Doug McGovern's signature interpretation is that of Alexander Gardner, who photographed Lee (and shot many other photographs credited to Mathew Brady). Both Norman and Doug lived in Hutchinson, Kansas. Both were primary caregivers for an elderly person. Both are amazingly kinesthetic and creative. Doug is a retired engineer. Norman taught industrial arts. Doug's workshop leaned toward the electronic (he has evolved into steam punk), while Norman built an electricity-free nineteenth-century workshop in his backyard. Although they no longer live in the same city, they can still book an occasional duo and share their passion for their historical subject and their inventions that support their performances.

It should go without saying, but here is a reminder: do not choose as a partner someone who is habitually negative. You know who they are. You may value them greatly, but their "honesty" is not the accurate critique that is useful to you. You will never please that person. The rest of the audience will, however, be very pleased, so choose someone who better represents the whole.

You must also be your own partner. Understanding yourself is very important. Do you have a passion for your historic era or topic but none for the huddled masses? If you pride yourself on being smarter than most people and are commonly heaping scorn on those who know less than you, you might do yourself, and them, a favor and consider going into a less interactive area of public history. For example, a form of museum theater where you present a script but do not take questions from the audience might be a better match. A historical performer respects audiences and does not patronize them. Do not talk down to children any more than you would talk down to their elders. And if you are inclined to talk down to elders, then cure yourself or move along. Likewise, as a historical performer, you must be aware of diversity in your audience that might not be visible. Do not presume, for example, that all audience members identify as Christians. An audience member might look white but identify as black. Some people who identify as tribal have blue eyes. Write your script with everyone in mind. If you do not know what is likely to offend a gay person or a southerner, find out before you alienate audience members. But more on that in chapter 3.

Historical performance enhances museum and historic site visitor experience. It engages audiences with past decision makers more effectively than any other learning method and in so doing has the potential to lead audience members to examine their own decision making. Historical performance is sneaky history because while it is educational, it is also interesting, and often it is fun. It involves emotions as well as facts. And it can be done in diverse settings.

To achieve a high level of skill, historical performers invest the time to find stories that will resonate with audiences and about which they themselves are passionate and invest time in understanding the context of past decisions. Historical performers will also find people who can help them reach their goal of taking audiences to another time and place. They will reinforce what audience members know, add new knowledge, and play for takeaways. Bottom line: What should audience members have learned well enough that they can tell someone else?

NOTES

1. Tessa Bridal, *Effective Exhibit Interpretation and Design* (Lanham, MD: AltaMira Press, 2013), 74.

2. Rob Jenkins, "The 4 Properties of Powerful Teachers," *Chronicle of Higher Education*, March 16, 2015, http://chronicle.com/article/The-4-Properties-of -Powerful/228483/.

3. "Storytelling: The Real Work of Museums," *Curator: The Museum Journal* 44, no. 1 (January 2001): 29.

4. "In Search of Lake Wobegon," *National Geographic Magazine*, December 2000.

5. Amelia Earhart: The Official Website, http://www.ameliaearhart.com/about/ quotes.html (accessed March 16, 2016). (Copyright is claimed to be by her estate, and no further source is given, although the quote is used a great deal elsewhere.)

2

Overcoming Fear of Research with Historians' Powerful Tools

This chapter is for aspiring historical performers who are having difficulty "getting into" research—those who have read all of the lists in the research chapter in *Telling History* and it is still not happening for them. If your wheels are just not getting traction, we need to move you from fear of research—or frustration with research—to pleasure in research. A student in a costumed historical interpretation class said, "I found that I was most fearful two days into the research and then again, just as I started my performance." Another student said that having created a character while a museum intern, she felt that she "did an adequate job, but after reading the book I was able to find new ways to add excitement, drama, and interest." However, the student also said that during the preparation for the performance for classmates, "I was worried that I would not know enough, particularly concerning the Q&A period. I studied and researched and found that I was becoming more anxious as I studied!"[1] The experiences of these students illustrate perfectly the concept that the more we learn, the more we learn how much we have yet to learn. We need to give ourselves permission not to know everything but rather to identify ourselves as part of several communities of ongoing learners. As important as research is, though, "research must not become procrastination. Too many insecure talents spend years in study and never actually write anything."[2] So let's get you out there researching, enjoying it, but letting go to share some of those splendid stories you find.

We are accustomed to looking at public speaking with trepidation—fear of public speaking has had a lot of publicity, but probably because fewer people are involved in serious research, we are less likely to hear from those who fear research. The internet has made sources such as local newspapers available to people in their own homes, but it has complicated searches because not all such sources are so readily available. Some individual has to put the source on the internet, and usually that is the result of the decision makers in an organization such as a library or historical society—it takes money to digitize sources. And those sources do not all fly onto the internet at once. It takes time to get the job done. So you might look for a small-town weekly newspaper from 1902 and not find it, but three months later it is online. So making allies of those who are involved in the decision making is important—they can tell you not to waste your time looking now but to check again in three months. Maybe they will even email you when it becomes available.

So let's sneak up on fear so we can deal with it and move on because research can be delightfully addictive—and with good reason. Once you find what sources work best for you, you just might be surprised to find yourself so involved with research that you have difficulty setting aside the research process to start writing. Once you start asking questions and the details come pouring in, you just can't wait to find out more. You know that there is more information right around the corner if only you keep looking. Don't believe it? Before fear and panic really set in and you let loose with a primal scream in proportion to the multitude of years since you had to write a paper in school, read on.

First, let's establish your identity as a researcher. You are a researcher, a historian, a scholar of your particular historic figure and that figure's historic context. So claim the labels. You might identify as a beginner, but you are, nonetheless, a professional (or an aspiring professional if you have not yet been paid to do a performance). You can learn the research skills used by historians, especially if you are patient with yourself and willing to seek help. You will be building relationships, and that takes time. Like any professional, you carefully collect tools: resources you will use each time you research. These include the questions you pose; materials you have at home; allies, such as professional librarians and archivists; other allies, including friends and other historical performers; internet sources, including search engines and databases; and the sources: primary and secondary. Think of it not as going on a fishing expedition for facts but rather as preparing yourself for a lifetime of enjoying fishing.

THE FIRST TOOL: MEANINGFUL QUESTIONS

To be a good historian is to be a good researcher, and before you can research, you need to figure out what it is you want to know. It's as simple as that. Humanities scholars (and history is a humanities discipline) know that the most important thinking that we do is to figure out what questions to ask. You need to know what your questions are before you can look for sources of answers and then sift through those sources so that you will recognize significant information among the dross. In other words, unless you know what gold looks like, don't tackle a mountain with a pickax. Only when historians know that they have significant questions do they ask the go-to-the-mountain question: "Where am I likely to find the answers to these questions?"

Before you seek the answers to your questions, it is useful to know that historians divide the places where they find answers (sources) into two categories: primary and secondary. Primary sources are recorded by an eyewitness, a contemporary account of the event. Secondary accounts are after-the-fact versions of the event(s).

And to know what it is that historians look for, it might help to know how they define history. Historians differ in their definitions of history. In his address to the American Historical Association in 1939, Carl L. Becker defined history as "the memory of things said and done."[3] As we have stated before and will again, Ride into History's definition is "the story of decisions we have made and the story of how we have explained those decisions," the latter being a bone thrown to historiography.

While you are sifting through information looking for answers to your questions, you will find the answers to questions you did not even know enough to ask. Those answers will give you an even greater understanding and even greater insights into your historic figure, but all of the questions begin with the most basic questions: Who, what, when, where, how, and, most importantly, why and what is the significance? Post these where you can routinely see them and add to them as your questions become more specific. There is another question, one often asked by adolescents: "Who cares?" It is your historical performance, your first-person narrative, that is going to answer that question because *they* will come to care.

It is important to understand that just because history happened in the past does not mean that all answers have been found or that all sources have disappeared into the void of time. Unfortunately, school textbooks simplify history. For example, a textbook might tell you that World War II began when the Japanese bombed the American naval fleet at Pearl Harbor on December 7, 1941. A question might be, "Why were so many troops, planes, and ships there if we were not at war?" The textbook is not going to tell you the answer, so where do you go from there for the backstory? This question has, of course, been answered. But the answer has varied greatly, depending on the interests of the person who asked the question and the sources they used in seeking the answer. New researchers bring new questions. For example, for the history of history, almost all of the writers of history were men, mostly well-educated men who were literate and had the leisure from work to spend their time writing. These men wrote of the men they admired. Hence, history was about men who were like them. When women began to write history, they asked questions about women. They asked questions that men said were not worth asking much less writing about. But other women cared about the answers to the women's questions, and gradually many men came around, too (or died out).

Traditionally, historians wrote about accomplishments—the war was won or a general won the war or the frontier was settled. Decisions were presumed to have been made by men and only a few men: those who left a written record. In reality, though, decisions made by many diverse people whose names have been lost to history have affected events that created our present and our future.

It is difficult to reach a single historic truth, especially when humans have a built-in "[universal] talent for deceiving each other."[4] Each witness to an event sees that event differently, even those who do not set out to lie. Think of a large crash coming from a room of children. "What happened?" No one was hurt, just a lamp broken. A parent interviews each child, and each child has a different explanation of what happened, usually one that does not involve her or his own guilt.

The process of doing history can appear to be deceptively simple, seeming not to require arcane language or jargon or even historical training. Historical performers, however, do more than simply locate facts and copy them into their notes. We are constantly evaluating our sources: Whose account of an event do we believe and why? Doing history requires an inquisitive mind willing to ask questions and then seeking answers to questions. Historical performance research requires diligence—detective work to answer the questions that will solve the mystery and then persistence and imagination to distill facts into a viable version of the story in the form of a first-person narrative. History methodology is about the questions we ask, the purposes to which we put information, and it is about careful investigation, balance, and the communication of a story.

Historical subjectivity is part of the arsenal of the traditional historian. "Subjectivity," according to Susan Crane of the University of Arizona, "always inflects the historian's choice of topic and evidence as well as the selection of an appropriate authorial voice. Although present at every step of historical research, historical subjectivity generally has been rendered obscure as part of the attempt to be objective." We tend to think about historians' subjectivity—their self, their personal choices, and their experiences—as surfacing when the writing, the interpretation process, begins, when the historian's voice begins to speak directly to the audience. Instead, however, that subjectivity is present from the time the historian chooses what questions to ask and what sources to use to answer those questions. "Historians—as agents, as historical actors—construct narratives about the past that would never exist without the same amount of self assertion, choice, desire, fortitude, and above all, writing, all of which must come from some body, a single person, namely the historian."[5] Charles F. Bryan, president and chief executive officer emeritus of the Virginia Historical Society and former council chair of the American Association of State and Local History, sees the role of historians as that of revisionists, "looking at familiar subjects from unique perspectives to come up with new ways of describing the past."[6]

Many people do not know that questions can be asked of historical sources. New questions can be asked of old sources. First, you will need a research plan. Do not wait for the perfect time to begin, as perfection rarely waits for you to begin anything let alone to brainstorm. We suggest you just start on the plan—grab paper and something with which to write. Panic! No paper in sight. The best way to move beyond panic is to take action, so look for index cards, which would be even better, but even a stack of old envelopes, the notepad from a motel, or the holiday gift of a pad of paper too cute to use for grocery lists would work, as would any stack of multiple pieces of paper or cards.

Not the computer, though—not yet. Computers encourage linear thinking, not the circular creative links that we want at this stage. At this stage, the questions should be more important to you than the answers. Trust us. You are going to start by creating notes about what you think you know about your historic figure and her or his surroundings in time and place. Either as you make a note for each fact that you think you know or when you come back to those notes later, write questions that you hope will lead you to more information about your historic figure, being sure to ask questions that will test your presumptive knowledge. For example, as something you know, you might write, "Calamity Jane was an outlaw." This becomes a hypothesis that you want to test. Then you might write the question, "What did Calamity Jane do that gave her the label of outlaw?"[7] Do not worry about writing a question for every statement. And some statements will have multiple questions, such as, "Where was Calamity Jane supposed to have broken the law?" "When did Calamity Jane break the law?" "Were there crime reports in newspapers that would substantiate her outlaw status?" "Was her outlaw status really about her breaking social mores rather than actual laws?"

Ask the big questions: "Why?" "What was the significance of this event, of that choice?" Also, seek the many small details that create pictures of the environment of your figure. What did they eat? What did they wear? How did what they wore affect their behavior and how they were perceived, and who was doing that perceiving? Seek commonalities of life. How is she like me? How will she be like some or all of my audience? This will help your audience connect with your historic figure, helping them understand the decisions she made that changed history. Do this for a few hours until you start to run out of questions. Gather your pieces of paper. Shuffle them and look for similarities and group facts and questions to make it easier to seek answers. These groupings will be useful to you as you create your research agenda and then later as you create your script.

Most people prefer today's comforts to yesterday's discomforts, but people like to project themselves into another time. You will give audience members enough information so that they can experience history vicariously through your first-person narrative. They do not want to be in the battle, but they like your description of the smell of the green grass under the horses' hooves and even appreciate your approximation of the sound of cannon fire. It all takes research to be able to take your audience to the time and place that your historic figure remembers. What did it smell like? What did it taste like? What were they thinking? Again and again, what led to the decisions they made?

Set aside your research groupings for a while but keep scraps of paper nearby. Add questions as they occur to you. A very useful tool that you may wish to examine at this point is *Nearby History: Exploring the Past Around You* by David E. Kyvig and Myron A. Marty. We have used all three editions over the years to clarify our research skills and sharpen our focus. The second chapter contains lists of questions grouped by topic that you can easily look over for ideas. For example, the list of family relationships questions includes, "Who was considered to be a member of the family?" In later chapters, they describe the types of sources you might seek as you do your own research. For example, where would you go to find out who was considered to be a member of a particular family? One list of questions is "Daily Living," which includes, for example, "In what kinds of social activities did the family engage?"[8]

THE SECOND TOOL: YOUR PERSONAL RESOURCES

What do you already have? What do you already know? We are going to address two very different types of resources: the things you need to keep you organized and the sources of information you have at home. First, organizing tools. Unless you are one of those who are not using paper, you will want a box, preferably a clear plastic box with a lid. You will save all kinds of materials as you come across them. File folders are useful, too, as you break your questions and answers down into stories. Keep in the box a few pencils, clips, blank paper (we like yellow pads and a clipboard), and books as you acquire them.

We are firm believers that the way to decrease the stress of researching and writing is in having the basic tools you need where you can find them at the point of use. Finding them now reduces stress later. Our space is shared—it is a large space, but multiple projects are going on simultaneously, and multiple boxes are scattered about, some in piles in front of the floor-to-ceiling bookcases. As we write this book, we enjoy the synergy of sharing, but it is also easy to be distracted by the larger project as well as other activity. And it is not just writing projects. Ann has to keep all the business aspects of Ride into History going and separate it from the ranch and other work business and Joyce's university class projects that get dragged into the shared work space. Let me say it again: organization is the key to reducing stress. A sense of calmness and ready-to-work attitude can easily flare into "I cannot find" (it could be anything), so frustration builds, anxiety flares, and physical stress systems go off in the mind and body as all other thoughts are put on hold until the thing is found and calmness slowly returns, but not only is physical time lost on the clock, but so, too, is the flow of thought. Even a wrong number call can cost the creative person ten to twenty minutes to resume the deep attention she or he had prior to the panic moment. Do not answer the phone; check messages later to take more control of your precious time. Joyce was required in two of her professional positions to note her activities in fifteen-minute intervals. Think "billable hours method." She hated it then, but now it is a very useful skill, especially when researching. This time awareness is also called mindfulness, and it lets her find ways to avoid a gap in thought. Here is her thought process: "For example, my cup is empty, so I think I need to fill it, but I want, not need, another cup of coffee, and if I left now, I would lose time better spent chatting with you. So mindfully, I will wait on the coffee until my alarm sounds and I know I'm at the end of my work session. Then I will stretch my body and as I fetch my coffee and think about how to say it more succinctly. I hate to waste time, so I try to use it to the maximum. Many little time wasters snare us, and we do not always know it—be vigilant. Look out for these little snares before they catch you."

Another useful tool or habit is to find a way for you to consistently take notes and indicate where you found the information. If you think lost car keys and a deadline cause stress, try finding that one crucial bit of information you need now—you photocopied it from one of the blue-covered books you returned to the library weeks ago, and now you do not recall the title. Yes, that photocopy was tucked into the unlabeled file folder left on the kitchen table last week.

Check other resources, such as information resources. Do you have an encyclopedia? A children's biography of your historic figure? Do you have a nonfiction book about your person and/or her or his era? Do you have a book

PHOTO 2.1
Make copies and record citations. Photo by authors.

about the history of the geographic region from which they come? Do you
have internet service? Do you know how to use the internet fruitfully, without
becoming hopelessly diverted?

Oral sources are not enough. They must be questioned. For example,
Joyce's grandfather told her repeatedly as they checked cattle from a horse-
drawn buggy, "Don't mortgage the land." He even had her repeat it so she
would remember that lesson (and others). Young Joyce took from that simple
phrase two erroneous lessons: 1) someday the land will be mine, and 2) our
family has never mortgaged the land. Let's take the last one first. Phrases
like this tend to be cautionary—prescriptive rather than descriptive. "If you
own the land, don't mortgage it—it is too hard to get it paid off." Joyce was
shocked to find deeds at the county courthouse that showed that her grandfather had mortgaged a few parcels of pasture. About the first lesson: that was
one she learned, then unlearned, only to "own" it again. Joyce's mother died
young. Her father was a bit of a "pill" and kept threatening to leave the farm
not to Joyce or her younger brother but rather to any of several friends. Before

he died, however, she and her brother and a lawyer prevailed so that there was equitable distribution, especially for Larry, who had farmed with his father for more than four decades. We recently saw a delightful play, *Miracle on South Division Street* with the same theme. A family fiercely defends the story about a statue of the Blessed Virgin Mary that the paterfamilias had constructed after Mary had appeared to him at his barbershop. Several years following his death, they discover that the statue was actually of his first love, and not only that, his daughter (now an adult with children who were dealing with all of this mythmaking and myth busting) was the daughter of his first love, not the daughter of their grandmother, but that the mother was Jewish. What difference is it going to make to that family to know a different truth?[9]

PHOTO 2.2
Both a primary source (older generation) and a secondary source (the book). Photo by authors.

The point is that primary sources may contradict each other. They come from real people with varying perspectives who tell what they want to tell and not what they do not want to tell. Even primary sources can have errors, such as numerical errors (1958 instead of 1858). A census taker might guess at the spelling of a name or get an age from an adult in the home who is embarrassed to say that he does not know how old his children are.

There is also a problem with lost information due to "improved" data storage. A letter sent via email is less likely to be available years from now than one written with pen and paper. Stories that are preserved only digitally (on computers) are as much in danger as is fragile newsprint.

Research is seeking stories, not just facts. Facts are the clues that we use to build stories. Historical performance is not oral history; it is a retelling of a gathering of stories—it is keeping history alive by keeping history fresh and human—real people making real decisions. An increase in knowledge leads to a decrease in fear. If the knowledge is false—for example, "We do not mort-

PHOTO 2.3
Anna Smith knew modern rifles, but learning to fire a black powder rifle made her even more an authority. Photo by authors.

gage the land"—it nonetheless provides us with a feeling of security until, that is, a contradiction takes away that security until we adjust our thinking based on the new knowledge and once more gain our feeling of authority.

THE THIRD TOOL: LIBRARIANS AND ARCHIVISTS

If you are a reluctant researcher, it may be because you have not yet found the tools that fit your learning style. Supportive librarians and archivists are like Indiana Jones combined with a personal trainer. Terri Summey of Emporia State University fits that description. She leaps over buildings in a single bound. She has a master's degree in history as well as in library science and a PhD in library and information management. She said to tell you that librarians went into their profession because they like to help people. Their passion is connecting people with information. Never think that you are bothering them if you need help. Remember the librarian's motto: the only dumb question is one that is never asked. And if it makes you feel any better, both of us have MLS (master of library science) degrees in addition to our subject matter doctorates, and we are very quick to ask questions of librarians. We can say that a lot has changed since we staffed reference desks, but the truth is that there is just a lot of "stuff" out there to wade through, and we need all the help we can get. Archivists in particular, those who have collections of unique items that exist nowhere else, are precious beyond belief. They are constantly going above and beyond. Ann, for example, was under contract to identify primary in two large collections sources by and about the women in a specific family. The Emporia State University archivist staff not only scanned everything she needed but also told her about two memoir manuscripts written by adults years after they lived with this family. Both memoirs focused on that family. Neither was of much value to the project, but one of those memoirs became a play that Ann wrote, produced, and directed.[10]

There are, however, lots of different specialties among librarians. Your small-town librarian might work part-time and have had only on-the-job training. Such persons will need you to lead them on services such as interlibrary loan, or you can encourage them to ask someone in their regional library organization. Maybe they do not know that if you give them the full citation (author, title of article [and journal if it's an article], or book title and publisher as well as date of publication, pages you want, and where you found the information), a library that has a copy of this material will loan it to the library near you. If the item is rare and never allowed to be checked out, the library that owns the material might photocopy the pages that are most important to you.

Dr. Summey points out that librarians know each other. They network. They go to conferences and exchange information. If they get stumped on a problem and the internet is not coming through on something for them, they will call a colleague and brainstorm together. Your team is expanding. You might not have the answer today, but give this new team time to tackle the problem, and you will have the answer.[11]

This is important when you want to research at an archive: to protect such vulnerable documents as handwritten letters, many archives want from you a letter of introduction that indicates your affiliation as well as your mission. What, specifically, do you want to search? What questions are you trying to answer? When will you arrive, and when will you leave? Have you been online and read the organization's policies?

Public archives like the National Archives require some identification and will create a photo identification card for you with an expiration date. One reason they want to know who you are and how to reach you is to follow up if they find something of interest after you leave. They are becoming part of your community of learners. There is also, sadly, the function of being able to follow-up if the document that you were using disappears: might it have accidentally left with you even though they did check for it among your papers as you left? It has happened that a supposedly respectable scholar has made off with whole volumes or has razored pages from a valuable volume. So be patient with the process of preserving archival collections for the long run.

Some archives need to minimize the number of people who just want to touch something that someone famous wrote. They might discourage a visit from someone who shows up at the door saying they want to see "anything Abraham Lincoln wrote." You will need to establish yourself as a serious scholar. And you are.

Although librarians should live to serve their clientele, an unfortunate few just do not quite get it.

THE FOURTH TOOL: OTHER ALLIES

Anyone who shares your interest or who owns a piece of your interest, such as the convention and visitors bureau of Atchison, Kansas, where the Amelia

Earhart Birthplace Museum draws visitors to local restaurants and motels, is a potential ally. They might not have specific knowledge about your historic figure, but they are probably able to use their network to introduce you to the person who can answer the question you have been trying to resolve. You want to meet those people who know people. Likewise, such places as the Earhart museum might be physically impressive, but it might be run on volunteer passion, not on professional historical or museum awareness. They might be doing their best to keep the memories alive, but analysis ("why" and "the significance of") will be undertaken by scholars from outside (thinking here of historian Susan Ware's *Still Missing: Amelia Earhart and the Search for Modern Feminism*), including you.

Another resource might be a friend or family member who is always curious about everything you are doing or who is willing to face down boredom for your sake and a free lunch. This is the person you want to take with you when you go to an archive to research. She or he will photocopy microfilm for you ("pages 33 to 89, please") or take citations to the county clerk who will pull the immense volume of records that your research assistant will photocopy. This person will also corroborate your Trail Stories as you describe your encounter with "interesting" motels and truculent public servants. *Rule: what makes you miserable can make a good story from a distance of time and place.*

You might even try posting your research topic on Facebook. Give people a chance to help you, to become involved in the excitement of uncovering your mysteries. You might even, with their help, find the proverbial needle in the haystack.

It might not make a lot of sense to you, but we feel you do need to know that occasional academic historians will resent you because they have spent a lot of money and time (usually at least six years to earn a doctorate after their four-year undergraduate degree) establishing credentials. You may need to prove yourself to them. They are very possessive of their knowledge. Even if they seem to be sharing with you, they do so sparingly because they are always writing a book and cannot give away their findings. You will have to wait until their book is published—whenever that is. You might be able to turn them into allies if you can prove that you have something to offer them and that you recognize their authority and appreciate their knowledge (be a dog and not a cat). Traditional historians are trained to be competitive. In seminars,

PHOTO 2.4
Learning to read a photograph at a Nebraska Youth Chautauqua Camp. Photo by
authors.

they learn to make obtuse statements and defend them against all comers,
whether or not they really believe what they are saying. Many history majors
have been debaters and become lawyers.

THE FIFTH TOOL: ONLINE RESOURCES

Information sources are constantly changing, which is why you want a librarian on your side. So we will mention a few here, but the bottom line is to find
your ally and do your homework based on their advice. Librarian Summey
says that her go-to-first online database is Google Scholar (https:www.google
.scholar.com) She describes it as "one-stop shopping." Google Scholar will let
you go online and see how much is available on your topic. Then, unless you
are affiliated with a university or have a state library card, you will need to go
to a research library, such as one at a public university, to look at the articles
themselves. Some services, like JSTOR, will let you subscribe directly for a fee
and buy permissions to download articles.

Once upon a time, researchers could go to a university library and look through volumes of the *America History and Life* index to find articles about their topics. Now researchers go online. Sounds good. Search from home. The problem is that now you must be affiliated with an institution. Otherwise, with some services, you cannot even try it from home. So let's go through Emporia State's library with Joyce's faculty status by our side (later, we can see if Ann's status as an alumnus of Emporia State will let her search or if she will have to cheat and use Joyce's password). Emporia State subscribes to a service that makes available to its scholars a wide range of databases. *American West*, for example, offers searchable full-text primary, or period, sources, including maps of book and map collector Everett D. Graff, whose collection is at the Newberry Library in Chicago. When we asked the database to search for "Calamity Jane," it brought up several items with which Joyce was familiar but also a "new" old one, *Hard Knocks: A Life Story of the Vanishing West*,[12] a memoir by Graff. She then asked it to find every time that "Calamity Jane" was mentioned in it. Scanning the resulting snippets, she could tell that the content was a little short on accuracy and long on mythology. On the other hand, some of the tales were new and might be interesting to follow up on but not now. So she downloaded the entire work to her computer. But do you get it? Do you understand? She did not have to go to Chicago to read this item. She could even print it or download it to her computer, which she could also do when she found "Carrying Concealed Weapons: Gendered Makeover in Calamity Jane" about the Doris Day movie of the 1950s in the online *America: History and Life* database of sources.[13] The last time she found something so interesting, she had to read it in Philadelphia, which was a pleasure for her but expensive and time consuming, so you don't want to go unless there are a good many such things to draw you to Philadelphia.

JSTOR indexes and provides complete text, mostly of material, articles, books, and citations written by college professors. Try JSTOR Web indexes sources. JSTOR indexes only academic journals, which share a very different level of information than Google. However, public use might be limited. For example, a college or university might pay a fee that says that only their faculty and students can use their subscription to JSTOR. As a history professor at Emporia State, Joyce has unlimited access to JSTOR as long as she goes through her university's portal to the internet. Ann, on the other hand, as an independent researcher not affiliated with a university, could in December

2016 pay a fee that allowed her to download three articles every fourteen days. A monthly fee of $19.50 allowed unlimited reading and downloading of articles as PDF files. An annual fee would allow her to download 120 articles if it were convenient for her to conduct most of her research within a few months instead of spreading it out over a year.

Ann was going to be away from her office. She wanted to use some of that "away" time to immerse herself in academic literature about Isabella Bird's *A Lady's Life in the Rocky Mountains* (1879) for a Kansas Humanities Council book talk she would be leading. She wondered how other scholars had approached Bird's memoir of traveling the Rockies on horseback. A trial of JSTOR let her download close to twenty articles, print them, and take them with her to peruse at her leisure. Here are a few of the wondrous sources she discovered (with abbreviated citations):

Domosh, Mona. "Toward a Feminist Historiography of Geography." *Transactions of the Institute of British Geographers*, 2015.
Herr, Elizabeth. "Women, Marital Status, and Work Opportunities in 1880 Colorado." *Journal of Economic History*, 1995.
Morin, Karen M. "British Women Travelers and Constructions of Racial Difference across the Nineteenth-Century American West." *Transactions of the Institute of British Geographers*, 1998.
———. "Peak Practices: Englishwomen's 'Heroic' Adventures in the Nineteenth-Century American West." *Annals of the Association of American Geographers*, 1999.
Valencius, Conevery Bolton. "Gender and the Economy of Health on the Santa Fe Trail." *Landscapes of Exposure: Knowledge and Illness in Modern Environments*, 2004.
West, Elliott. "Heathens and Angels: Childhood in the Rocky Mountain Mining Towns." *Western Historical Quarterly*, 1983.

Maybe this wealth will encourage one of you to portray the intrepid author and explorer Isabella Lucy Bird, who was also the first woman elected a fellow of the Royal Geographical Society—and encourage all of you to try JSTOR as an access point to knowledge being created by scholars.

The National Archives website is very useful but has many multilayered internal sites. For example, what pops up first is helpful information on how to search it and many instructions. We suggest you take the time to read it because doing so will save you time and decrease your frustration. For example, Joyce has her undergraduate college students locate the initial Homestead Act of 1862 in the National Archives. Her goal was to get them to the handwritten document signed by President Abraham Lincoln, which contains several crucial details left out of most summaries of the act. For example, the summaries in most textbooks indicate or suggest that to homestead under the act, you had to be male, while the document itself alternates "he or she" with "she or he." Secondary sources also play up "free land" without describing the hard work and/or military service that was required. Free? Really? Every semester, she hears whines and howls as the students protest that they cannot find this primary source document. What is happening is that they resist reading the instructions. It is not organized in the more common, simplified Google- or Wikipedia-style website but rather is a real research site demanding a level of skill that is typical of many tools out there to help historians and researchers. It takes more than two minutes. This attitude does not bode well for digging, so learn from this little story about this website, as it really is a treasure trove of primary source historical information. Take your time. Before you sit down at your computer, use the bathroom and get your cup of coffee. Be ready to ignore incoming electronic communications. Another challenge for many younger scholars is that they did not learn to read cursive. It is very sad that they cannot read Lincoln's signature or the text of anything that was prepared before the advent of typewriters.

These, too, are favorite scholarly sites:

- The Library of Congress website has a wide variety of subsites to get to know.
- The National Digital Newspapers has a program: Chronicling America: Historic American Newspapers (http://chroniclesgamerica.loc.gov).
- State historical societies have been microfilming newspapers and scanning articles and creating searchable websites.

Rule: don't let it overwhelm you; focus on your topic. Keep in front of you the list of questions you are trying to answer. Don't be led astray—when you see something enticing that is not immediately relevant, make a note of it or print a page but go back to your question.

THE SIXTH TOOL: CUSTOM SOURCES

If a community is very fortunate, they will have tools created by local people to answer local research needs. Often, these are created and maintained by and for genealogists. For example, Robert and Lois Hodge indexed Lyon County, Kansas, newspapers from the newspapers' beginnings. They distributed the paper indexes to area libraries. The Flint Hills Genealogical Society, in turn, digitized the list of obituaries from the Hodges' indexes.

We have researched at libraries that have card indexes to local obituaries—very helpful, but one does need to go the library to use the index, which will tell you the location of the obituary: in which newspaper(s) on what date(s). Presumably, with enough love and money, some of this information has been put online. If you do not find the information you need online, call the area library and ask if they can help you find the information you need. *Caution: the person you reach might not know the answer.* They might be very sincere and confident but newly hired and of limited experience, so do not accept a dead end. Ask them to pass along your query to another reference librarian (if there is one) or someone (perhaps a library volunteer) who does genealogy. If you do not hear back within two days, call again and find out who has your question.

PHOTO 2.5
Using an obituary. Photo by authors.

Caution: not every death results in a newspaper notice. When you die, for example, if your friends and/or family get permission from the powers-that-be to bury your unembalmed body on rural family property among the graves of your horses and, as you wished, they have a wake just for your family and Facebook friends and you said you did not want an obituary, there won't be an obituary. For one thing, some newspapers now charge for obituaries like they do for advertising. This does not mean, however, that newspapers all around the world will not trumpet the news of your passing. And even if you are not as famous as you think you are, they might still use your unorthodox means of body removal to discuss local burial ordinances or cross-cultural death rituals. So, information about an individual's life and death might be in an obituary and/or a news article or not in a newspaper at all. Another thought: there had to *be* a newspaper for a newspaper to report your death and a witness to your body to tell one of several possible stories about how you/the body came to be at this place. And if it was not an unusual death (we are thinking if you died of cholera in the 1800s and no one was with you when it happened), then it was like the tree fell in the forest with no ears to hear. A dearth of witnesses and printed news sources made it relatively easy for individuals to re-create their identity. Eleanor Pruitt Stewart, for example, took charge of the script of her life. She wrote a book in which she described herself as a widow and her second husband as a bachelor when, in fact, she was divorced and he was a widower.[14]

Why do you want to find obituaries? An obituary usually tells little or nothing about the actual death except the date, which might be useful. It tells you which family members predeceased you and who is still living. It might also give you clues about family relationships. An elderly woman dies, for example. The names of six children are given, but their father is not mentioned. The absence of his name is telling. There was no doubt some ill will between them or at least on her part. The researcher must decide whether this information is important to lead her or him to contact the children and ask about the missing name—not just the name, of course, but why it is missing.

IN SUMMARY AND A FEW MORE THOUGHTS

Research is incredibly fun when you are the one setting the parameters of what you are seeking. As a historian you get to pose your own questions. Forget the drudgery that might have accompanied a school assignment to do research. You are choosing your topic, and you will use your research to craft something important, something useful that will give people pleasure and that will help other historians in their own research. You will fully understand why a dog can focus on nothing else when a squirrel is nearby, because you will drop everything when you see a "new" photo of your historic figure or their home or anything having to do with them. We historians are passionate about our niche. If you have ever had a lengthy conversation with a genealogist then you have met the consummate researcher, the "dig-until-I-die" commitment that is always key to doing the research that results in a strong performance.

As a new researcher you are not starting cold—you are building on skills you use every day. We all routinely do research as we seek information. Whether or not you are aware of it, at any given moment as you listen to a media source (radio, television, or get your news via the computer) or read a print media source (newspaper, news magazine, or from your computer) you are gaining historical information. If you look up a phone number or an address you are doing research. If you access the internet for information you are doing research. Likewise, if you consult a book, manuscript, a map, or a photograph you are gathering data. Whatever the interest, everyone routinely seeks and finds information on a daily basis, we just tend not to give it the academic label of "research."

As you research, look for good stories. What is a good story? Think about yourself—what do you like in a story? Then expand that list while thinking about audience members: What do you know about the people most likely to be attending your historical performances, and what do they like in the stories they read or watch or hear? Then expand to think about others who might be in attendance. As you research, look for stories that will show (as opposed to tell) what you determine to be the most important ideas about your historic figures and their context.

In our workshops, people have brainstormed the following themes and subjects with which some audience members are likely to connect:

- Animals (everyone likes stories about cats, dogs, and horses)
- Conflict (with others, self, and/or nature)
- Overcoming adversity
- Adventure
- Suspense
- Gore and/or violence

- Romance
- Friendship
- Details of daily life
- People who have things in common with me
- Humor
- Aliens (maybe mystery?)

Be aware. Be open to new thoughts. You might have an idea about your person informed by prior knowledge and a source contradicts what you thought you knew. This move is to the more formal focus on a goal to search efforts, adding to or building on the informal research that you probably have already done in the past in your daily interests and inquiries that will help you determine what you want to seek and definitely what you do *not* want to spend time searching for. Remember that it is your agenda; therefore, you want to find data, tidbits, trivia, and the bigger answers to your ponderings, wonderings, and questions that you, as the seeker, want to know. In the classroom setting, the research agenda is often set by the class parameters, and thus the procedures and the outcomes are focused on class survival and a need for a grade. As an independent researcher, you are in the ideal situation: you are working on researching for your historical performance piece—you are in charge of your agenda, you want to satisfy your personal curiosity, and you formulate your questions and then start looking for clues. This search builds on what you know or are interested in as it becomes more thorough and systematic. As you gather ideas and information about your topic, you will probably become more demanding and more clearly oriented on your goals. Remember that at first, everything is new and has a "wow" factor because you are learning. As you gain more familiarity with the material, you will see more repetitions and patterns. You may even start to say, "Wait this says . . . but the last thing I read said. . . ." When that happens, you have become a discerning researcher.

While research can be invigorating, it can, admittedly, also be frustrating. If ever you ask yourself, "Why am I putting myself through this?" remember the "seven ways that history is essential," as identified by the History Relevance Campaign, and feel proud of your role, especially the role you will play when enough of your research is completed that you can corral some stories and share them with an audience. Here are the seven ways identified by the campaign:

1. IDENTITY History nurtures personal identity in an intercultural world. History enables people to discover their own place in the stories of their families, communities, and nation. They learn the stories of the many individuals and groups that have come before them and shaped the world in which they live. There are stories of freedom and equality, injustice and struggle, loss and achievement, and courage and triumph. Through these varied stories, they create systems of personal values that guide their approach to life and relationships with others.

2. CRITICAL SKILLS History teaches critical twenty-first-century skills and independent thinking. The practice of history teaches research, judgment of the accuracy and reliability of sources, validation of facts, awareness of multiple perspectives and biases, analysis of conflicting evidence, sequencing to discern causes, synthesis to present a coherent interpretation, clear and persuasive written and oral communication, and other skills that have been identified as critical to a successful and productive life in the twenty-first century.

3. VITAL PLACES TO LIVE AND WORK History lays the groundwork for strong, resilient communities. No place really becomes a community until it is wrapped in human memory: family stories, tribal traditions, civic commemorations. No place is a community until it has awareness of its history. Our connections and commitment to one another are strengthened when we share stories and experiences.

4. ECONOMIC DEVELOPMENT History is a catalyst for economic growth. People are drawn to communities that have preserved a strong sense of historical identity and character. Cultural heritage is a demonstrated economic asset and an essential component of any vibrant local economy, providing an infrastructure that attracts talent and enhances business development.

5. ENGAGED CITIZENS History helps people craft better solutions. At the heart of democracy is the practice of individuals coming together to express views and take action. By bringing history into discussions about contemporary issues, we can better understand the origins of and multiple perspectives on the challenges facing our communities and nation. This can clarify misperceptions, reveal complexities, temper volatile viewpoints, open people to new possibilities, and lead to more effective solutions for today's challenges.

6. LEADERSHIP History inspires local and global leaders. History provides leaders with inspiration and role models for meeting the complex challenges that face our communities, nation, and the world. It may be a parent, grandparent or distant ancestor, a local or national hero, or someone famous or

someone unknown. Their stories reveal how they met the challenges of their day, which can give new leaders the courage and wisdom to confront the challenges of our time.

7. LEGACY History, saved and preserved, is the foundation for future generations. History is crucial to preserving democracy for the future by explaining our shared past. Through the preservation of authentic, meaningful places, documents, artifacts, images, and stories, we leave a foundation upon which future Americans can build. Without the preservation of our histories, future citizens will have no grounding in what it means to be an American.[15]

Go, research, and be proud of the legacy that *you* are creating and the leadership you are providing. We will see you again in chapter 3.

NOTES

1. Survey by the authors involving costumed historic interpretation students at the University of Central Oklahoma, August 2015.

2. Robert McKee, *Story: Substance, Structure, Style, and the Principles of Screenwriting* (New York: HarperCollins, 1997), 75.

3. Carl L. Becker, "Everyman His Own Historian," American Historical Association Review Presidential Address, *American Historical Review* 37, no. 2 (January 1932): 221–36, https://www.historians.org/about-aha-and-membership/aha-history-and -archives/presidential-addresses/carl-l-becker (accessed July 31, 2017).

4. Yudhijit Bhattacharjee, "Why We Lie," *National Geographic* 231, no. 62 (June 2017): 38.

5. Susan A. Crane, "Historical Subjectivity: A Review Essay," *Journal of Modern History* 78, no. 2 (June 2006): 434, https://doi.org/10.1086/505803 (accessed July 23, 2017).

6. Charles F. Bryan Jr., *Imperfect Past: History in a New Light* (Manakin-Sabot, VA: Dementi Milestone Publishing, 2015), quoted by Bob Beatty, "From the Editor," *History News: The Magazine of the American Association for State and Local History* 71, no. 4 (2016): 2

7. Joyce Thierer, "How to Choose a Historic Figure to Portray," in *Telling History: A Manual for Performers and Presenters of First-Person Narratives* (Lanham, MD: AltaMira Press, 2010), 35–46.

8. David E. Kyvig and Myron A. Marty, *Nearby History: Exploring the Past Around You*, 3rd ed. (Lanham, MD: AltaMira Press, 2010), 22, 25.

9. Tom Dudzick, *Miracle on South Division Street* (Playscripts Inc.).

10. L. Morris, "The Little Girl across the Street." Typescript memoir of Emporia State University Library and Archive.

11. Terri Summey, "Emotional Intelligence as a Framework for Reference and Information Competencies," poster session, Emporia State University Research and Creativity Day, April 27, 2017; conversation with authors, July 29, 2017 (authors have notes). Contact Dr. Summey at 620-341-5058 or Tsummey@emporia.edu.

12. Everett D. Graff, *Hard Knocks: A Life Story of the Vanishing West* (1915), accessed through the Newberry Library's American West database, July 30, 2017, http://www.americanwest.amdigital.co.uk.emporiastate.idm.oclc.org/Documents/Images/Graff_4789/97#Chapters.

13. Tamar Jeffers McDonald, "Carrying Concealed Weapons: Gendered Makeover in Calamity Jane," *Journal of Popular Film and Television*, Winter 2007.

14. Susanne K. George, *The Adventures of The Woman Homesteader: The Life and Letters of Elinore Pruitt Stewart* (Lincoln: University of Nebraska Press, 1992), found the documents and did chronological calculations that led her to construct an account of Elinore Pruitt Stewart's life that was even more impressive than that Stewart wrote for publication in *Letters of a Woman Homesteader* (Boston: Houghton Mifflin, 1913).

15. History Relevance Campaign, https://www.historyrelevance.com/value-history-statement (accessed July 31, 2017).

Designing Your Performance

"While research provides material it's no substitute for creativity."[1] As we said in the preface, this chapter is more for performers than for presenting organizations—and more for performers who have been working on their writing for some time and need to reframe their effort. But, presenting organizations, know that your performers have given great thought to your audiences. Think of performance as a present. The performer thinks about your audience members, even if they are strangers to the performer, and spends time selecting just the right gift, the right stories, for your audience, a gift that ends up expressing the highest hopes and values of your organization as well as those of the historic figure, the audience, and the performer.

As the performer-to-be, you have done your research, learning far more about your historic person and her or his context than you will use in any given performance. You now have authority. But you want more. You want confidence in delivering a well-constructed presentation. That confidence is what will let you wear the mantle of authority comfortably—maybe even with a bit of flare. You know that you know a lot. You know that no one can know everything. And you want the comfort that comes in knowing that you are able to share what you know in a way that pleases others. In this chapter, we discuss the power that you have in designing performances. You select stories, you shape them, and you structure your entrance and exit to fit a setting that will support your stories. And as you select, shape, and structure, you do so with your own ability and interests in mind as well as the interests of a broad range of audiences.

First-person narratives are amazingly empowering. You know this. Pauline Sharp portrays her grandmother, Lucy Tayiah Eads, the only woman elected chief of the Kaw Nation, serving from 1922 to 1934. Pauline was recently juried into the Kansas Alliance of Professional Historical Performers. "Never in my wildest dreams did I ever think I would find the courage to do this."[2] It is the stories that make us do it. As a performer, you connect with each audience, but even more, the stories you have crafted and delivered in a compelling way connect with the audience. You share the power of the stories with your audience members. If you have not yet experienced it, you have seen it in other historical performers. It is the power to make a difference in people's lives by sharing with them your understanding of historical truth that motivates you to bring history's stories to life through historical performance instead of through another means of sharing history's stories.

Leslie Bedford describes storytelling as the most authentic thing about museums: "Stories are the most fundamental way we learn. . . . They teach without preaching, encouraging both personal reflection and public discussion. Stories inspire wonder and awe; they allow a listener to imagine another time and place, to find the universal in the particular, and to feel empathy for others. They preserve individual and collective memory and speak to both the adult and the child."[3]

In *Telling History*, Joyce takes readers through the process of creating a script, including sorting and prioritizing information, determining the setting for the performance, converting information into stories, and organizing the stories and transitions. In this book, we presume that you have begun that process, perhaps even taken your show on the road a few times, and that you are thinking about how to modify your performance for the audiences you have had and to increase your bookings by diversifying your possible audiences, helping more people understand that they would like to experience your performances or those of other historical performers.

Perhaps, though, you are still surrounded by piles and files of research findings and your fears are keeping you from making a commitment to perform on a particular date. You are stuck in limbo between researching and sharing. You fear the stage, especially beyond the edge of the stage, which might as well be the edge of the earth, where, as we all suspect, "there will be monsters." After all, you have never been there before, so how do you know there are *not* monsters? And if others have been there and returned, well, *they* are not *you*. So before we address anything else, let's take on those monsters head-on. After all, the pen *is* mightier than the sword, so we *are* well armed.

WRITING FOR THE KLONGS

A klong has been described as "a sudden rush of shit to the heart," a blood-chilling, heart-stopping moment as you realize your own utter failure.[4] It has happened to both of us a time or two, and we are guessing that you, too, know the feeling: life is perking along just fine, and then you suddenly discover that you failed someone in a big way. You forgot your daughter's college graduation ceremony after promising her that you would be there. Or, as an example more appropriate for this chapter, you suddenly realize or remember that most members of your audience are vegetarians and you have begun to tell them, in character, how to kill, slaughter, and use all of the parts of a buffalo. *Telling History* has business practices that should decrease the likelihood of scheduling catastrophes, so we have already taken care of double booking or not showing up for a booked performance. Here, we deal with terrors about the performance itself. Our goal is to make your future in historical performance klong free.

You have done your research, so you know the most likely places where your person might be encountering a group of people in their day—and your audience today will take the role of that audience "back then." Where are you meeting? When are you meeting? What are the circumstances? You are the one who determines that. As a historical performer who writes your own script, you are in control. As historical performers, we have so much power that we can afford to give some of the good stuff back to the audience. Imagination gives us the empathy that helps us love our subject and our audience. That means that we put our "all" into creating and delivering a performance. We pour love out to the audience, and they love us back.

If you have a few "what-ifs" buzzing at you, that is not entirely a bad thing because it makes you more likely to prepare carefully and have an edginess to your performance that is very realistic: after all, most of us are performing people who were risk takers of one sort or another, so we are risk takers portraying risk takers. It's all good. And a performance without energy is a dull performance. But only fools do not examine their risks before taking them.

PHOTO 3.1
An appreciative Chautauqua audience. Photo by authors.

And we are not fools, so we include our concerns in the initial design of our performances. If you have no such concerns, skip over this but know that the advice is here in case the monster bites you in the butt when your back is turned. It is useful to face in daylight the worst that can happen and examine that worst thing closely.

Often, a "worst thing" has to do with fear. Fear of what? Fear of being unable to speak? Fear of forgetting something you were going to say? Fear of an intimidating and therefore totally distracting audience member? Fear of totally running out of energy midway through? Fear of not being able to answer questions? Let's lay it all out: Fear of peeing in your pants or other physical distresses? Fear of having "no one" in your audience? Fear of the audience walking out on you? Fear of the sound equipment not being provided or not working?

What is that worst thing for you? "I will make a fool of myself onstage." Write your worst thing or things predicting failure on a piece of paper and tear the messages into tiny pieces and toss them into the trash (not recycling—

you do not want them to pop up again). Repeat this process as often as necessary. Or project your worst fear(s) onto an inanimate object, such as a cute plush toy sabertooth tiger, nothing you are likely to see embodied in your living room. Hug that sabertooth cat and for the fun of it name it after your worst fear. Now that fear is not so scary, is it? Examine your fear minutely. Imagine how that worst thing would come to pass. Then reflect on how likely it is that that worst thing will happen? Will the likelihood vary? In other words, as you are writing your script, you do not need to worry about being so hoarse that an audience cannot hear you—unless you are chronically hoarse, in which case start figuring out how to use throat sprays and lozenges and by all means get your own sound system so you can depend on it. Such fears that are related to logistics (Will I have enough time to go to the bathroom or eat before my performance? Have I packed enough handkerchiefs?) can be prepared ahead of time and headed off at the pass. "Fear," according to Carla Marie Manly, "is two-faced; we are accustomed to seeing only one aspect of fear—its frightening side. When we smile at our fears and look at them with curiosity, we gain control over the fear—and fear loses its power over us."[5] "Without nervousness you might not have the optimal amount of adrenal to perform effectively."[6]

Remember that the fact that you write your own script means that you can deal in advance with any of those worst things that could happen. During filming of *Bionic Blonde*, the leading male actor, who was to have resumed his own fighting stunts, broke his arm. He (and the director) came up with the idea of issuing him with what looked like a period cast and to continue filming, having written the injury into the script.[7]

We were going to say that historical performers are lucky because we get to tell the audience who they are. It is not, however, about luck. It is our craft. We write the script, so we determine the setting. We get to describe the space where we meet the audience. Is it a saloon? Is it Rachel Carson's yard in Silver Spring, Maryland? Is it a classroom? A conference center? Inside our home? At a theater? At our homestead along the Santa Fe Trail? In the employees' break room? A campfire?

We also decide who our audience is. Are they friends? Members of the local garden club? History students? Physics students? Our grandchildren? Members of the public who have come to hear a lecture? Sojourners west who need a place to stay along the trail? Coworkers? Our military unit?

When in history is this meeting of historic figure and audience to our musings happening? During one of the most significant events in our life? Shortly after that event? After all but the final significant event (our death)? (Have we mentioned that we never, ever die onstage or appear as ghosts? We will leave that to other forms of costumed historical interpretation.)

We decide how we enter the space where the audience awaits us. How will we (always as our historic figure) greet our audience? The audience is not passive. Its members are part of our play. We give them cues as to their response to us. Do we recognize them immediately? Do we know they have been awaiting our arrival? Are we late? Where are we coming from? Where are we going from here?

About the moving onstage and off, we've been reading Viola Spolin's *Theater Games for the Lone Actor.* One of her games is "Exits and Entrances," in which you "present yourself to whomever is present in a room when you enter and when you exit." She says, "Each entrance or exit must be so framed that those present are fully involved (connected) with you at that moment. If you barge in or out without such full involvement, you didn't make it. . . ." Then she has her students analyze their entrances and exits: "Which . . . truly had full involvement and which were only attempts at getting attention?"[8]

That engaged movement onstage and off has become a Ride into History trademark, and we want to help you understand why it is effective and therefore important. For one thing, such involvement from even before you reach the stage helps dispel nervousness because you are focused on the audience instead of yourself. There is great power in a good entrance—the right entrance to introduce the essence of your historic figure to your audience, real and in their role. Be real—be your historic figure focusing on her or his audience at that other place and time. Imagine yourself in an audience seeing your historic figure make each of the following entrances:

- Standing onstage while the audience enters and is seated.
- Walking onstage after the audience is seated.
- Coming onstage after a formal introduction to you as a historical performer.
- Coming onstage after a formal introduction to your historic figure.
- Coming from the back of the audience walking toward the stage, stopping to greet people as the historic figure.
- Running in from the back or the side of the auditorium.

- Starting your narrative offstage to "someone" there, your character not knowing that the audience hears you.
- Having a musical entrée to your performance.

Experiment with these in your head, then try a few with a small group of friends or colleagues. Analyze what worked for them and for you. What seemed natural, and at what points were you pulled out of character to struggle with what you were going to say or do next?

Rule: when that worst thing happens, if that worst thing happens (and remember, it is not likely that it will), it must happen to your historic figure and not to you. This works for anticipated events, but it also works for spontaneous events that are difficult to anticipate, originating from forces beyond your control. Projectile vomiting by a child in the first row of bleachers? Really? When you are truly in character, it is just a matter of staying in character. What would Amelia Earhart have done? She would graciously offer to help clean up, then bring her audience's attention away from the mess with a

PHOTO 3.2
Trying out a new approach on a friendly but honest audience. Photo by authors.

compelling story. Never mind the bit of splatter on your boots—you can deal with that later. A tornado siren sounds during a carnival (when you thought the Tilt-a-Whirl noise was enough of a challenge)? In character, you lead the audience into the nearest shelter and distract a now larger audience with a compelling story. Most things can be handled by staying in character and focusing on your audience. There is a "we're all in this together" sense of camaraderie in which the sponsors appreciate the calm mastery of your craft, which makes you flexible and unflappable.

But what about those other fears—the ones that you do anticipate and the ones that are related to your own perceived shortcomings? If you can anticipate a fear, you can anticipate the means to head off the fear. Again, this is your script, your knowledge, and *you are in charge.*

CRAFTING A SETTING THAT WORKS FOR YOU

The first and most important task you have is to craft the setting to your advantage. Determine a time and place when a worst thing might have happened—or is feared to about to happen—to your historic figure or composite character. This will provide you with a liminal time when things are not as they usually are. At such a time, your historic figure might be more willing to speak more freely than usual. Maybe you will confess to your audience that "this is a most difficult time for me as you know, so we might as well talk about it." In Amelia Earhart's case, she had wrecked her plane taking off on the second leg of her flight around the world at the equator and was now back in the United States waiting for it to be prepared. She has to give a lot of talks to make enough money to repair the plane, but she also has to be ready to go as soon as it is fixed. This being a liminal time allows her to run into the auditorium late, wearing scuffed-up aviator garb instead of the dress and shoes that she would ordinarily have worn when giving one of the talks that was a primary source of her income. It also lets Ann have a few seconds to gather her thoughts onstage while laying down her pack and reaching into the pocket of her leather jacket to switch on her wireless microphone. "[Takes a couple of breaths.] Well, I *am* Amelia Earhart, and this *is* April 14, 1937, so we are in [a pause while Amelia pictures the sign on the edge of town], we are in Wichita. So I am at the right place at the right time. A little late. And I do apologize, but my itinerary says I am in India today, not back in my home state of Kansas [or wherever]."

Help the audience immediately engage with your historic figure by presenting them with a time in history when your character was angry, sad, or scared to the point of tears, when the historic figure cannot help but share the story of that emotion with the audience before moving on to explain how we got to this place. Go with it. Make sure, of course, that you have a handkerchief appropriate to your era (or tissues if you are in the latter half of the twentieth century). Practice dabbing at your eyes and blowing your nose in front of the mirror. How would your historic figure handle that challenge?

We do not know if Norman Joy's selection of setting for his audiences to meet General Robert E. Lee had anything to do with a fear, but it is an excellent example of a liminal space in time and place. Lee has spent his entire adult life in the military, the first thirty-two years in the U.S. Army, then as commander of the Confederate Army of Northern Virginia during the Civil War, always in uniform. When we meet him, he is not sure what his future holds, no longer sure of his identity. He apologizes to us, his family, for his lack of a plan. He does not even know if he has clothing appropriate for whatever it is he will be doing today or tomorrow. He is in his home—a place where he has always been known for his absences, not his presence. So do you understand what is happening here? No matter what happens to historical performer Joy, we know him as "General Lee" or, rather "civilian Lee," who is going through a very bad time. If he should break down and weep, it will be Lee who does so, understandably. It will be part of the performance. If he apologizes and leaves the "room," it will be Lee leaving, not Joy, and the audience remains comfortable, trusting the performance to continue—which it must. The show, as we know, must go on.

We have had such things happen to young people and once to an adult, all first-timers doing what would probably be a one-time local history performance. In two of the three cases, the audience presumed it was staged. The first was a young person portraying a newspaper editor who said his wife had recently died. When shortly thereafter the editor began crying, it was relatively simple to go onstage and help him (really her) off, reminding the audience about that recent death and saying that we hoped he would be able to come back and visit with them again. After about eight more performers went on, the editor went on, and we almost did not get him offstage, he had so much to say. We were worried that there would not be time for everyone to go onstage again to take questions.

Many audience members still do not realize that when Dianne, the owner of a shooting preserve, who was making sure there was a rifle for the governor when he arrived and still had to bake a cake for dinner, faced the audience squarely and said, "I just cannot do this"; it was the historical performer, not the historic figure speaker (Flossie). It fit the script and what some of them knew of this person's life, but in truth the temporary historian had said she would try—and she did try, and then she spoke her feelings and left the stage. Tears followed, but the audience thought they were Flossie's tears, not Dianne's.

A third performance was one that would have been great if we had pulled it off. As it was, it did at least save the ego of a young performer (we think). A very young (fourth-grade) lieutenant colonel was having difficulty onstage during the dress rehearsal. We told him that, if necessary, when he was on-stage and unable to find his stories in his head, he could reach into his left pocket to feel the piece of paper that would remind him to mumble "shell shock." He could then exit the stage, and after everyone else had crossed in character, he could read his script from backstage, using a handheld wireless microphone. The officer's voice confidently coming over the theater's speakers would be an interesting change of format. He read his script well, but even out in the hallway, we could hear audience members getting restless. It turned out they could not hear and were waiting for something to happen. Unfortunately, our otherwise crackerjack sound tech had forgotten about the change. It took what felt like an eon to find her, to announce something from the stage that put the audience back in their seats, and to have the young historian read it again. At least he did get to perform—and he went onstage with his colleagues for the question-and-answer session.

Ann's first performance was several years after Joyce's, and like Joyce, she had no drama experience, but she had observed Joyce's process in creating Calamity Jane and the processes of two graduate students whom Joyce recruited to do composite characters. (Joyce was forty when she began performing, and Ann was forty-two, so we had some life experience to throw into the mix.) Anyway, Ann decided to present an 1894 Kansas suffragist to the Chase County Craft Festival audience. Advantages: she was familiar with primary sources from the era as well as having done some research into nineteenth-century gender roles, and had found stories that would surprise and please the anticipated audience, including one that involved the belief among members of the late nineteenth-century medical establishment that riding astride caused a loss of virginity, and with little time to prepare, she had to know more than her audience members about her topic, spending much time on research. However, as she started threading her stories into a script and picturing how she wanted the audience to react to each story, it occurred to her that she could very well be setting herself up for harassment from smart alecks who wanted to represent the antisuffrage contingent. If she proclaimed, "1894 will go down in history as the year that the men of Kansas gave the women of the most progressive state in the nation the right to vote in state and national elections!" would there be those who disagreed just to be ornery? How to deal with the possibility of one or more hecklers? She did not want to turn her performance into a debate. Nor did she want to give up the stage to audience members, even though with direct address they were "part of" the play.

Ann's solution was to tell the audience members that they were all members of the Kansas Equal Suffrage Association. This would put hecklers out of business, but even though men were members of the association, they of course would not want to be like the livery stable owner who told her that "it is no more proper for a woman to vote than it is for one to ride by herself on horseback across the countryside." "It is such a relief to be among like-minded people, especially after the day I have had."

YOU ARE IN CHARGE

Anticipate your worst thing and write it out of existence. Are you afraid you will go blank and not remember your first line? Don't worry about it—prepare for it. Another rule: *Your first line, or any line, can be anything related to your character or her or his historic context. Say something. Your audience does not know that the line, or story, you just used is not the one you intended to use. Stay calm, say something, and recalibrate*—take another turn, and eventually you will make it back to where you wanted to be. In the meantime, practice that first line over and over just before you go on.

Another way to prepare for the possibility of forgetting your opening: give the person who will introduce you a written script (a good idea no matter what). Write into that introduction a bit of dialogue, a prompt that will get you off and talking: "Thank you so much for making time for us, Madam Walker. We especially look forward to hearing your thoughts on philanthropy." The reply to which might be, "Thank you for your kind words, and

Table 3.1. Entrances—How Ride Gets Onstage and Why Each Entrance Is Used

Historic Figure	Entrance	Reason for Entrance
Grower	Tribal flute music plays during entry. Walks on with digging stick, turns, and greets audience with "Hi-ho. I am Grower of the people of the south wind."	Music suggests the village, her people, nearby.
Civil War soldier	Music "Just before the battle, Mother," fades, and Jo's voice comes up as she walks onstage looking down at saddle soap can and rag, muttering, "Go, don't go; go, don't go." Shares her quandary with audience, her neighbors.	Jo's decision-making is front and center, and her dilemma foreshadows her telling of her parents' decision-making.
Julia Archibald Holmes	Julia stands casually by an 1850s saddle as the "president" of the literary society introduces her as Julia Holmes of Washington, D.C., the first woman to climb to the top of Pike's Peak (she enters with the emcee).	Stories are framed by Julia's life after Kansas Territory— her identity as a poet; Ann no longer feared stage fright.
"Settling in the Territory"	Mary Fix walks into the space calling for her daughter Rosa. Finding travelers, she invites them to rest and assures the men that her husband and sons will soon be up from the field for supper. She will prepare a simple meal for a minimal fee, and it is so *good* to see another woman.	Establishes rapport while describing isolated setting and her familial context.
Calamity Jane	Roars into the space, usually from side of stage or behind the audience, with her saddle on her shoulder, demanding of an audience member, "I see you have a writing utensil. Are you a reporter?!"	Great energy! Be in command of the space! Overwhelm the audience that terrifies you!
"Elizabeth Hampstead"	Starts speaking offstage: "To think that a man like that can vote for president and I cannot, just because I am a woman. And now, what am I going to do with this side saddle!?" Moves onstage, carrying the saddle, and sees the audience, moment of realization, then:, "Oh, hello! You must be members of the Kansas Equal Suffrage Association come to greet me before my lecture this evening!"	Ann's first character and first theater experience; beginning backstage before seeing the audience decreased fear—and she knows she will have no hecklers because they are all "like-minded people."
"Cattle Tales"	Georgiana Jackson stomps onto stage, throws her leather chaps down, comments on her antipathy toward the banker, then notices there are potential buyers for her stock (the audience), so apologizes.	We want to know how she came to be so angry at the banker and what choices she will make.
"How Can You Keep 'Em Down on the Farm"	We sometimes use a recording of the World War I song before Joyce strides in with her iron hoe and talks about her grandson fighting in France and how even the malicious tractor he had them buy might not be enough to convince him to come back to farming.	Establishes parallels between soldiers' struggles "over there" and those on the home front; we are neighbors.

Historic Figure	Entrance	Reason for Entrance
Amelia Earhart	Amelia earned her living giving talks, so this is just another one, with the emcee introducing her, but she has not yet shown up. "I hope she is not lost." Earhart *runs* into the space, probably from behind the audience, usually slamming a door to emphasize coming into the building.	Running = energy *and* allows gasping for air in front of the audience, which will disguise nervousness.
Rachel Carson	The "President of the Silver Springs Garden Club" welcomes members and guests and tells them why they are all in Rachel Carson's front yard, also thanking the early comers for writing out questions for Miss Carson. We hear Rachel calling "Roger! Roger!" before we see her. The emcee hands the cards with questions to Carson, who speaks a bit about Roger, then peruses the questions, putting them in order.	After Carson's best-known book was published, she was very ill with cancer, not leaving home. Roger was her adopted thirteen-year-old great nephew, so we are also establishing early on that she has a family.

I do intend to tell you what I think about philanthropy, but first I need to tell you how an incident in my childhood led me to. . . ," or you start in on philanthropy and loop back to your childhood: "And that is why it is so important for me to help children now that I have the means to do so."

Another option, one that we do not recommend for professionals, is to arrange to have someone come onstage as a reporter to interview you. Do not, however, write that reporter into your script if you are a professional or plan to make some or all of your living from historical performance because costs and date conflicts will limit your bookings and income. Besides, you want your audience to have the experience of you addressing them directly, without a surrogate. If, on the other hand, you have a groupie who will be traveling with you, at least initially, it is okay to arrange a cue that will bring them onstage or speaking from the front row with a list of questions. You could even subtly make your setting a press conference.

Joyce's very first performance, from which Ride into History grew, was born from fear. She was teaching college classes while completing a doctoral degree that would let her be a "real" university professor. She was contracted to give a series of lectures to earn some summer money to secondary school teachers. Every time she thought about being in front of those teachers, however, she thought of them ignoring her and disrespecting her knowledge as her own teachers had when she was a student. The solution was to meet them as Calamity Jane on horseback. Careful scripting meant that she could involve them while remaining in charge.

In Ann's case, a very realistic fear of an equestrian embarrassment while on side saddle inspired her to write into her script that her 1894 suffragist had "not ridden horseback for a good many years . . . and then I rode [pause and whisper confidentially] astride." That way, if the A-frame Western side saddle designed for nineteenth-century high-withered horses started shifting on her barrel-shaped horse, she could jump off and continue from the ground with no pride lost. It happened to Elizabeth, not to Ann. It was planned, you know.

Horse as Teddy Bear

We were sitting at a very long table in the basement of the Admire Methodist Church, enjoying breakfast cooked by the church's men's group to raise funds for local projects. The subject of the upcoming annual North Lyon County Historical Performance Camp came up. A stranger leaned forward from a few seats away and asked what we were talking about. We explained that we were going to be interpreting the nearby town of Allen by having the audience walk up and down Main Street to meet the historic figures. She proclaimed, "I want to do that!" Her only stipulation was that she get help finding a story that would let her ride up on her horse, Teddy Bear. The woman and her soon-to-be-retired-from-the-army husband had recently purchased an acreage two miles from Allen, and they were eager to learn the area's history. Most of our audience members enjoy horses, so we were quite pleased with the proposition that our troupe include a teddy bear.

Oh, yes—the peeing-in-your-pants fear? Make sure your costume has room for something absorbent. And if you have a cold, be sure to not only treat your throat but also have a stash of era-appropriate nose wipes on hand.[9] Now, enough about fear. Be confident, but first, be prepared. Think about the possibility, prepare for it, and get on with preparing something really wonderful for your audience.

WRITE YOUR AUDIENCE INTO A LIMINAL SETTING

In creating something really wonderful for her audience, instead of writing her historic figure into a liminal state, Teresa Bachman placed her *audience* in that liminal place. Bachman was "Gladys the Riveter," who worked on Boeing

B-29s during World War II. Her audience was a group of new hires whom she was orienting. In addition to studying secondary sources, Bachman had interviewed her great aunt Gladys to create the composite character based on her relatives' experiences (three sisters worked in the plant) and visited the plant. She understood the setting that she wanted. She knew when and where she and the audience would meet and what roles each would play.

Like Calamity Jane, there was no doubt that Gladys was in charge when she arrived in front of her audience. Scratch that. Actually, Bachman made no "entrance." Her audience entered to see Gladys in blue coveralls and a red bandana on a ladder with a very loud rivet gun that Bachman had recorded at a Boeing plant. To encounter her audience, she had only to stop riveting (while someone pulled the plug on the "shop" noise), turn around, and greet the new hires, coming down from her ladder and picking up a clipboard with her list of everything they needed to know—and more than was on the official list. Gladys told them that while they should be commended for wanting to help with the war effort and save the lives of American soldiers, the new hires should also know that the gloves they would be given were too large and therefore more dangerous than working without gloves and that their supervisor was dangerous—avoid being alone with him. They should also know that male workers resented that the women were there at all, much less that they were paid as much as men.

All Teresa had to do if she panicked was to look at the clipboard. And if the clipboard had disappeared, well, what would Gladys do? Her responsibility was orienting the new hires, so she could begin anywhere in the process of telling them what they needed to know. And goodness knows, they would need all the help they could get from her. No one need know because no one else had a copy of what was on the clipboard—or what was on Gladys's mind.

Rule number three (you have heard this from us before, but it is a good one): *if you stop and look thoughtful, your audience will think that it is your historic figure thinking and that you are a very realistic actor, not that you have forgotten where you were going.* Always allow some silence. Even if you don't need it to remember something, audience members will appreciate it because it gives them a chance to catch up. Your pacing should include speeding up, slowing down, *and* silence. Imagine Amelia Earhart describing her solo flight across the Atlantic as she scans the audience in three sections—right, center, and left—ending in a new section of the audience

PHOTO 3.3
Asking for help and getting it. Photo by authors.

with each word emphasized: "[looking right] Just when I *thought* [one beat, another beat, then scan toward center] that everything that *could* go wrong [3/4 beat, scan to left] *had* gone wrong [back to center, tap leather jacket on shoulder three beats while looking up], I had a leak in the fuel gauge, fuel dripping down on me. . . ." This word pacing was not born of cleverness. It was born from a fear of getting the phrasing wrong. This was one of those stories where Ann wanted to use exact wording to build suspense. Rhythm was important. She could have said very quickly, "Just when I thought that everything that could go wrong had gone wrong," but fortunately, because she feared that she would invert the phrases to make something nonsensical, "Just when I thought that everything that had gone wrong could go wrong," she practiced it really slowly and heard the magic that resulted from slowing the pacing and allowing carefully spaced silence.

It does not take much silence to create suspense. Imagine. You are sitting in a small auditorium. The emcee has praised to the roof the amazing accomplishments of the speaker, who is still out of sight. The emcee gives the cue:

"Please join me in welcoming [our most accomplished speaker]." Thunderous applause, but nothing happens. No speaker.

Actually, something does happen to a count of two. Suspense happens. The emcee says, "We thought we heard her come in," and sends someone out to look for the speaker. This is not rolling out the way it "always" does. The speaker always strides out onto the stage long before this point. Where is the speaker? Has something happened to the speaker?

Suspense = excitement = engagement. Use it. You are in control of the audience's experience. If you are convinced that you are going to break down onstage, use it. Just be sure that from the audience's perspective, it is the historic figure coming in late, not you. The historic figure should apologize and explain what is going on just now in her or his life.

Maybe your scenario does not involve a formal speaking engagement. Maybe the introduction or the playbill helped the audience understand that they are in an outdoor setting. Audience members are waiting for the person who will transport them to their next stop. They are in danger but not at the moment. They hear a wagon creak, horses snort, and harness jingle. They begin to think their conveyance is near, but it seems to have stopped. Then they hear someone reassuring the horses. They hear what sounds like someone blowing their nose. Then someone strides into our space (the stage) and begins to address us as people who are fleeing. That person, however, loses control of emotion and speaks instead as one who has just suffered a great loss. Who is this? What was their loss? Suspense.

COMPELLING STORIES COME FROM CHOICES

You have researched until you have exhausted your sources, or the resources with which to pursue more sources (hoping the material from a particular archive will be digitized and online soon so that you do not need to invest in flights, ground transportation, meals, and lodging). You have found the kernel of stories that you are convinced will connect with audiences. It is time to decide what information you will include in your monologue. What will make it to the stage and into your audience's ears, and what will end up, as they say in the movie editing business, on the cutting room floor?

Actually, the creative process of a historical performer during the script-writing stage might be less like that of a film editor than that of a sculptor. First, you are a modeler of clay, selecting handfuls of material and fashioning them to fit your vision, and then you are more like the sculptor of marble or wood, removing excess until the form you envision is revealed (and because it is no more than about fifty minutes long, without the discussion, there will be a lot of excess).

As we said in chapter 2, no matter who is in your audience, many (and, hopefully, most) will like the same content that you enjoy in a story or the content that your trial audience likes. The list includes humor, adventure, conflict, animals, and romance. Be bold, be brave, but be useful. We often talk about script writing, but what you are doing is learning stories as much as it is writing a script.

And as we said in chapter 1, every performance has three components: the performer, the message, and the audience. Sometimes, we think of the performer as the star of the show ("Doesn't she play beautifully?!"). This is because for too many people, their only experience with the arts is attending children's school offerings or watching contests on television, the culture of fandom. Ideally, however, it is the message, the story, the music that brings

PHOTO 3.4
What will interest your audience? Photo by authors.

the performer and the audience together. And for the performer, the most important thing is that she or he convey that message—interpret that message so
well that the audience forgets the performer and is transported by the message,
what Samuel Taylor Coleridge called "the willing suspension of disbelief."[10]

People who study the humanities are all about questions. What more can
I learn about the decisions that this individual made *and* about the context
within which she or he made those decisions? Who were the people around
her, and what decisions were they making that affected her choices? The more
we understand the people we portray, the more we really "get" their decisions
and the more we feel *their* emotions instead of our own petty fear of the audience. In other words, at some point, the decision of what stories to tell must
become that of our historic figure. I must become Amelia deciding whether
members of this audience, these very young people she sees in front of her,
are old enough to understand her description of the wounded soldiers who
inspired her to volunteer as a nursing aide during World War I.

An actor being interviewed on National Public Radio insisted that her
character had *no* choices; she *had* to do the things she did.[11] That may be true
of a fictional character, but it is not true of real people. We might not like the
choices that we have, but we have choices (consider Toni Morrison's novel
Beloved, based on a true event in which a woman who had escaped slavery
and then is recaptured attempts to kill her children and herself[12]).

A friend of ours (we will call her Gloria) was complaining because her son
(we will call him John) was "making" her move. She had had a series of "small
strokes," and he was worried about her because she lived about four hours
away from him. John wanted Gloria to move from her home in a university
city to the tiny rural town at the other end of the state where he lived with
his family. It was going to work, he thought, because she could afford to buy
the nicest house in town with room enough for all of her research materials
and built-in bookcases for the books that continued to arrive —most of them
on history, politics, and geography. Even the nicest senior living facility—the
best one in the state with impressive programming for retired professors (we
will call it Eagles Nest)—could not provide enough room for the objects that
gave our friend her identity as a scholar. Gloria kept saying that she had no
choice in the matter. We quickly figured out that what she was doing was
abdicating control and blaming her son. We reminded her that she did have
a choice: she could go along with John's suggestion, or she could resist and

stay in her current home. It really was her choice to stay or go. She was also choosing whether to keep her library, how safe she wanted to be, and how important it was for her to provide John with peace of mind. She could move to Eagles Nest, where she would be physically safe and remain in the university town with friends nearby, but she would need to give up her library. If she moved to be closer to John, she would be able to take all of her research, and by letting John take care of her, she would be a very generous mother to a son who had not been actively involved in her life for a good many years. We all have choices in our lives. We might dislike making a choice, or we might choose to give the choice to others, but even the latter is a choice. If we abdicate a decision, we are still making a choice—the choice to abdicate.

Ride into History's Definition of History

History is the story of the decisions we have made over time, and it is the story of how we have explained those decisions.

Finding the place where our historic figures made important decisions and figuring out how they made them, how their decision-making processes are similar to and different from our own, and how their decisions changed history—makes good stories. It helps us all think about our own decisions and their ramifications.

WRITING KINDLY FOR AN AUDIENCE

Don't talk like (most) college professors. Generally, historians who teach in colleges use three styles of oral presentation. The first is reading, which they use primarily when presenting papers at a conference of their peers. They literally step in front of their audience and rapidly read an esoteric/just-the-facts-ma'am paper for about fifteen minutes with little or no audience eye contact. There will be three or four such papers presented during a session of an hour or an hour and a half, followed by discussion (often challenges to the professors' findings) for as long as there is time in the session.

Those same academics traditionally use a lecture format in their classroom. The professor looks down at notes or up at a PowerPoint and occasionally seems to notice that there are students in the room. We think it safe to say that most college students do not wonder where their teachers came from or what training they had to have. They presume that like their high school teachers, college professors took education courses. And some students peevishly complain that college teachers do not teach "right." They expect to be taught the same way their high school teachers had taught them—the way that teacher education students are learning to teach. The students do not understand that a college teacher is an expert in their subject matter, not an expert in teaching.

Chautauquans are historical performers who come out of the academic (college) tradition. The Chautauqua tradition is text based, which means that works written, say, a century or more ago are either spoken from behind a podium, as would be a speech, or memorized, especially if the Chautauquan is on the drama faculty. As a historical performer, however, you are creating a space in which you, as your historic figure, will be talking with the audience, not lecturing at them. There is a flow to the spoken word that differs from the flow of the written word, even written dialogue.

A major difference between written and spoken text is that written text, even audio-recorded text, can be "replayed." If you have ever spaced out while reading or been surprised by the mention of a character you do not remember encountering in a book, you know that you can always flip back through the pages until the problem is solved—you read the paragraphs you missed, or you locate the earlier mention of the name and then you settle back into the story. Even during a classroom lecture with an informal professor, you might have permission—and the gall—to raise your hand, interrupting the flow of the lecture, and say, "Excuse me, but you just mentioned XYZ and I have no idea what XYZ is," hoping that it was not in the assigned reading.

It is hoped that when you are performing, no one will thusly interrupt you, especially if you have worked into your introduction that you will take questions afterward. But we need to build into our performances explanations of unfamiliar words and repetitions of important phrases, especially if someone coughs or comes into the room at a crucial time. Ann built into her Amelia Earhart script the date of her setting and even her name—twice, in addition to the buildup that the emcee's introduction provides, to accommodate the person who comes in late and misses the introduction?"

If you are like Ann, you will write down every word that you intend to say and then, with experience, change individual parts out until you no longer have a written script that reads like she sounds. If you are like Joyce, you will use key words to remember stories and not actually write the script out until you have done many performances and have a script that you know is a "keeper." No one is going to ask you for a copy of your script, so do not worry about having one presentable to a member of the public. The only script that is important is the one you share verbally with the audience, the first-person stories you tell, and you want those stories to sound natural, as recalled from memory.

Surprise, but do *not* shock for the sake of shocking. Amelia Earhart had an agreement with her publicist/husband George Palmer Putnam: he could book her for as many talks as he could get into a week, but she got to say what she liked, and what she liked sometimes discomfited her audience. She told the Daughters of the Revolution, for example (having warned them in advance), that if they were going to openly support war, then they should be in the trenches fighting next to men. Women should be drafted, she said. She also wrote that because the doors of aviation were closing to women— for example, the pilots' union "protecting" women by barring them from flying after dark or in bad weather—those women approaching aviation's door would best take an ax with them to open it. She questioned the hue and cry that resulted when women died flying, compared to far less ruckus when a man died.

Jeff MacGregor describes Lin-Manuel Miranda, creator of the musical *Hamilton*: "The show is successful because the show is so good, and the show is so good largely because of Lin-Manuel Miranda. His secret is that he writes in service of character, to advance the story. He doesn't write merely to be clever, to show off. Without having to contrive event or fabricate plot he breathes life into history and Alexander Hamilton, animates him, stands him up and makes him human for a couple of hours."[13] His father says that what he most admires about his son is his *humility*, not his genius.

RESPECTING THE AUDIENCE *AND* THE HISTORIC FIGURE

One reason we are sold on the three-part Chautauqua format—monologue, audience discussion with the historic figure, and finally, audience discussion with the scholar—is that it allows us as scholars to address our contemporary audiences in their contemporary awareness. Amelia Earhart was a very early celebrity. She was so popular that she was able to earn her living by giving

talks and writing about aviation and her record-setting flights. She was not
paid to fly (opportunities were very limited for all aviators but especially for
women). The media fully cooperated—they loved to write about Earhart, but
they did not pry. Her publicist-husband controlled her image, advising her,
for example, to smile with her mouth closed so that the gap between her front
upper teeth did not show.

The first time Ann performed biologist/author/environmentalist Rachel
Carson for a workshop audience, she got feedback from her (Ann's) mother:
"You did not mention her family. Didn't she have a family?" In every audience, we could imagine there would be a significant portion who, like Ann's
mom, are interested in who it is that the historic figure cared about and who
cared for her. Who sustained her in her endeavors? What were her responsibilities? Ann had to admit to her mother that she had wimped out. When
Ann set out to learn about Rachel Carson and share her stories, Ann did not
know that Ray (as she was known to her close friends) housed and fed most of
her family of birth from the time she was in graduate school: her mother, father, sister, brother, nieces, great nieces, and grandnephew all lived with her,
sometimes all at once. Ann also did not know that Carson's primary relationships were with women. And at the time of that first performance (in 2004
in Kansas), Ann had not figured out what to do with that information, wanting to honor Carson's obvious preference for the closet. Luckily, Dorothy
Freeman's granddaughter Martha edited letters that Carson exchanged with
Freeman: intimate, touching letters that give us insight into that relationship
as well as others.[14] As Rachel, Ann refers to Dorothy as "a dear friend," but
Ann as Dr. Birney can now describe what she has learned about the joys and
challenges of being "Ray" in particular and the joys and challenges of other
lesbians in the early and mid-twentieth century. Your performance will give
you the opportunity to be brave and be bold about introducing ideas that we
are discussing now but have been hidden because of choices made by those
who wrote the stories in the past.

If you are going to interpret film stars Greta Garbo or Rock Hudson or
novelist/anthropologist Zora Neal Hurston, will you create an audience with
which she or he can be honest? You are in control. Feel free to make the audience into friends who know and understand the pressures and pleasures of
their lives—or fill in the things that they would not have talked about during
the discussion time when you as the historian have the floor.

One of the great helps we have recently acquired is a series of books put out by our publisher, the American Association of State and Local History, in partnership with publishers Rowman & Littlefield. The series was created "to help practitioners expand their interpretation to be more inclusive of the range of American history." The series begins with an overview volume, then monographs on Native American history and culture; Prohibition; African American history and culture; lesbian, gay, bisexual, and transgender history; and slavery. Each book is written for people who are not scholars of the topic (actually, museum professionals are the intended audience, but if that is not your identity, feel free to crash the party) and begins with a historical overview that is useful when putting your historic figure in context.[15]

WRITING FOR THE PUBLIC GAZE

Let's face it, because soon you will be literally facing "it." If you are worried about being onstage before the public, know that this is true of many actors. And *you* have the advantage of being able to write your script in a way that will make being onstage easier. What we have discovered over the years is that even if you break down and call out, "I just can't do this!" the audience presumes you are on script, not having an onstage meltdown. And that's the worst that can happen, not the most likely thing to happen. What is more likely is that you will go out onstage, terrified, but you will smile at your audience, and they will read your expression of terror (knees knocking, maybe?) as "energy."

Messages that we received from family, peers, and teachers might have defined us in one way, but we really do have the opportunity, through art meeting history, to re-create ourselves and to take the audience with us on that journey. Therefore, name your fear and announce your current goal to friendly, supportive colleagues. This normalizes any fear you might have. And fear *is* normal. We really are hardwired to choose flight or fight. Fear can protect us as individuals and has preserved humans for a hundred thousand years. In the modern world, however, fear has its limits: "Fear can work against us by making us immobilized and constrained. Much of this has its roots in neurobiology—in the 'fight and flight' instinct. However, most of our fears don't serve to protect us from actual threats. Instead, we become accustomed to being in a chronic state of irrational fear based upon imaginings and worries about the future. The worry and anxiety only debilitate us and make matters worse. When the self-preservation instinct becomes over-utilized, we often freeze without realizing that we are frozen."[16]

Joyce declares that she is an expert on negative messages and responses. Intellectually, she knows that the messages should be innocuous; she has internalized the smallest "that was stupid!" Everyone misplaces keys at some point. She knows this. When others lose keys, it is a minor event. When Joyce does so, she hears, "You are an idiot!" From the outside, it might seem that she is uttering the message only as an aside to herself, but in her brain, it reverberates like cymbals, yelled, with exclamation points. Joyce knows it is a very disruptive negative message, so she has learned to snarl at this fear and push onward, replacing a hurtful message with an encouraging one: "It's not easy, but it is better than cowering." When she took the risk and did that first Calamity Jane performance on horseback, the rewards were immediate and immense, and she is still reaping them. And her historical performances have made her a better instructor/professor and give her deep empathy for others who panic. Fear is learned. When there are only positive responses to your performances, it can be dialed down and then lessened with practice in neutral or safe ways. It is all about conditioning.

WRITE SUBTLE

Make a list of information that you want to share, what Ann calls "dumb" things—not important to the universe but somehow should not be left out. An example is Amelia Earhart's middle name. It was not worth making a big deal about "My first name was from my grandmother Otis, my middle name, Mary, was my grandmother Earhart's." Yawn. But thinking about when it is that middle names are used led to incorporating Earhart's middle name into the sled story that introduced Amelia's occasional resistance to proper society. After all, who uses middle names? Some figures of authority. Why? As a reprimand—to emphasize the gravity of a situation. The first few times Ann took on Amelia's grandmother's voice, it felt very risky to Ann (what if the audience had no idea why her voice changed?), but with the right preparation, it worked. "My grandmother was a proper Victorian lady, and she knew exactly what a boy should do and exactly what a girl should do, and those two things were generally very different. . . . Inevitably grandmother would appear on the porch. 'Amelia *Mary*! *How* many *times* have I *told* you, Dear?'". Some audience members smile and nod, having experienced just such a dressing-down from an authority figure in their own lives—and/or recently administered one themself. Amelia's final story is about her solo flight across the Atlantic Ocean. Early on, Amelia says that she was flying over the North Atlantic, "so I knew I would have bad weather." But her starting and stopping points were probably not crucial to audience members. It was the perils of the flight that were more memorable, so they were covered by, "I knew I had enough fuel to go from Newfoundland to Paris like this [indicates straight line from audience left to right], but this [up and down, creating a series of peaks] was a much longer flight and would take more fuel."

Remember that any story you tell should give us insight into the personal traits and historic contexts that led to the decisions she or he made. Those stories should build on each other, leading to the most gripping decision and its outcome.

Joyce's first script was written longhand with pencil and/or pen and on everything from index cards to pads of paper, a paper napkin, backs of envelopes, and a torn piece of a brown grocery bag. These were then organized and cut with scissors and taped together, a process that created an unsightly mess with photocopied parts in between. The kitchen table was out of commission for eating until the scroll was complete. She then converted the scroll into a script of sorts. When the first-person narrative was told, it came out flowingly. No one sees the process of creation, and the birth of anything can be a messy event after a long gestation.

Seven scripts later, Joyce found that there tends to be some continuity in her process. Familiarity with the system reduces stress. Thus, some thoughts from Joyce about it. First, knowing your needs and proclivities will reduce stress and impede the old childhood messages interrupting the flow. Any distraction will seduce her mind away from her process. A cup of coffee at hand and more coffee in a carafe nearby lets the thoughts flow uninterrupted. She also keeps near her feet a clipboard with paper that looks different than the paper with which she is working. When an aberrant but worthwhile thought about another project (or even something for the grocery list) pushes its way to the forefront of consciousness, she can jot a note without completely losing focus on the task at hand. (As she wrote the last two paragraphs, she put the following on a list: "order horse ration, bird seed, read thesis ch., write ref ltr.")

By this time (which might be after several performances), Joyce is transferring her script from taped-together scroll to computer. This, too, begins as a

PHOTO 3.5
Which stories shall I tell? Photo by authors.

loose process. As her thoughts pour out and her mind goes much faster than her fingers, she ignores the red underlining that attempts to call her attention to misspelled words. Only when inspiration has taken a break does she go back to correct grammar and misspellings. When creating a first-person narrative, she says, it is more important to get the thoughts and images down than to have a perfect draft that only you will read. Remember that you are not turning anything in for a grade. Breathe out and reduce you stress. Breathe in and go back to writing.

MAY YOUR AUDIENCES BE PLENTIFUL

Many times sponsors have said, "I hope we have a good audience," and we have assured the sponsors that for us, a good audience is an attentive, appreciative audience, an engaged audience, and that it is our job to see that it happens. After all, we are paid by the performance, not by the number of audience members. It is easier to get energy from fifty people than five, but we are not prima donnas; rather, we work with the audience we are given. The sponsor promotes the program after we provide the standard materials. In fact, one of our occasional presenting organizations uses their own contract instead of ours, and in that contract, they say that we are not to advertise the event.

On the other hand, that over which we have more control than the numbers in our audience is the number of performances we book. Advertising is critical, but networking is even more so. Go to history and library conferences. When you have made some money, invest some of it in a booth at a conference. Want to perform for schools? Find out where the school librarians gather. Want to perform at museums? Go to your state museum association conference, then the regional organization, and finally a national conference, such as the American Association of State and Local History. Not only talk with people who stop by your booth but also take your card with you to sessions that might attract people who would hire you.

What do you do when you have stories you really want to share but they will not be appropriate for your usual audience—how do you find the audience for your stories? Search online. Find, for example, professional organizations. Also talk with convention and visitors bureau staff who help such organizations find local entertainment for their meetings. This includes tapping into "hot topics" and anniversaries. For example, U.S. history programming will have been focusing on World War I in 2017 and 2018, those being the centennial year for U.S. participation in the "war to end all wars."

You will also want to know what is being taught in schools so that you can link your performance to the curriculum. You can be engaging and relevant to both children and adults. Enjoy yourself, and the audience will also enjoy the experience that you are sharing.

Compelling Stories Come from Choices

1. Do your research—know the stories and facts that your audience might know, but you should know much, much more.
2. Shape each story in a way to keep audience members wondering what comes next.
3. Select stories that reveal, through your character's behavior as she or he makes a decision, something about her or his personality.
4. Select stories that illustrate the historic contexts in which your character made difficult decisions.
5. Choose stories that will speak to the audiences you are most likely to encounter.
6. Determine the setting (place, time/day, and audience role) and how you will convey this information to the audience in a natural manner.
7. Be ready to add and subtract stories and change your setting as your audiences change.
8. Do not write or talk down to your audiences (no cutesy language for children).
9. Always remember that you are in control of your process as well as your product.
10. Love your audience and love your historic figure.

NOTES

1. Robert McKee, *Story: Substance, Structure, Style, and the Principles of Screenwriting* (New York: HarperCollins, 1997), 75.

2. Pauline Sharp, note to the authors, June 30, 2017.

3. Leslie Bedford, "Storytelling: The Real Work of Museums," *Curator: The Museum Journal* 44, no. 1 (January 2001): 33.

4. Tom Honig, "KLONG—A Word for Modern Life," *Santa Cruz Observer*, May 16, 2011, http://www.tomhonig.com/santa_cruz_observed/2011/05/klong.html (accessed September 12, 2017).

5. Carla Marie Manly, *The Fear Handbook*, http://www.drcarlamanly.com/fearHandbook.php (accessed July 25, 2017).

6. Susan Dunhaupt, conversation with the authors, July 26, 2017 (notes with authors).

7. "'Atomic Blonde' Director Brings Stuntman Skills to His 'Punk Rock Spy Thriller,'" *NPR Weekend Edition*, July 30, 2017, http://www.npr.org/programs/weekend-edition-sunday/2017/07/30/540359324/weekend-edition-sunday-for-july-30-2017.

8. Viola Spolin, *Theater Games for the Lone Actor* (Evanston, IL: Northwestern University Press, 2001), 104–5.

9. Paper tissues in small packages were available in the 1930s but were not ubiquitous until after World War II, according to Mary Bellis, "History of Kleenex Tissue," https://www.thoughtco.com/history-of-kleenex-tissue-1992033. Updated April 17, 2017 (accessed July 18, 2017).

10. "Samuel Taylor Coleridge: *Biographia Literaria* (1817)," chapter 14, http://www.english.upenn.edu/~mgamer/Etexts/biographia.html (accessed August 21, 2015).

11. "Florence Pugh on Her Role in 'Lady Macbeth,'" *Weekend Edition*, July 16, 2017, http://www.npr.org/2017/07/16/537509464/florence-pugh-on-her-role-in-lady-macbeth.

12. Toni Morrison, *Beloved* (New York: Knopf, 1987).

13. Jeff MacGregor, "The Maestro," *Smithsonian* 46, no. 8 (December 2015): 86.

14. Martha Freeman, ed., *Always, Rachel: The Letters of Rachel Carson and Dorothy Freeman, 1952–1964* (Boston: Beacon Press, 1995).

15. Julia Rose, *Interpreting Difficult History at Museums and Historic Sites* (Lanham, MD: Rowman & Littlefield, 2016). The following were published by Rowman & Littlefield for the American Association of State and Local History's Interpreting History series, copyrighted in 2015: *Interpreting African American History and Culture at Museums and Historic Sites* by Max van Balgooy, *Interpreting Native American History and Culture at Museums and Historic Sites* by Raney Bench, *Interpreting LGBT History at Museums and Historic Sites* by Susan Ferentinos, *Interpreting Slavery at Museums and Historic Sites* by Kristin L. Gallas and James DeWolf Perry, and *Interpreting the Prohibition Era at Museums and Historic Sites* by Jason D. Lantzer.

16. Manly, *The Fear Handbook*.

4

Performance

It's All about the Audience When There's No Fourth Wall

People who have seen us perform and do not know us well proclaim that *they* would not be able to get up in front of an audience as we do and talk for forty-five minutes, then take questions for another twenty to thirty minutes or so. "I would die!" we have heard people pronounce. Actually, such drama is not as far-fetched as we might think, considering that death is linked to public speaking in more ways than one, but the chances of the performer dying on-stage are greatly exaggerated. Death—and even great embarrassment—is also unlikely because audiences are by and large friendly.

It is true that one cannot do what one cannot imagine doing. So someone might say, "I could never do what you do," and they might be wrong. They just have not yet tried to do what we do or had our experience with wonderful audiences. Our job, therefore, wishing as we do to inspire more people to become historical performers, is not only to model really good historical performances but also to ask people to stretch their imaginations to believe that neither of us is, in real life, an extrovert. It's true—in general, both of us have always preferred to stay at home with a good book than go to a party. Yes, even that Calamity Jane person who comes whooping onto stage and gets in the faces of audience members. Calamity may have been a party person but not so Joyce. Yet these introverts, these somewhat shy people, have gradually become comfortable in front of an audience. So maybe others can too.

A significant characteristic of historical performance is that it is direct address. There is no invisible fourth wall at the front of the stage between you and the audience as there is in most plays. The audience is part of the play. People you do not know will have a role in your performance—and not a passive role. It might seem scary, but it really means that you will have collaborators—partners in your performance.

In this excerpt from Joyce's performance as her great-great grandmother in "Coming to Kansas Territory," she greets the audience as she comes onstage. She even walks into the audience to establish their very active role. She will gradually tell them more about themselves: they have been traveling west with the goal of settling on good land, they have wagons and livestock, and they do not have a milk cow or fresh eggs. View the video on YouTube at "Mary Fix: Someday" (https://www.youtube.com/watch?v=hFvcRgnuV0U).

What made us put ourselves in front of audience after audience, almost thirty years of audiences (in 1997, we averaged, each of us, four performances a week), and almost as many years of workshop attendees? We do it because it is important. Bringing the stories of the people to the people, especially the stories of women, is important. And we say, with both pride and humility, we do it well. We keep doing it because there are still not enough people performing history's stories. We also keep doing it because we enjoy it. We are confident in our competence, which brings us pleasure. As Pearl S. Buck said, "The secret of joy in work is contained in one word—excellence. To know how to do something well is to enjoy it."[1]

For many people, though, there seem to be barriers to even getting on the stage much less achieving excellence. And we want more people to have the pleasure of historical performance that we and our audiences have enjoyed. So, once the research and scripting are largely completed, what are the barriers, and how might one overcome them? Preparation is key. Preparation plus some attention to the subject of fear will have you and/or your staff onstage, enjoying telling stories in character to a wide variety of engaged audiences. We outlined the steps to learning your stories, developing your look, and going into character in *Telling History*.[2] This chapter is for reluctant performers (and those who are coaching the reluctant performer)—performers who seem to have hit a wall. That wall is often the fear of performing, not an inability to perform.

PHOTO 4.1
Enthralled by Joyce Thierer as Calamity Jane. Photo by authors.

In our experience, fear is usually about the audience. We fear that our performance will not go well between us and the audience. Then the presenting organization, the people who brought us in, will not be pleased. Fear escalates. Anticipation is all about negatives, not the positives. We *know* we are going to fail.

But for now, put the anticipated fear on pause. We assure you that we are going to discuss fear, but before we do go into the fear factor and explain that the audience is the best part of the experience, let's go through some preparatory steps and make sure you are really, truly prepared by doing what we call "the dumb stuff," the nitty-gritty.

PREPARING FOR THE PERFORMANCE: THE NECESSARY BUT NUMBING STUFF

Good preparation is required for a good performance. The major portion of your preparation is, of course, your research, story-crafting, and building your look. These processes are arduous, but they are also fun, providing many celebratory moments: a primary source discovered, a word sequence shaped, a piece of vintage clothing surfacing in the nick of time. "Eureka!" And the adrenaline flows. To us, even marketing can be fun because it requires creativity.

On the other hand, running your own business also requires a lot of "dumb stuff." You want to be practicing, but instead you are making calls and revising news releases. "Dumb stuff" includes the communication that makes sure that your expectations are aligned with those of the presenting organization. Knowing that you as a performer are on the same page as your presenter goes a long way to making you confident when you arrive on-site. Know also, however, that until you are on-site, you can never really "know" that you and the presenting organization's staff have the same mental picture for where you will park, what time you will arrive, and what you need for sound equipment. Two major factors that you cannot control are likely to hinder that understanding: 1) the person who reads and signs the contract in September is not the person implementing the contract the next summer, the latter likely being a volunteer who has never done "this kind of thing" before, and 2) what the staff person knows/thinks might shift over time—after all, who reads the contract more than once, if then? This is why we construct our contract to look like a checklist that the presenting organization can use to make sure they are ready for us. Our hope is that it will actually be referred to during preparations. We recommend following up with a telephone call the week before the performance. Make up some excuse to call and casually go over the entire list with them to make sure that nothing crucial has changed.

We were once on the phone with two communities who had booked us for festivals coming up in the next few months. We had talked earlier several times and extensively to each of their event planners before sending contracts, invoices, and publicity material. Each community's file, however, was incomplete. Two days earlier, a new-to-us convention and visitors bureau staffer in the cattle trail community had left a message asking if we wanted to be involved in their festival. "Involved?! We have three performers filling three hours! Do they want *more*?" And, by the way, why had they not signed our contract? We left a message telling her that we were already working with their event coordinator. The contract event coordinator called to apologize— they had a change in executive directors and could not find our contract, would we send a copy? And, yes, they were still counting on us.

We received another phone call the next day from someone we had worked with years ago, the acting executive director, taking the place of the recently released director. She told us that the event coordinator was spending most of his time with his wife in a distant hospital where they were facing surgery for their now one-month-old child, who had been born at twenty-seven weeks and had a hole in his heart. This story brought us, the performers, together with them, the staff members. Theoretically, we knew that we were on the same team, but now we were emotionally engaged. We are, with empathy and professionalism, going to bend over backward to help this community. We want the individual staff members, no longer strangers, to be successful. Stories connect people. Emotions connect people. We know this for audiences, but now we are the audience.

The pioneer festival museum staffer in the second community had been hedging on assigning fixed performance times. Nor had she signed the contract. She said each time we heard from her that she just did not know yet when during the four hours of the afternoon she would have Joyce do her two performances. We began to understand just how little true communication was going on when she emailed that she hoped Joyce would stay "in costume" between her performances because "everyone does" and they have always used hay bale seating, so what is our concern about comfortable seating for the audience? We called her. It turns out that she did not realize that Joyce's performances were an hour long, not the fifteen minutes that their other costumed performers were doing. We had heard that their museum director, their founder, their heart and soul, had recently died, and we presumed they were all reeling. They were not taking in new information as well as they would have if they were not also dealing with the mega-message "How are we going to do this without Cathy?" Joyce compromised with the museum so that she could better accommodate their format, and in turn they are not expecting her to be there the entire four hours. We reminded her that we needed her to sign and return the contract.

Those two phone calls, to the cattle trail festival and the pioneer festival, likely headed off two days of performances from hell. Touching base is crucial, especially with presenters with whom you have not worked before. To reduce stress, you find out as much as possible ahead of time and confirm a week before. It is part of doing your best for your audience. If you don't have to worry about these things, you can focus on getting into character, making a smoother transition from "you" to your historic figure. Many of these things will be in your contract if you have one. If you don't have a contract, it's only because you are doing this for your "home" organization. Whenever you work for an organization that does not employ you or for which you do not regularly volunteer, you need a contract that has the following items:

- Where (e.g., what building, indoors/outdoors, east side of the gallery or west side of the building)
- When (date and time, including completion time if there is a firm one; setup time, including microphone check at a time when the venue is quiet)
- Title of the performance ("Cattle Tales," "Amelia Earhart, Live!")
- Event (Amelia Earhart Festival)
- In addition to the monologue, will there be time for discussion? Any other add-ons? (Judging the antique automobile show to award the Amelia Earhart Prize? Going live on radio before the event—in character, out of character, or both?)
- Sound (Will a microphone be necessary? Who will provide it? We prefer a wireless lapel microphone, with brand-new batteries specified.)
- Lighting (This might help determine where the performance should be held—keeping in mind the sun's arc at different times of the year.)
- Seating (How will the audience's comfort be taken into consideration? If they aren't comfortable, the performer won't be comfortable.)
- How much you will be paid and when? (This fee should include travel.)
- What happens if there is a need to cancel?

Each of the above can seem so simple that it hardly bears our mention. However, consider that we have performed for libraries, for example, that do not have performance spaces, not even a large meeting room with flexible seating. On one occasion, we did not find out that we would *not* be performing at the library until we were writing the contract and came to the place where we said specifically the performance will be. We call it the "at" clause. We almost did not bother to confirm. *Of course* it would be "at" the library. The library was the presenting organization. They were the ones paying us. Imagine our surprise, then, when we called to double-check and heard something to the tune of, "Oh, yes. I just confirmed that we are going to be in the courthouse." And where is that? "Where the mall used to be." We asked for a street address.

Imagine finding out about the different venue only when you reported at the library in a town that was new to you an hour before your performance was scheduled. It takes twenty minutes to find someone who knows which program you are talking about (the relevant staff, of course, being at the site awaiting your arrival). Then it takes you another fifteen minutes to get directions and drive across town. Stress mounts as you start unloading sound equipment. You are at the address but see no sign that says which door you should be entering, and some are locked. None are marked with a flyer about your program. You find an unlocked door and head swiftly down a hallway with your cart of equipment until you find an open door with someone in it—a city office! A very nice person says that she *thinks* the library is using the city council chambers this afternoon and gives you elaborate directions. You are grateful when she then offers to walk you to your destination even though she moves much slower than you would like to go. You are now twenty minutes out, and you still need to find the specific room, make two more trips for equipment and your few props, set up the sound equipment, and change into your look. Lesson 1: confirm the location of the program. Lesson 2: always get a cell phone number (and ask if it works on-site). Lesson 3: be very calm and cordial with the staff who are very glad to see you. If you show your anxiety, they will be anxious. You do not want the herd to stampede.

Don't discuss who was at fault. Just convey what you will need now in order to give them the best program you can under the circumstances. Acknowledge that best-laid plans can go awry. As the stress and fear build, your usual adrenaline due to anticipation of the performance—more excitement than fear—switches and becomes negative. You feel frozen with fear. "I am going to die" starts to take over your mind, threatening to replace those wonderful stories.

But you won't die, and one reason is because you are going to be paid and need that check to pay for gas, your sound system, your research excursions, and new tires, not to mention food and health insurance. You won't die because you are a professional and want the best for the presenting organization that is paying you and for their audience that will soon be *your* audience. We have known people who were volunteering their time and hit a rough spot and bailed, walking out on the presenting organization. Bad weather? We can deal with it. Thin audience? A good audience is even one person who is interested in what we have to say. That's what it means to be a professional.

Chapter 6 of *Telling History*, "The Business of Doing Freelance,"[3] takes you through these and other contract considerations. If you are a freelance performer, spend some time with that information. If you want to be treated with respect, you need to treat yourself with respect. Your knowledge, your time, your skills, and the investment you have made in your performance, including your look, are valuable. In our society, we measure value with dollars. To be taken seriously (and, we hate to say it, this is especially true of women), you must charge appropriately. And you must know how to organize yourself to market your product (performances) and to accept pay (charge appropriately to your costs, deliver the product as you promised the presenting organization, and pay your taxes). This is why you charge a fee—not because you hate what you do but because you have to work so hard to get to meet the audience. (And opportunity cost—being on the road means you are not able to otherwise earn money to make your house payment.) The audience is your reward. And guess why? Because they are really going to appreciate the gift you give them once you get the hard work done. The band Kansas has said that they work for free and charge only for travel.

The presenting organization provides your audience, which is a good thing, but that same organization can sometimes also feel like a forest that you need to walk through (think *Wizard of Oz*) to get to that audience. Trees of all kinds reach out to grab you as you walk through the forest: "We need a W-9." "Can you also do an assisted living center during that hour between the library and the school?" "Will it be okay if we put you up with someone who smokes?" "Don't charge us a food fee because we'll provide your food (at our time and what we want to feed you)."

Would you ask someone to align your car for free? To repair your sewer line for free? To teach your children without being paid? To give you a dental exam without being paid? You have acquired knowledge and tools. You have expended hundreds of hours doing research and deciding which stories work best with which audiences. You continue to do these things to be the best you can be. It is a craft. It is an art. Help people learn the value by charging them a reasonable fee that reflects their share of your preparation *plus* travel. Besides, pay gives you an extra modicum of patience. Like service providers, we are providing a service to the organizations that provide consumers for our product. When we know we will go home with a decent check (translation: dignity), we can put up with a lot. Likewise, if you are a presenting organization and have hired people for your site or people you selected to volunteer as costumed interpreters, you have a relationship that includes their respect for your mission and your appreciation of their skill and enthusiasm.

Back to the list. You have prepared well. So why are you feeling queasy when you picture yourself in front of the audience? Jennifer, who attended one of our workshops, said quite some time later that going into her first performance for a "real" audience of friends, she was confident that she knew what she was talking about, but she kept getting lost in the details of her historic figure's life. Her performance was, she felt, a failure. However, having long before embraced the mission of getting her historic figure's story before the public, she pushed forward with that mission. She wrote a biography and published it. She created a dandy website on which she states, as she called to our attention, that she has created a first-person narrative. "I am finally starting to feel confident with my script," she wrote to us, "but, my nerves still keep me from giving a performance. However, I am working up to it and am planning to do something this fall."[4] Jennifer did a fine short performance during the workshop. Why is she so challenged now?

This chapter is dedicated to Jennifer. We have you front and center in our minds as we "talk" this through, friend. First of all, know that you are not alone in being afraid.

The more you know in advance, the more fear and stress are reduced. You cannot control everything. You can, however, do your best to prepare for anything and then control your response to the unexpected. Remember that you are a partner with the presenting organization's staff. Tell them what you need from them to do your best for their audience—but only what you really need. You are a professional, not a prima donna. What is failure? What is success? One story told well and received with pleasure is a success.

Ann's mantra before taking a risk (or a booking) is, "What's the worst that can happen?" It's not just words; it's a prompt to think this through. And, chances are, the worst is very unlikely to happen, and if it does, it can be dealt with. How do you deal with "the worst that can happen?" Pilots have an answer: the three C's—call, confess, and comply. Isn't it reassuring to know that "the worst" happens often enough that others have a procedure and a mnemonic device to deal with it?

Let's say you have your first performance scheduled and you know what stories you want to tell. You also know why you are telling those stories to

It Happens

This is Joyce. It was a recent gig. I had a substantial, healthy breakfast.
I reviewed my script. I was on-site at 9:00, two hours before my first
performance of the day. I had had an extremely well-received performance
in another community two evenings before, and I was basking in my
glory. And even with all of these positives, I soon found myself in a slowly
unwinding nightmare of things I could not control. I couldn't get my sound
to work. Panic! After twenty-eight years of performing, I can still panic! I
kept thinking to myself, "I am a professional. I am a professional. I can get
through this."

I was convinced that the fault was mine. I spent an hour and a half
trying to get consistent sound, trying everything I could think of, even
calling the "home office." "Touching base" brought no solutions, but it
did reduce my stress. First, there was no sound. It turned out that a switch
had to be thrown to activate the outlet. My local handler had not used
that outlet before. Even with power at the outlet, however, I could not
get consistent sound. Four people were tweaking—putting their hands
all over—my delicate system. They were turning knobs and playing with
antennae. Their anxiety was overwhelming me. I wanted to scream, "I
am a professional. I have been using this sound system for twenty years.
Leave me alone, dammit!" But I did not! Three people were vying for my
attention. With one, I was playing counselor. I wanted to send them all
away, but they sincerely wanted my experience at their site to be good
for me as well as the performance to be good for their public. Rain was
imminent, and I was not yet in Calamity Jane's clothes. For a short time, I
switched to their sound system, which did not allow me to move around
as I had anticipated. The small microphone had no windscreen. I ended
up using my unamplified voice, which was fine because the turnout was
small, and I just walked out into them. I was juggling sound while being
Calamity Jane. It was, indeed, a calamity from the get-go. I just wanted
to sit down and cry after that first of two performances. I *am*, however, a
professional. And we figured out afterward that it was their extension cord
that was at fault.

P.S. Both small audiences were pleased, as was the presenting
organization. They never knew that my performance was only a "six" from
my perspective.

this particular audience. You have learned far more about your historic figure and that person's historical context than you will have time to tell during
your monologue, but you know that audience members' questions will enable
you to add other stories during the discussion. And you know how to move
comfortably from the historic figure to the historian of that figure so that
whatever questions you are asked you can answer in the appropriate voice.
Your "look" may not be perfect, but it is a strong representation of what your
historic figure would have worn, and you know where you want to take it
next—what articles of clothing you will add as you find them and/or get the
money to acquire them.

You have a contract and invoice if you are performing for an organization other than the one for which you work if you are employed by a museum or historic site. You know where you will stage your performance,
when you will perform, who is providing the sound system and wireless
lapel microphone, and when you will need to test the microphone. All anticipated needs are met. And you are, nonetheless, so nervous that you are
not sure that you can do this thing.

PREPARING FOR FEAR

First of all, know that you are in good company if you fear speaking in front
of an audience. Biologist Glenn Croston calls public speaking "the thing
we fear more than death" because surveys indicate that our fear of death
is overshadowed only by our fear of public speaking.[5] The fear of public
speaking is so pervasive that comedians have joked about it for almost a
century and a half. Mark Twain: "There are two types of speakers: those
who get nervous and those who are liars." And Jerry Seinfeld has weighed
in: "According to most studies, people's number one fear is public speaking.
Number two is death. Death is number two. Does that sound right? This
means to the average person, if you go to a funeral, you're better off in the
casket than doing the eulogy."[6]

Summar McGee, a sixteen-year-old history student at the Mississippi
School for Mathematics and Science in Columbus, had that sense that public
speaking was directly linked to death. Of course, it helped that the first-
person narrative that she had been researching for the past year was going to
be performed in a cemetery. In the fall, she could scarcely talk in class, and
here she was that next spring, expected to "be" a woman in 1843. "'I asked

Mr. Yarborough, 'Every time I perform, what if I die?'" Summar said. "And he said that would be the best performance he ever saw."[7]

Why Do We Fear?

The fact that your misery has lots of company might not be reassuring just now, but hang on because scientists have come to the rescue with a very interesting explanation about why we are afraid to speak in public: fear of death. Yes, there is a biological explanation for our fear, and it really does involve death.

Humans who lived to evolve did so only because we so feared death that we did not risk setting ourselves apart from our peers by such abnormal behaviors as speaking up. According to Croston, "Humans evolved over the last few million years in a world filled with risks like large predators and starvation. . . . Anything that threatens our status in our social group, like the threat of ostracism, feels like a very great risk to us."[8] "When faced with standing up in front of a group, we break into a sweat because we [fear] rejection. And at a primal level . . . , we are not merely afraid of being embarrassed, or judged. . . . We fear ostracism . . . because not so long ago getting kicked out of the group probably really was a death sentence."[9]

Performing gender and stepping outside of stereotypes is an example of a threatening situation. Gender has been defined as a social performance that we do from the time we are socialized as toddlers. Women are often stuck not knowing how to please an audience while interpreting "real history." "Nice" women are presumed to be boring (although their stories need not be), while wild women are not suitable for much of the public gaze. Susan B. Anthony characterized this as the challenge of the dancing bear: men on the territorial frontier would turn out to see (rather than hear) suffragists speak just because it was a scandal for a woman to speak in public, never mind what she said.

Many men want to play "bad man," desiring to swagger with the authority that is given to men in general. These men are eager to be onstage. Little boys in classrooms raise their hands even though they do not have a question—they reach upward for attention. Women seek authority from written texts, from the authorities—their authority originates in others, not from within. Men are more comfortable in the public sphere—they own the stage. Whether it is a bar microphone or a computer lab, it is theirs. Women claiming such ownership are critiqued as unladylike.

You are a woman. You are performing. How do you counter this? What Joyce does with Calamity Jane is to attract the audience with the promise of wickedness—what is the Wild West if not wicked? We know nothing about Calamity Jane except that she was part of the West and maybe that she wore buckskins and carried a rifle and rode a horse. Joyce invites the audience into her confidence as she describes how she was complicit in encouraging journalists to create the myths that overshadowed the "proper women's roles" that she also played.

What Is Fear?

Fear stimuli trigger fight-or-flight responses, which have saved us humans for eons and continue to save us in horrifying situations. Fear is a well-adapted response for survival. Fear is the loss of a sense of an internal locus of control. You feel that you are at the mercy of your environment. When it is extreme, you try to fight or to flee, but if you can't, you might freeze—maybe the danger will pass you by. As you can imagine, though, the reactions just do not work for historical performance, so we must find better ways of coping with our fear.

The amygdala of the brain is the source of emotions. It is the fight, flight, or freeze center when it comes to fear as well as where we find empathy and sadness and, yes, joy. Important to know is that the amygdala can be reprogrammed to reduce and/or remove fear impulses. We can condition our neural pathways to reduce fear.[10] How do we carry out this conditioning? Begin by coping and gradually work up to enjoying your performance, practicing in a safe place, with an audience member or members who encourage your work. When you have accomplished your goal, oxytocin, the hormone that encourages us to love babies and puppies, will flow between you and your audience.[11] That song about belonging to "a mutual admiration society" was written by someone who had experienced oxytocin.

Audience members want to create a relationship, to know that the performer cares about them, just as they quickly learn to care about the performer (really the historic figure). Direct address, or looking (or seeming to look) audience members in the eyes, is a first step. Practice your opening. There is a reason speakers often tell a joke at the beginning of a talk: to relax not only the audience but also the speaker. As Amelia Earhart, Ann tells a self-deprecating story about a newspaperman who critiqued her messy hair

("He said I should take a comb into the cockpit with me . . . and use it before I came out.") Tour guides often break the ice by asking visitors where they are from, indicating a desire to establish a relationship.

You cannot let your fear of performing interfere with the historic figure's story. You must set yourself aside and focus on the message and getting that message to the audience. The only time you show fear to your audience is as your historic figure remembering a fearful time. Your historic figure is *never* afraid of their audience—this you can control by controlling the setting (see also chapter 3).

How Can We Deal with Fear?

Some of our local performers, including very young people, told us how they deal with fear. "J": "I try not to look at anyone" is extreme but actually works. We suggest picking several points right over audience members' shoulders, one each at stage left, right, and center. One approach would be for you to, when you first go out, scan the audience benignly, looking at each of those spots. The audience will feel that you are greeting everyone in the room and not know you are not looking at any one person. "C" says that he finds "a person I know and just talk to them and them only." The problem, though, is that that person might feel uncomfortable with so much energy directed at them, and the rest of the audience will feel neglected. "K" combined these responses by saying that she finds "one audience member immediately and just talks to them first. Then [I] look out and see the rest of the audience."

A former student had been advised by a speech teacher, "First time talking in front of a crowd, I made sure I was prepared, that I had practiced. The speech teacher taught us to outline our presentation." One likes to "watch performers before me to calm myself. I like to go down my checklist: I got my lines, I got my clothes, I'm good." They describe their experiences with fear: "[I] went to the bathroom over and over waiting to go on until my guts quit signaling me/confusing me." Another fear was "that I [would] sound stupid, that I would forget what I needed to say. That my mind would go blank."

That blankness can happen. If you have not yet had the experience of going into a room in your home and wondering why you were there, you are likely either very young or have always lived in a single room. What do you do when that happens? Do you retrace your steps to get your chain of thought back? Do you think your character would have had a similar experience in her or his life? The point is that when your mind goes blank, take an alternative route. You know who your historic figure is and what the setting is. Greet the audience appropriately—maybe not with the exact words you had originally planned but with words appropriate to any occasion, such as a nice, slow "Good evening" (if it is, indeed, evening). *Stay in character and own your space.* Seize on anything you remember about the setting and/or the stories you were going to tell and get started: "I don't have to tell you that these times are both difficult and inspirational" (true of just about any era). At some point, all of your practicing will pay off, and you can backtrack as necessary. It will seem perfectly natural, and because you are addressing the audience directly and not reading from notes or quoting a script memorized word for word, the audience will accept your informality.

What's the worst that can happen? Pill bugs (we grew up calling them roly-pollies) curl up into a tight ball when they feel threatened, rather like tiny armadillos. It is very effective protection for them. And there might have been times in your life when you crawled into what seemed to be a secure place and curled up into a ball to disappear while you sought a means to control your situation. If as a child you poked pill bugs or watched armadillos, it would be logical for you to imitate them when you felt out of control. However, what was a logical response for you then does not work onstage. Granted, it *would* be an attention grabber. You stagger onto the stage, croak out a few words, and then curl up on the stage floor in a fetal position. "What," the audience wonders, "will happen next?" Have we said yet that you cannot die onstage? Not in a first-person narrative. Don't do it. Besides, someone will call 911. (they should, anyway). And you do not want first responders upstaging you. It would be hard to get the audience back after that.

Perhaps that is the worst thing that can happen. But it will not happen. Standing and speaking in front of an audience will not result in death, nor will schmoozing in costume at a mall opening. No matter how uncomfortable initially, these are not appropriate times to be "scared to death." Driving all night to get someplace instead of spending time and money on a motel might lead to death. Standing in front of even the worst possible audience will result only in getting paid, not in your death. Curling up in a ball before presenting will probably cancel the getting-paid part, though, so let's make sure that that *will not happen.* We must find a way to deal with fear other than death, fight, flight, or freezing. As Croston reminds us, "Nobody is killed or maimed because they gave a bad speech."[12]

If you have prepared, the worst that can happen is very likely due to things beyond your control. You have a flat tire en route to the event. The festival has placed you so close to the Tilt-a-Whirl that your microphone picks up the noise of the machine and the people screaming. A baby is crying. Teachers are talking in the back of the classroom. A tornado warning drives everyone into the basement of the courthouse. Think about these possibilities and what you might do. Will you leave plenty early and carry road insurance that will bring someone promptly to change the tire and/or bring a new one? Will you rent a car if your own is "iffy"? Will you invite your audience to move in closer so they can hear you better? Will you entertain and educate those taking shelter from the tornado? (They will welcome the distraction—start telling stories to a few, and chances are that more will start listening.)

Dialing Down Fear

Joyce is the designated worrier in her family. She has been through some serious hardships that she just might have taken personally, seemingly endless negative messages from key individuals in her young life that she internalized. She had speech therapy and learning challenges. She should be the last person to be a public speaker. She should be totally constrained by social anxiety.

She also, however, comes from an oral culture. Her mother encouraged her storytelling. Her spouse tolerates her verbal processing (sometimes). Joyce protests, "How can I know what I think until I say it out loud?" Her intelligence and her mother's patience and a few really fine teachers in high school helped her adapt to her learning style. As a result, she had the grand experience of everything involved in earning not only two master's degrees but also a PhD. She says, "To be honest, I had a huge fear factor and stress and pressure to research, write, and present (defend) my dissertation. I got overwhelmed with negative messages and the stress and anxiety built. It was not easy (still is not), but I have learned to snarl at my fear and push onward, better than cowering." Fear is learned and can be dialed down. We train our horses to be "bombproof" so they won't shy if someone snaps a blanket in front of them, a plastic bag blows under them, or some fools fire black powder musket "blanks" without warning us. It's very important when we go out in public that our horses are not a danger to others or themselves. We do this training by exposing them gradually and repeatedly to noises and situations that would ordinarily seem threatening until they are calm. It works for people too.

Mental practice + physical practice = success. Visualize yourself doing each step. Practice telling each story. Practice the transitions between the stories. Even though in our primordial past and in our middle school experience we feared ostracism as something that would cost us our physical or social lives, as adults we logically know that if we are invited to do a performance to an adult audience that has volunteered to attend, we are among friends, among like-minded people.

The audience's attention banishes fear and reinforces the hard work you put into doing the research, script writing, and practicing—all this pays off, so allow yourself to enjoy the moments. Maintain dignity, stay in character, tell the best stories, and have fun with the audience. Don't call attention to what you perceive of as problems but keep going back to the stories.

Two Lessons from Dr. D.: Practice for the Inevitable and Appear Calm

One of Ann's former faculty colleagues used to practice visualizing the worst that could happen to her: her mother's death. She knew that eventually her bedridden mother would not be there when she got home from teaching graduate students. Dr. D. would open the door to their apartment, and there would be no one to give her a cheery greeting and ask how her day went. So, she told Ann, in her mind she practiced her mother not being there. She would walk the five or so blocks home, picturing her apartment without her mother, how different her routine would be without her, her only relative. Ann cried subtly during this story, but Dr. D. was very matter-of-fact. She was also the person who told Ann that the reason she had, ten years before, let Ann enroll one week late for a five-week summer class was because she had so confidently asked to do so. Ann says that she remembers being terrified and literally quaking.

Retired airline pilot Ron Nielsen says, "People ask me, 'What's the most important thing for me to do to get over my fear?'" His answer: "Book a flight" and/or take one of his classes.[13] Our answer to you is: book a performance. That's how to get over performance anxiety. One performance at a time, but there has to be a first performance and immediately a second. Your goal should be that you get at least one future performance each time you perform—maybe not an immediate booking but at least interested contacts with whom you can follow up. We invite people who have come to one of our workshops to return for a tune-up. It not only has the benefit of giving them the opportunity to perform after having more time than a weekend workshop to prepare, but also stresses to "newbies" that historical performance is a process, not something that you are likely to do the day after the workshop. People ask how long we prepare before we do a performance, and we say that we are still preparing for all of our historic figures; it is ongoing when you want to be the best you can be. But knowing that we can never be perfect does not keep us from sharing what we are able to share.

Another thing you can do to decrease your anxiety is to change hats: present a performance instead of being the performer. Experiencing the other side is invaluable. Offer to find a program for an organization to which you belong or offer to do it for a community event. Find a historical performer to present. Do most of the preparations yourself, including introducing the program. Delegate only those things that still allow you to be involved every step of the way. It will increase your empathy—and your usefulness—to all of those presenting organizations that will be bringing

PHOTO 4.2
George Washington Carver (Paxton Williams) and a member of his fan club. Photo by authors.

you in, especially those for which your performance will be their very first such project. You will quickly get a reputation as a team player.

Embrace Fear

Amelia Earhart said, "Fear is usually a lack of understanding."[14] Amelia's friend and Eleanor's husband, Franklin Delano Roosevelt, said, "The only thing we have to fear is fear itself."[15]

Fear can freeze us. But fear, President Roosevelt, sir, can also be our friend. Fear can give us the appearance of energy and can save us from freezing. We can harness fear when we let go of our own egos and focus on 1) the messages that we want to convey and 2) the audience's desires and needs. Fearful or not, our primary responsibility is the audience. Our goal is to help audience members understand the historic context of the person we are portraying as well as how that person's decisions affected history.

And embrace fear because fear gives performers certain advantages. Professional public speaker Natalie Sisson asks us to consider the advantage that others' fear of public speaking gives those of us who are willing to put our bodies and words in front of other folks. First, she says, people are impressed with those who are public speakers because they think that they could never do it. You must, therefore, be brave and be a leader if you are a public speaker. Second, when you are in front of a group, your message travels beyond those in the room to their acquaintances and friends. These people include what we call the "virtual audience," those who wanted to come and could not but are thinking about what you might be saying and hoping to make your next performance. Third, "being in front of an audience can feel vulnerable and exposed, the audience picks up on this and if you communicate a genuine message effectively, you will gain their trust." Fourth, there might be others who would like to do as you do, but their fear will keep them from doing so, thereby reducing your competition. And, finally, "taking on any challenge is empowering as you redefine how great you are. . . . Every time you speak and improve, it's a boost of confidence."[16]

On her way down the fast way from the world's highest bungee platform Yubing Zhang was also on her way to discovering that "Life begins at the end of your comfort zone" and "It's never as scary as it looks." After taking up public speaking, for the first time ever she told her mother that she loved her. And she is still alive and on YouTube.17 Where is your comfort zone? If performing in costume onstage has not been your comfort zone, that does not mean that it cannot become your comfort zone. The name Eleanor Roosevelt is familiar to most adults. What most people probably do not know is that she was emotionally abused as a child and had to struggle to find that strong social force with which we are familiar. She describes facing down her fears: "Painfully, step by step, I learned to stare down each of my fears, conquer it, attain hard-earned courage to go on to the next. Only then was I truly free. Of all the knowledge that we acquire in life, this is the most difficult. But it is also the most rewarding. With each victory no matter how great the cost or how agonizing at the time, there came increased confidence and strength to help meet the next fear."[18]

Finally, if you can feel fear, chances are that you can feel other emotions that enable you to empathize with your historic figure and with your audience. Your audience will know and appreciate this. Of course, they will think it is the historic figure empathizing with them because you have seen that that person is more present than you yourself are. It might surprise you, but moving away from behind the podium, becoming vulnerable to your audience, and really putting yourself (your historic figure) in an emotionally vulnerable setting actually increases your comfort by increasing what you thought of as your comfort zone. Getting closer physically to your audience tells them that you want to be near them, that you care about them, that you need their empathy. You might be terrified, but if you act as though you are comfortable with your audience, you will become comfortable. And, of course, whatever happens, whatever you feel, stay in character until you make the transition to the scholar during the discussion.

Making Fear Work for You

Perhaps it would be useful to divide our fears into two groups: those fears based on our experience and those fears based on anticipated possibilities that we have not (yet) experienced. In other words, if, like Jennifer, you perceive that you "bombed" at public speaking (and never felt the adrenaline of having an audience be "with" you), you have a very real reason to fear public speaking. On the other hand, if you have not spoken in public at all and have only that cellular memory that suggests that you flee rather than risk ostracism by your peers, it might be easier for you to convince yourself that public speaking will not cause your demise.

Try writing down your fears on tiny pieces of paper, then burning them or placing them into the trash (do not recycle them—we want them destroyed!).

If you learn best with your body, assign each of the stories you will routinely use while in character to a knuckle or a crease on one of your hands. Hide your script or your notes from your script in a pocket or inside a hatband. Even if you only do it metaphorically, it will give you a place to seek in your mind for that "next story." You know the stories because you have been working so long and so hard on this project. Stop worrying about exact story and word sequence and just start talking with the audience. When you reach your set time or get the signal that it is time to wrap up (Calamity Jane has someone call into the room that her horse has come untied), you will have told the audience more than they knew about your historic figure—and maybe about themselves too.

Not Fear but Energy!

In the preface, we briefly described how Joyce overcame her fear of teachers by becoming Calamity Jane before meeting with them. This is a success story, but we should confess that for the first several times that we performed in schools, Joyce got the heebie-jeebies. And the first time we performed in her old grade school, it was touch-and-go as to whether we could keep her in her adult persona long enough to rescue young Joyce from expecting an encounter with her fourth-grade teacher, who until her death had a very difficult time believing that Kansas State University "gave" her a doctoral degree.

"My first performances I set my bar pretty low: get myself on stage, let the audience enjoy the story, let the story unfold." When fear surfaced, she shoved it back down because the story must be told. The story was more important than her fear. The fear is always with her, but the adrenaline is an advantage, as it gives her performance an edge. "Energetic" is frequently used to describe our performances. Early on, we thought of ourselves as "fearful" rather than "energetic," but we gratefully accepted the alternative interpretation. The audience does not need to know that a large part of that energy is fear.

If you are breathing fast due to nervousness, build your breathlessness into your script (You had to run to get here? You saw something disturbing as you came in?). We know that when we are afraid, our bodies become tense as our mind chooses between fight and flight. What happens if instead of greeting our audience with a grimace, we greet them with a grin? Instead of rushing into our first story, we scan the audience, bathing them in the good feelings we have toward them (not fear but best wishes).

"Fidget." That's a new word for us, new as a noun, that is. Special education teachers in a school where we were performing told us that they provided such objects as Velcro under a desk for students who need a place to
channel their nervous energy. A bucket held an assortment of small objects,
fidgets from which the children could choose. You know that prop that historical performers are likely to have onstage with them? Chautauquan Doug
Watson plays with a rope onstage, never quite throwing out Will Rogers's
lasso but always just about to do so. Joyce carries a horse bridle for Calamity Jane, and when she is a tribal earth lodge woman in 1803, the buffalo
scapula hoe that she made is never far away. Be careful, though, that your
"fidget" does not become a distraction. Recently, we juried a new performer
who will probably "go pro." He carried a bugle while he talked. He did not
know how to play it, but he certainly played *with* it, a little chain on the
brass instrument clanking constantly.

BECOME YOUR HISTORIC FIGURE

We have always found it reassuring to know that it is not really us on that
stage. Unless you are playing to a home audience, people will not know you
and will not be there to support *you*. They will be there to learn about the person you are portraying. And you will be you during only the last of three parts
of the historical performance. That should feel reassuring. You are focusing
on the performance and the audience.

In addition to the three parts of a historical performance (the monologue,
questions in character, and questions as the scholar), there are three components to any performance: the performer, the message, and the audience.
Each is crucial, but in historical performance, it is very important that the performer's own identity be eclipsed by that of the person she or he is becoming.
If the performer is too much oneself that she or he is trying to portray a character in a role instead of losing oneself in a role, the performance becomes
about the performer and not about the message or the audience.

If the performance becomes a parlor game, one where the audience admires first and foremost the amount of information you have memorized,
you have failed. You want them instead to forget about you and focus on
your historic figure. They should not marvel at how you can remember details
from the historic figure's childhood because if they see you as your historic

figure, they would expect that knowledge. The best compliment is that you took them back in time so that they forgot you were not your historic figure.

Honestly portray your historic figure. Your research should lead you to an understanding of their personality. You cannot show fear onstage if they would not, and they would not—or you should not let them. People wish to know about others who had interesting lives. They want to live vicariously—and to be inspired to take their own risks. And people who lived interesting lives are able to talk about those lives. Strong women might be humble, but they are not ones to waste their own time or that of their real-life audiences by being wimpy. If you respect your historic figures, respect their strength. It might be a quiet strength, but there is some reason for them to be talking to an audience, and that reason must be honored.

Your choice of historic figure and your choice of the historic setting on which your historic figure will meet your audience will help determine your character's relationship with your audience. You are in control of this choice and also in control of how to interpret that person. Theresa Mitchell, Emporia State University professor and speech coach, offers some help. She wrote a manual of exercises for actors to help them identify tension and reduce stress.[19] "Creative energy that can be channeled into dynamic character choices is more accessible during relaxed states."[20] Her warm-up exercises lead us from one life role to the next, culminating in choosing which of your life experiences you want to take to a given character. "When playing a character, ask yourself, 'What do I want?' It can be an overall objective for the action of the play, a scene objective, or a moment-to-moment objective. . . . Ask, 'What is preventing me from getting what I want?'" It helps you create dramatic action in your character because you feel in control.[21]

All of us can probably think of an actor or two (or ten) who are always themselves onstage. They are very successful because their appearance and personalities fit many roles, and they are well liked. They do not, however, "become" the person they are portraying. They are, instead, no matter the setting, always themselves, just interacting with different people and a different script on a different set. An actor told us recently that she felt a shift in her acting when she changed from "putting on a role" to "finding the role within myself and sharing it."[22] Profound. Find where that historic figure resonates with you. You have probably read a novel that pulled you into another world and temporarily changed your perspective. Give yourself up to your historic figure, suspend disbelief, and you, too, can be brave onstage. You have the advantage of choosing someone you admire, a person who has faults but whom you genuinely admire.

Find places in your script that give you the opportunity to slow time while you spend the time to look across the audience, seeming to take in each person with your eyes and your voice, bringing your audience to you and making that connection that will lower your anxiety. For example, as Amelia Earhart describing her solo flight across the Atlantic Ocean, Ann builds suspense and brings in the audience by looking from left to right across the audience as she says, "And then . . . just as I thought . . . that everything that could go wrong . . . had gone wrong. . . . [back to center, looks up while tapping hard three times with the first two fingers of right hand the left shoulder of leather jacket] there was a leak in the fuel gauge overhead."

Know more than the average person about your person. Know more than the average person knows about her or his historical context. Have friends ask you questions about your historic figure until you are comfortable answering them in character or as the scholar, whichever is most appropriate—or some of each. Audience member: "Amelia, where did you crash?" Amelia: "As I said earlier, I wrecked the Electra taking off from Honolulu, and I am waiting for the plane to be repaired so I can attempt again my flight around the world at the equator." Ann (taking off leather jacket and shifting wireless microphone transmitter from inside jacket pocket to jodhpurs pocket): "Amelia can't answer that because it has not yet happened on April 7, 1937, but I really am Ann Birney, and I can take you forward in time if you would like to know what happened to Amelia." The deeper your knowledge, the more you will enjoy your audiences, but always remember that you cannot know it all.

LOVE YOUR AUDIENCE

The audience is on your side. It is very important not only to know this but also to *believe* it. Audience members want you to succeed because they want to learn and to enjoy, and they believe that you are just the person to entertain and teach them. How could you be afraid of people who want you to succeed?

Conversely, even though the audience is on your side, the fact is that the audience really doesn't care about you yourself—except, of course, for family and friends who are there to support you. Most of your audiences care about

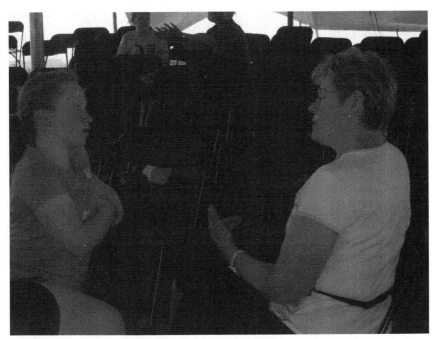

PHOTO 4.3
One-on-one coaching under the Chautauqua tent. Photo by authors.

your presentation. They do not know you. Again, they want to learn and to enjoy. They want you to embody the person you are portraying. And that is the person you want them to meet, enjoy, and admire.

Historical performers should think of themselves as one with the audience. We are each, as said in a National Association of Interpreters article, part of a community of people who are interested in the topic they are presenting. "Interpreters are less the authoritative dispensers of truth, than they are enthusiastic believers in the search, seeing themselves as part of a larger community, not above that community."[23] While we wear the mantle of authority, we are always eager to learn more, as symbolized by the humility that lines our metaphorical cape. A question is a reason to dig deeper, to continue to research, and perhaps to correspond with the questioner, strengthening the community of scholars.

Build trust with the audience: people want to like you, they come anticipating that they will like you, and they trust you not to challenge them, but when you do, they listen because by that time they like you. Joyce does break the fourth wall immediately with Calamity Jane, whooping as she comes into the room or onto the stage, "What's the matter, ain't you never seen a proper woman come into a room before?" The audience laughs appreciatively because she is exactly as she should be. Then she asks an individual who has pen and paper or something in a shirt pocket or who has been planted by a representative of the presenting organization, "Are you a reporter?" Depending on how she or he answers (usually "no"), she says, "Good 'cause I ain't got no use for reporters, and I'll tell you why," or if it is an affirmative response, she snorts and then says, "Well, I ain't got no use for reporters, and I'll tell you why." There are three of these intimate direct addresses (the other two to small groups), and after those, the first stories are told, and she has the audience in the palm of her hands. They love Calamity even though (because?) she as good as tells them that she is going to lie to them.

Maybe fear of speaking comes from a misunderstanding of audiences. Think of your own attitude as a member of an audience. Why are you there? Hopefully, it is because you look forward to the performance with pleasure. That is the kind of audience you want and the kind you should expect. Identifying with the audience helps overcome shyness: these are *my* students, *my* audience. *My* people are accepting of me as the authority. They are with me for the duration. They choose to be with me.

If someone leaves or falls asleep, though, it is about them and not about you. They need to go to the bathroom, the program was scheduled during their usual naptime right after lunch, or they had an appointment but came to see as much of your program as they could.

Some individuals might be resistant when you present a perspective that they were not taught in middle school history. They might prefer, for instance, the mythic gunfight reenactment at a Western historic site. The gunfight occurs three times a day, at, say, 10 AM, 2 PM, and 4 PM, and of course those who are killed get up and walk away at the end. Julia Rose discusses how to work with individuals who find some aspects of history "difficult," honoring the individual to allow learning to occur. If their worldview is challenged, they need time to reflect, to think. That happens during a performance and the discussion that follows. A performance has the advantage of slowly unfolding a story so that the audience has the opportunity to experience a new truth. The performer shows how something that is a new concept to many audience members (e.g., "women fought in the Civil War") is very possible. Motivations for the historic figure's choices are revealed so that they can be understood, and they relate to decisions made by audience members.

Going back to Amelia Earhart's suggestion that understanding will overcome fear, go over with the presenting organization's representative the following questions about the audience for your upcoming performance:

- What are the characteristics of the people who are likely to be in your audience (ages, knowledge levels)?
- Will the audience be physically comfortable considering the following: seated, not facing the sun, and lighting working against or with you?
- Will audience members be able to hear ambient noise, occasional street noise, amplification possibilities, quality of amplification, and amplification for audience questions and for introduction?
- How can we best introduce the historic figure? Introduce the historic figure (*not* the performer), time travel (no cell phones), and help the audience anticipate.

If you anticipate the positive, the audience's pleasure in your performance, and your pleasure in their pleasure, you start to override fear. It's rather like starting the love with your audience ahead of time. They won't know it, but it will make a difference.

You will hear over and over about contemporary attention spans, but take away distractions and tell good stories, and you will amaze teachers and other members of presenting organizations with how long your audiences willingly focus. We have no problem holding for close to an hour the attention of a physically comfortable audience who can hear the program (amplification and/or no ambient [background] noise).

We talked earlier (repeatedly) about the importance of respecting your audience. Stanislavski cautions actors to "think more about other people and less about yourselves. Be concerned for everybody else's mood, everybody else's work and less for your own, then things will go right." "*Love the art in yourself, not yourself in art.*"[25]

PHOTO 4.4
Santa Fe Trail Association members time travel in extreme heat to learn about survey-
ing. Photo by authors.

But could you take it another step and actually show fondness for your
audience? Unless your script calls for something wildly different, bathe your
audience in gold light with your eyes. Look at them with fondness. Show them
that you like them, that you (as your historic figure) appreciate their being
here. It is part of what Konstantin Stanislavski called "that curious mixture of
discipline and spontaneity that characterises all good art."[26]

We talked earlier about the willing suspension of disbelief. Stanislavski
talks about being credible: "thinking, wanting, striving, behaving truthfully,
in logical sequence in a human way, within the character, and in complete
parallel to it."[27] Stanislavski proposes "the secret of 'if'" as a stimulus—the actor should imagine the character in various scenarios.[28] How would she react
if X happened? Actually, this is played out in the improv that is our question-
and-answer in character, the second portion of the performance. What would
Amelia Earhart do if someone asked her about her parents: "Is it true that
your father was an alcoholic?" What would she do if asked about her wreck

on Honolulu? What if she was asked about her husband's motives—"Isn't he pushing you too hard? Are you sure you are ready for this flight around the world? Is it all about the money?"

Remember that you have already performed for friends. You are even better now. Allow your consciousness to operate on multiple levels. There is no scared child in you, only the competent adult who is your historic figure.

Practice until you have become that person: Do they walk, stride, skip, glide, stomp onto the stage? Stanislavski advised his students to "create a physical life" for their role. "The most difficult thing to do," he said, "is to execute the simplest physical objectives like a real human being." In other words, if you as your character are trying to remember something, what would they be doing as they tried to remember? How long would it take them? Or, as was the case with Stanislavski's students, would their characters walk along a street in the same way that actors walk across stage? We don't need to learn to act, but we need to learn to act in a way that is natural for our characters and their setting.[29]

Love for your message and your audience will give you the power to overcome what fear you may feel and create a setting in which you inspire a willing suspension of disbelief.

No matter where you perform, whether you are in your own home giving your first performance for family and friends, standing on a riser on the street corner of a historic district, or in a 500-seat theater, wherever you perform is a stage. And the audience is there to enjoy, to hear what you have to say. They are relaxed and looking forward to your performance, to meeting your historic figure, and you should be looking forward to sharing with them what they came for.

As we mentioned earlier, neither of us has theater experience. Joyce was in her rural high school's play one year, and Ann helped out with one of the light boards for the Omaha Magic Theatre's production of Megan Terry's *Babes in the Big House*. In fact, Ann's next-younger sister was her family's designated actor, dancer, and graceful child. When Ann did her first performance for Ride into History at age forty-two, her mother proclaimed afterward, "I didn't know you could do that! Susan must have rubbed off on you." Ann was a literature major in college and so had read plays and attended several. But she accepted the fact that she was too shy to be onstage and never thought about going solo except in front of classes of graduate students. So if we can do it, so can you. You can find it in yourself if you want it badly enough, if you are passionate about sharing your historic figure's stories, and if you are willing to trust and love your audiences.

NOTES

1. Pearl Buck. *The Joy of Children* (New York: John Day, 1964).

2. Joyce Thierer, *Telling History: A Manual for Performers and Presenters of First-Person Narratives* (Lanham, MD: AltaMira Press, 2010).

3. Ibid.

4. We are not sharing the will-be performer's name because we believe that she will be performing soon and her identity as someone who can perform should be her primary identity, not that of someone who is struggling to perform.

5. Glenn Croston, "The Thing We Fear More Than Death: Why Predators Are Responsible for Our Fear of Public Speaking," November 29, 2012, https://www.psychologytoday.com/blog/the-real-story-risk/201211/the-thing-we-fear-more-death.

6. Jerry Weissman, "Another Humorous View on the Fear of Public Speaking," *Forbes*, June 17, 2014, http://www.forbes.com/sites/jerryweissman/2014/06/17/another-humorous-view-on-the-fear-of-public-speaking/#3f10eaa67729.

7. Elissa Nadworny, "Through Performance, Mississippi Students Honor Long-Forgotten Locals," May 25, 2015, http://www.npr.org/sections/ed/2015/04/17/400363343/through-performance-mississippi-students-honor-long-forgotten-locals.

8. Croston, citing Robert Sussman and Donna Hart, *Man the Hunted*, in "The Thing We Fear More Than Death."

9. Glenn Croston, *The Real Story of Risk: Adventures in a Hazardous World* (Amherst, NY: Prometheus Books, 2012), 233.

10. Michael Lewis et al., *Handbook of Emotions*, 3rd ed. (New York: Guilford Press, 2008), 161–62.

11. Croston, *The Real Story of Risk*, 225–30.

12. Ibid., 235.

13. Danny Hajek, "Hollywood Jet Gives Fearful Fliers the Courage to Soar," *NPR Morning Edition*, May 17, 2016, http://www.npr.org/2016/05/17/478234178/hollywood-jet-gives-fearful-fliers-the-courage-to-soar.

14. Amelia Earhart, "Miss Earhart's Adventure on the Floor of the Sea," *Hearst's International-Cosmopolitan*, November 1929, 102.

15. Franklin Delano Roosevelt, First Inaugural Address, 1933.

16. Natalie Sisson, "Five Reasons Why the Fear of Public Speaking Is Great for You," *ForbesWoman*, October 9, 2012, http://www.forbes.com/sites/work-in -progress/2012/10/09/five-reasons-why-the-fear-of-public-speaking-is-great-for -you/#2ede0ad1168f.

17. Yubing Zhang, "Life Begins at the End of Your Comfort Zone," Tedxstanford, Tedx Talks June 18, 2015, https://www.youtube.com/watch?v=cmN4xOGkxGo.

18. Eleanor Roosevelt, *You Learn by Living* (Philadelphia: Westminster Press, 1960), 25, in Susan Daniels and Michael M. Piechowski, *Living with Intensity: Understanding the Sensitivity, Excitability, and Emotional Development of Gifted Children, Adolescents, and Adults* (Scottsdale, AZ: Great Potential Press, 2009), 24.

19. Theresa Mitchell, *Movement from Person to Actor to Character* (Lanham, MD: Scarecrow Press, 1998), 23.

20. Ibid., 22.

21. Ibid., 79.

22. Susan Dunhaupt, conversation with the authors, July 29, 2016; notes in possession of authors.

23. Will LaPage, "The Ethical Interpreter," *Legacy: The Magazine of the National Association for Interpretation*, March–April 2016, 9.

24. Julia Rose, *Interpreting Difficult History at Museums and Historic Sites* (Lanham, MD: Rowman & Littlefield, 2016)

25. Konstantin Stanislavski, *An Actor's Work: A Student's Diary* (New York: Routledge, 2008), 558–59.

26. Ibid., ix.

27. Ibid., 19.

28. Ibid., 51.

29. Constantin Stanislavski, *Creating a Role* (New York: Routledge, 1961), 131–38.

5

Sharing the Mantle
of Authority

Young People Interpret History

In this chapter, we discuss two reasons young people should be involved in interpreting history and why young people should interpret local history in particular. We describe some models for involving young people in historical performance, and, finally, we lay out specifically how we implement historical performance camps that provide an opportunity for young people to explore and share history. If you have questions, do not hesitate to email us at ridehist@satelephone.com, and we'll set up a time to visit by phone. And, of course, you can always bring us in to model the process for you. We will even help you write the grant.

WHY YOUNG PEOPLE?

The answer to "why young people?" is that interpreting history is 1) good for young people and 2) as good for the community, short and long range, as it is for the youngsters. "Good for youth development" is perhaps the most obvious, so let's address that aspect first.

The Portland Children's Museum has a gallery called the "Play It Again Theater." It includes a stage and costumes—an opportunity for children ages four to twelve to indulge their fantasies or, as the museum says, an opportunity for parents to help their children develop four of what Ellen Galinsky describes as "the seven essential life skills." Those four skills are communication, making connections (creativity and learning), focus and self-control, and perspective taking. Those are all great skills to learn while young, and historical performance certainly gives young people the opportunity to grow in those four skills, but our young people also find themselves involved in "self-directed engaged learning," another of Galinsky's seven skills.[1] Lillee and Sophia, both age ten but at different camps, said that being in control was a favorite part of camp. They got to choose their characters, do their own research, and decide what stories to tell. For both of them, this was different than their prior theater experience. Jim surprised his mother, who had challenged him to try Youth Chautauqua Camp in and around playing baseball. He liked it. Why? Because, he told her, he could call the adults by their first names and go to the bathroom when he needed to. Respect is key—we have learned that the more respect we can ask from and give to young people, the more confidence they display in the choices they make.

We began our historical performance careers as scriptwriter/performers of first-person narratives, doing solo shows. We did not expect to share—and did not even *imagine* ourselves sharing—our process with prospective historical performers. Things do, however, have a way of changing, especially when road trips provide hours of verbal processing time. As we said in the "Dreams and Plans" chapter of *Telling History*, during one of our shared road trips we discussed how much we had learned about ourselves from performing as someone else. And how having become intimate with our heroes, we had also become more confident and willing to take risk in our daily lives.[2] It occurred to us that adolescents would appreciate the process that we had been enjoying, getting to choose a new identity, stepping into someone else's life, and leaving our own quirks and dilemmas behind, if only for a short time.

As young people try to define for themselves who they are, very often they feel as though most of the defining is being done by the adults around them and then by their peers. Even when they try out for a play, someone else is casting them—determining who their alter ego will be based on what the director sees in them, not based on what they hope to find in themselves. It is, then, a scary pleasure for a child of nine through fourteen to *choose* who they are going to be. Identity is important for the young historians, but in camp the focus is the stories, not the actors. The young people get to decide who tells the story, which enhances empathy and identity. The more they focus away from themselves, the more self-confident they become.

"I WOULD CHOOSE THIS"

Lillee, age ten, has been in several plays. She likes being in plays, but in plays she is given words to say and told how to act. In history camp, "I was responsible for myself." Research was more fun than she thought it would be, but what she really enjoyed, she said, was creating her story. Lillee had chosen a local historic figure named Blanche Paulson. There was a problem, though. There were two Blanche Paulsons in the area, born within a few decades of each other. She had photographs of cemetery stones, an undated newspaper "Woman of the Week" interview with one of the women, and a few other clues. Which was *her* Blanche Paulson? Lillee focused her considerable energy on coaxing clues until they spoke to her, and after the Lyon County Archives staff gave us the newspaper article's date, Lillee was off and running, with an enhanced appreciation for complete citations.

PHOTO TRAIL STORY 5.1
Lillee, age ten, likes being responsible for herself. Photo by Ann Birney.

A month later in another community, Sophia, also age ten, said that next year if the annual traveling children's theater was at the same time as history camp, "I would choose this," surprising her mother with her fervor. Her reasons were similar to Lillee's: although she had enjoyed both for two years, as a historical performer she had ownership of her character, her stories, and even her "look." She acknowledged a great deal of help from colleagues, but in the end the decisions were hers. The story she wanted to interpret, for example, was associated with a man, but she did not want to be a man, so she chose to interpret a female relative who could tell the same story, differently, talking about the man.

As they go through the process of creating a performance for an audience, they also assume the identity of historian/researchers, scriptwriter, and actor, gradually assuming the mantle of the expert.[3] They do all this in a safe environment. We will *not* let them fail, and they know it. For one thing, success has a broad definition, one that they define for themselves. Dare to give young people responsibility for the mission; that is, "Share the stories of the community with the community." Note that this mission does not say, "Teach stories to youngsters." Why not? Because of the pleasure of a discovery process that leads to their ownership—not top down but bottom up, spreading out; not opening the skull and dumping in information but letting the young person become engrossed in the struggles that lead to the joy of discovery; not "the role you assume now is your role for life" but a laboratory for trying out possibilities with stories as the focus.

There is a major transformation that occurs when young people realize that they are probably going to know more about their historic figure and/or event than any other person under that tent. This is not simply a "cute kid" exercise; rather, it is an important opportunity for adults to learn from the past, thanks to young people who dedicate significant time to give their community the gift of the stories. A teacher of gifted children told us that talking with one of our troupe members about his experience with our camps was one of the greatest factors in the decision to invite him to join her program.

WHY COMMUNITY DEVELOPMENT?

Trite but true: young people are our future. If we want our libraries and museums and arts organizations supported in the future, those organizations need to be involved with young people now. Many organizations have great children's programs. But too many invite the children to come at 2:00, present them with a terrific learning/doing opportunity, feed them a cookie, and then send them home. Too few give them ownership in the organization and make them feel a part of that museum, that art center. How many young people know that there are "hidden" rooms in the back of the library and in the back of the museum and that real people do real work "back there," work that they, themselves, might aspire to one day, work that they will want to support with their donations because they have a sense of what a wondrous job such employees do?

TRAIL STORY 5.2

LOUDLY AND PROUDLY: "AN ARCHIVIST!"

In Grand Island, Nebraska, our camp's base was a community college, but we worked closely with the Stuhr Museum archivist, who not only brought a list of local historic figures but also had had a volunteer put together a folder of primary materials for each of the local figures. We transported the young people, a few at a time, to the museum so that they could actually go into the back room of the archives and see the source of their information and meet the other people who had been instrumental in preparing for the campers. It was a camp tradition, and we knew that young people liked to see those hidden places. One girl overwhelmed us, though, when she loudly and proudly declared that she had found her calling: she was going to be an archivist! Local historians not only had found someone interested in local history but also someone who wanted to spend her life doing what they did.

When a young person contacts a community member and says that she or he or wants to know about the shell case art that the older person's father brought back from World War I, the telegraph key that their father used in the railroad depot, or her or his mother's paintings, it does not make any difference that this young person is not the grandchild of that particular community member. A bridge is being built. That child might not have grandparents in that community, or that grandparent might not have grand-children living nearby, but the generations are interested in each other. That older person will be in the audience not only to see how the younger person has interpreted the information but also to support that younger person—and out of curiosity about what else will be happening. A young historian had questions about the portable child-sized cooling table in the museum: Who used it, and how? How was it cleaned? The mortician who had donated the equipment came to the library to explain those things and to describe the man who had been his predecessor and had donated the folding table.

There is often a sense among older people who value family stories and "stuff" that no one else cares about "the old things," "the old ways," or "what my people contributed to this place." When young people show a genuine interest in and an enthusiasm for stuff and stories, a link is formed, a gratitude expressed. For some reason, people with limited experience with young people equate enthusiasm with destructiveness. However, we are working not with four-year-olds but with fourteen-year-olds, people who have learned to control their bodies (one of Galinksy's life skills) or at least to be aware when reminded. For example, one dedicated volunteer at a county museum did not want young people coming to research at "her" small, cluttered research library, so she compromised by creating a file for each historic figure and committed to coming to the first day of the camp. She was, however, so impressed with the young people that it seemed she formed a genuine fondness for each and all of them and came to camp every day in spite of transportation challenges created by a physical disability. She was of immense help. And she said that the young people gave her hope for the future—someone else cared, someone who just might be here after she was no longer. This we have heard in many communities, this gratitude for the young people's dedication to their mission.

In reality, we know that the children involved in our camps might leave the community, but in the meantime they are teaching their parents and neighbors to care about local history. Even if the ties that those parents have to the local historic figures are geographical instead of genealogical, they have a sense of how the decisions made by those people have affected their families today.

Having offspring involved in an event means that young parents and their other children can be involved. Families make it to sporting events. They attend recitals. They want to cheer on their children. When children become involved in an organization, so do those young parents whom our civic organizations are always trying to reach. The young parents are always too busy earning a living and parenting to leave their families to become involved with the arts association or the museum. But if their children are involved and they can go together to help out, then they are multitasking, which is a good thing when it means more family time, not less. We learned a great deal from an extended project with the Flint Hills Girl Scout Council that involved forming a Latina troop and conducting oral histories.[4] One thing we learned was that the parents really valued family time. The fathers wanted their daughters at home when the fathers got home from work. So evening events included a potluck supper, and everyone was invited. Make it easy for families—have a potluck with the basics already provided so they don't have to feed families before the performance; they can "just" pack up and go. Or have a civic organization sell inexpensive meals.

WHY *LOCAL* HISTORY[5]?

Why do we recommend that you focus on local history instead of having young people select national figures? Because the local stories must be told, and if they are not told locally, they will be lost. That is the other community development answer. The youth development answer is that, typically, the young historian has the opportunity to truly become known as *the* expert, an expert with a community of encouragement.

And if you are working with a museum or historic site, without a story an artifact is merely an oddity, a thing to gaze on. Tell a story about an artifact, especially in first person, and that artifact glows with import. We still remember the artifacts the young people chose in our first Night at the Museum camp at the Santa Fe Trail Center near Larned, Kansas. There were Mexican trade goods, Wichita pottery earthenware, a wagon grease bucket and chain, a cradle, a deck of cards, a shell casing, an early slide projector, and a set of wood-carving tools. But it is not the objects that we remember as much as the magic infused into those objects by the enthusiasm of the young storytellers. Their focus was not only on the object but also on the historical context, a context with which members of the audience were familiar to a varying degree, and that familiarity led to an affective association. "I remember . . . " or "That was over by where we used to. . . ." Even newcomers to the community make associations: "I wonder if that is the father of the fellow who owns the service station." Ties to place are strengthened, bonds of shared connection. Audience members share not only a shared text (the text of the stories being told and the text about how the stories were told) but also an increasingly shared place and people over time. You do not have to have lived in your community 100 years ago or had family members who lived there 100 years ago to "own" your community's stories and want them nurtured. National figures and national events, on the other hand, tend to evoke a more cerebral connection: "I think I remember studying that in American History class."

Even myths that cannot be confirmed are worth saving because there is a reason they are part of our local story. What does the perpetuation of the story about the siege and attempted robbery of the Mexicans carrying gold to Westport on the Santa Fe Trail east of Council Grove say about the people who have perpetuated it? That we like adventure? That we yearn for riches (what happened to that gold?)? That killing is intriguing when it happened a long time ago to people we don't know? How about that we like a good story?

We (Joyce and Ann and Ride into History) define history as the story of choices that have been made over time and the story of how we have explained those choices. This means that because we are all constantly making choices, we are all making history. We learn from our collective mistakes and take hope from our successes. And what better place to start than nearby, where we know that everyone is quite ordinary, just like us, where surely we can identify with the motivations for their decisions? Nearby is also where the primary sources exist. If we are fortunate, someone remembers the person who interests us. National figures usually have books upon books written about them. Anyone researching one of those people (think Amelia Earhart or Abraham Lincoln) must dedicate months if not years to wading through simply the secondary sources, never mind going to multiple archives to use primary sources to decide which of the many stories that have been told we want to tell. In *Telling History*, we advised that if you want significant income from a historic figure and you are not under long-term contract to a historic site associated with that person, your historic figures need to be ones who are pleasantly familiar to a wide audience.[6] However, young people and local historical performance troupes have the luxury of speaking within their local culture about familiar local events while putting them within a larger historical context. (Were hoboes a constant presence because this was the Great Depression?) We also know that, just as all politics is personal, all history is local. When in the film *Amelia* Eugene Vidal is made to comment on how far Amelia Earhart has come from her "humble beginnings," people who know Earhart's story or know of her family and where she grew up and people who have visited the Amelia Earhart Birthplace Museum know that her beginnings were humble only if everyone from Kansas is from "humble beginnings" because her grandparents were royalty in Atchison, Kansas—Judge Alfred Otis was on the bank and gas company boards and helped found the railroad. They had a governor in the family.

Students in school ask, "Why do I have to know this?" In camp, it becomes obvious. Young people trust us to give them the tools they need to carry out their mission. They learn that part of being a historian (their *identity*) is knowing the importance of primary sources and how secondary sources are useful and that both should be checked. We did not go through the requirements for each grade when structuring the camp; we simply decided what skills were necessary and/or useful to accomplishing our goal: helping young people interpret the community's stories for the community.

We ask, "Who knows the difference between a primary and a secondary source?" A few hands go up. We ask, "When did you learn this? What grade?" We ask those who did not raise their hands, "Are you ready to learn something you don't usually get to learn until ———th grade?" The information becomes very special. Older colleagues (seventh graders) are passing down their knowledge, knowledge not owned by most of the elders either because even older college history professors were not introduced to this crucial but fallible dichotomy—we simply knew that a source created at the time was generally more reliable than one re-created some time later and that we should have three sources.

Race and gender: this is one area where children have an advantage. We suggest to adults, especially those adults who are portraying well-known individuals, that they bear some resemblance to that person. But young people get a pass. They need not resemble the person they are interpreting. The audience is already suspending disbelief that redheaded, fair-skinned Mallory, female, age twelve and skinny as a rail, is Army Air Corps pilot Robert ("my friends call me Beefy") Clayton. If Clayton had been black and talked about being trained to fly at Tuskegee, it would not have been that much more of a stretch for the audience to see Mallory portraying him. It really is about the stories. The audience is so grateful that someone is telling Great Aunt Myrtle's stories that they are less than fussy about the size, shape, and skin color of the teller. However, the person who actually remembers Myrtle might correct the choice of look or of words. "You said it was August, but she would never wear black shoes and gloves after Memorial Day and before Labor Day." "Great Aunt Myrtle would never have said 'You guys.'"

Dark-skinned D'Andre portrayed a light-skinned architect. D'Andre was impressive in his suit and bowler hat. But it was his detailed knowledge of the house that he as George Frank designed for his parents that impressed his audience. No one asked, "Was George Frank black?" any more than they asked, "Was George Frank twelve years old?" On the other hand, some audience members want to know about any personal connections a young historian might have with her or his historic figures, so the question "Why did you choose the person you chose?" is a common one. Does D'Andre want to be an architect, or does he just enjoy beautiful buildings?

MODELS FOR INVOLVING YOUNG PEOPLE IN HISTORICAL PERFORMANCE

We must confess that when we started out, it really was with the idea that historical performance, first-person narratives, would be great for kids. We had not even begun thinking about the impact that this form of community service by young people would have on their communities. Therefore, we determined that if we wanted to reach young people, we needed to reach their teachers.[7] We had what we thought was the brilliant idea of teaching teachers to integrate historical performance into their curricula. But first, we had to develop teacher credentials by doing such a unit ourselves.

We proposed a two-week intersession course for third, fourth, and fifth graders at the laboratory school at Emporia State University. Naively (but eventually helpfully), we spent most of several weeks learning educational jargon so that we could justify our proposal. Our proposal was accepted, although we really had the feeling that the two teacher/administrators to whom we gave our pitch had no idea what we were really talking about—or just did not care—when we slipped in references to educational theory. They wanted a quality experience for their intersessions. And we did not realize that the other "classes" were mostly field trips.

We used everything we learned, but one of the theories we found especially useful was Dorothy Heathcote's "Mantle of the Expert."[8] We applied that theory by creating a frame story for the seven girls who chose to participate in the intersession class. We told them that a museum was desperately in need of stimulating programming and that they had been brought in to solve the problem. They created a name for their consulting service and described their mission. Then they went about creating programming that they themselves would enjoy. We gave them carte blanche in choosing a character. It was memorable. We had a Sacagawea who hated history but liked to act, so she reluctantly became a historian so she could perform. We had an only child who created a composite Oregon Trail traveler with a large family. We had a child with many siblings who created a composite character whose sisters and brothers all died on the Oregon Trail (our only requirement was that they communicate how children actually died on the trail). We had an accused and convicted Salem witch's daughter, herself jailed for witchcraft. We had baseball catcher Dottie Hinson, made famous by the movie *A League of Their Own*.

It was a good thing we had two weeks with the girls, because as we planned we kept adding goals. For example, in 1994, one of our concerns was that girls were not having access to and training with technology. So we determined that the performances would be videotaped and that it would be done by the same girls who were performing, so they would have to take turns filming, presenting each other, getting into costume and character backstage, and, of course, being onstage in character. And somehow they also found time and energy to write a musical review of the entire two weeks with which they surprised us.

The intersession went well, so we made ourselves available for paid teacher in-services.[9] The workshops were well attended. The teachers expressed great appreciation, especially for the sample performances. But with a very few exceptions, the teachers did not implement our suggestions. Evaluations indicated that they were not convinced that they could model a performance for their students—and that if they tried to do so, they would lose control over their classrooms.

The only solution we could see was that we had to be the models. We had to model a first-person narrative for the students and then model for the teachers how to take students through the process of creating their own first-person narratives. We helped teachers write grants to the now defunct Kansas Arts Commission,[10] grants that let us perform for whole-school assemblies and then be in residence to engage the students and model our process for the teachers. That approach worked well, although too many teachers still treated us as having magical powers that they could not emulate.

Usually, the camps are sponsored by organizations other than schools, often museums or libraries. Kansas and Nebraska humanities councils have hired us to provide camps to enhance Chautauquas. Teachers can certainly adapt this for classroom use, and we will use some examples of school residencies that have worked much like camps. There are, however, two significant differences: first, schools exist primarily for youth development, while we are about youth helping with community development, and, second, we use a more informal setting that acknowledges the young people as community volunteers—they are learning so that they can teach. They are not required to be in history camp, and we are grateful that they choose to spend a week with us. Our model also worked nicely, though, for twenty-one third through seventh graders in a Montessori school who researched the Kansas/Missouri border conflict, the area now interpreted as Freedom's Frontier. We had to catch them up on the historical context—creating a border down the center of the classroom and then having individual students or groups of two represent the main players in the conflict: pro-slavery Missourians moving into Kansas Territory to vote for whether it should enter the Union as a slave state, antislavery New Englanders moving into the territory to vote for a free state, enslaved people on both sides of the border hoping to escape slavery, and tribal people who were being removed and not allowed to vote. We took an early Kansas history book with us, a two-volume, two-ton book with tiny print. The young historians were delighted to see something so old. They were glad we had an "app," a magnifying glass, that helped them access the information. They traveled as a group to the Kansas City Public Library, where the Missouri Valley Special Collections staff provided the same level of service as they did for any other researchers who had called ahead with requests (more on that in chapter 2). The teachers arranged for the young people to perform at a high school's smaller theater. Immediately after his performance, one of the older boys, whose parents and the teacher had coun-seled long and hard about how to motivate him, turned to his teacher and asked if they could do their next unit the same way. His teacher did not have to think before saying, "Yes!"

We remember very clearly the first time we mentioned the five W's and the "how" in a classroom. Most heads swiveled to look at their teacher. They were amazed that this was information that was used in the real world, not simply something their teacher made up to test them on. Their teacher was *relevant*, and she loved it.

A very practical reason for museums and libraries to be the sponsor of a camp is that they tend to have under their roof the primary sources for lo-cal history. We want young people to experience handling actual letters and newspapers (or at least microfilm). We want them to have a sense of where the original document that has been digitized is kept and cared for, that be-fore it became ones and zeroes it started its life as paper and ink, a real letter written by a real person that someone decided should be kept.

The above presumes that a staff member takes primary responsibility for organizing and conducting the camp. On the other hand, volunteers who want this to happen can make it happen. They can partner with a historic site or museum, a library, an arts council, or a teacher or can set up a one-week summer camp or integrate the process into language arts and/or social stud-ies curricula.

So how can you make that happen even when you are working with a school where the primary (if not only) mission *is* to educate the children? Now we focus on teaching *how* to learn instead of only teaching that which someone else has decided should be learned. This process of learning is now recognized as crucial to the young people who will lead us in twenty, thirty, or forty years.

Regarding learning styles, as we said above, we had steeped ourselves in Howard Gardner, Barbara Clark, and a few others when we made that initial pitch to conduct an intersession class. It came in very handy for us under-standing ourselves and each other, so we also include the young historians in the "secret." We (Joyce and Ann) tend to favor different ways of learning. Joyce remembers what she hears, including detail at accelerated speeds. Ann, on the other hand, will forget most of what she is told if she doesn't write it down. Don't ask Joyce to read written directions. Written directions are for emergencies. She would rather figure out how to assemble a bookcase with screwdriver in hand. We share our learning-style preferences and ask youngers and elders how they prefer to learn. Maybe they like to talk out loud while marching or make a song of something they want to learn. We try to include various learning styles in our presentations and give youngsters the opportunity to work to their best styles. That's one reason to have both quiet space and loud, moving around space for our camps. More on that later.

We want the process of research to be exciting. We are, indeed, detectives working together, teasing out clues individually and collectively. We are seeking. We are anticipating. When one person yells triumphantly, "I found my obituary!" everyone cheers. We are on a common mission—to sleuth out those stories and share them. Primary sources are treasured. A history textbook becomes a tool to get historical context that is suddenly relevant.

Adults will probably be the ones who provide structure for the camps or residencies, even when a troupe is ongoing. At least, we have not yet had experience with a group of young people doing it on their own. But young or old, Table 5.1 lists some of the formats we have used.

Table 5.1.   Models for Youth Historical Performance Camps

Models	Typical Participants	Immediate Outcome	Long-Range Outcome
Youth Chautauqua	Fourth through eighth graders, "elders" help	Stage performances of about five minutes plus questions and answers	Friends Young family involvement Ongoing?
Night at the Museum	Fourth through eighth graders, staff and volunteers	Series of fast-paced museum tours highlighting artifacts	Brings visitors back Young family involvement Ongoing?
School residency	Fourth graders and up	Performance for colleagues and/or for younger students and/or for families and friends	Meets educational standards Tradition?
Community troupe	Fourth graders and up	Short stage performance for public	Performances can be expanded into longer solos and/or can be used at festivals and civic organization programs; troupe is ongoing, readily adapts to adult historian/actors

Camp makes school more relevant. What young people use in one setting they can apply in another. The concepts of primary and secondary resources, and the five W's and the "how" are useful tools that they use in this mission of taking the community's stories to the community. They are not simply something that must be memorized to move to the next grade.

Children have limited and varying control over the use of their time. We have had young people go to extreme measures to make the camp work for them. For example, while most young people are signed up for camp by their parents, occasionally we get a youngster who overcomes barriers put in place by parents. We have had parents announce that the youngster cannot perform on the last day because the family has another commitment. This is heartbreaking because not only has the young performer put a great deal of work into the character (and staff have likewise invested energy in that performance), but the young historian is also by then part of a troupe. It is as though the best catcher is absent for a baseball game. The game goes on, but the team feels the absence, and the player regrets letting the team down. This is an argument for having more than one performance opportunity. It is, as we keep saying, a process, not a single product.

The primary difference between a Youth Chautauqua Camp or Night at the Museum and our other formats for using first-person narrative is not so much the age of the performers as the length of the performance and the interactiveness of the process.

In both, there is "alone time" to ponder what you have learned about the historic figure and era and consider how to shape it for an audience, but with the weeklong camp there are five days of opportunities to get feedback from colleagues of all ages.

This is a fine one-time event. However, it is an even better ongoing program. If you are going to do it one time, you should probably bring us in and/or send a few staff members or volunteers to one of our workshops. This is because it takes *a lot* of work and can be overwhelming, even the transition from having us there and then doing it on your own the next year. But museums and historic sites have done so and found it rewarding.

You are creating a community of learners, a community of sharers. You will have a troupe of learner/sharers who will take their stories out into the community to other organizations that in turn become part of your community of learning. Once you have decided that a historical performance camp will help you build community, create legacy, and, if you are at or working with a museum or historic site, enhance the experience of visitors, you are ready to start putting the process in motion.

A STEP-BY-STEP GUIDE TO CREATING YOUR OWN HISTORICAL PERFORMANCE CAMP

We are all young when we are doing something for the first time (including producing a historical performance camp). You bring some amazing skills and resources to the project, but part of you is only four years old—eager but aware of your state of ignorance. So the first thing you need to do to prepare is to cut yourself some slack as a newbie. In fact, one of the best reasons to produce an event a *second* time is because you have learned so much from doing the first one. It is also a good reason to share what you know, which is, of course, what we are doing here. A summary of the steps listed in the following sections is provided in appendix A, which gives you a place to indicate who will take responsibility for each step as well as when it should be done.

Form Your Committee

You will want allies to share the responsibility and share their ideas. Your committee should be small and agile and meet as a whole very seldom if ever. That way, they are more likely to say "yes." Include representatives of organizations that will want to sponsor the project, such as the library and museum. You will want a genealogist who has researched local history and knows online sources for the things that young people care about the most: "How many sisters and brothers did I have? What were their names?" You will want someone who knows all of the "old folks" in town or how to find them. You will want someone who is very creative, who thinks outside the box. You will want someone who knows parents and teachers (maybe a school social worker?). You will want someone who knows performance venues and costume sources (community theater?). And you will want someone who is a publicity machine. And again, not everyone on the committee needs to come to every meeting. Some people are atrocious in a meeting but good at what they do. Maybe the historic figure list maker(s) will have only working meetings. Don't beat yourself up if people don't want to come to meetings. Instead, be glad that they are willing to do the work by the date you have stipulated and to fill you in on how it's going. Hopefully, some of these same allies will also help out during the camp as elders. Appendix B shows some of the duties that you and your cohorts will be sharing.

Write Your Mission, Decide Your Goals, and Determine Your Theme

You and your committee should take time to make sure that everyone is on the same page as to why you are doing this as well as what you are doing. The very first thing you should do, though, after you have gathered some people to work with you is to write down and post where you and your committee can see readily just why it is that you are producing this fine program. It is *not* "because we are blooming crazy" or "because I could not get anyone else to do it," although there may be a little bit of that. And maybe you are hoping that you will prove your worth to someone whose attention you have been trying to attract and they will hire you or that your community will rise higher in the "best communities to raise families" survey. There is something else that has inspired you to do this.

What is your mission? What are your goals? Why will other people and organizations want to sign on with you? And don't worry about the difference between goals and outcomes—just get it all out there. Then figure out how you will know if you have been successful. Often, this means numbers. "If we have six young people and six elders participate and an audience of twenty-five to fifty and they all have a great time and better appreciate local history and they want to do it again, we will have been successful." Your brief mission statement should be something like, "Share the stories of the community with the community." Note that it does not say, "Teach stories to youngsters." Why not? Because the camp should involve a discovery process that leads to ownership—not top down but rather bottom up, spreading out. It should involve, potentially, your entire community—not opening the skull and dumping in information but rather involving young and old alike in the process of discovery, including the discovery of the talent of sharing and excitement.

Then make some notes about the worst things that can happen. Get this out of the way early on. Be wild and crazy and list several things. Then indicate how likely it is that any of those things could happen and, if it seems at all likely, prepare for them, then forget about them for the time being. You can't be ready for everything, but most of what we think are worst things are *not* the worst things. The worst things are a tornado when you have not thought about where to go, food poisoning, or your young historian/performers bailing on you when the audience has been invited. The very worst thing is when the media interviews participants and the young historians say that they had a miserable time. None of those has happened to us, but think about those worst things, control the ones you can control, plan for the others (weather), decide where the buck will stop, and begin having fun because that is, after all, the bottom line: having fun with history.

TRAIL STORY 5.3

THE SHOW MUST GO ON

The mission boils down to just this: the stories must be told. So the show must go on. This makes a great chant when overcoming adversity. We did not have that chant yet in Manhattan, Kansas, when it rained so heavily in such a short time that some of our young historians were grabbing poles and standing on chairs to help taller people release water that was pooling on the Chautauqua tent roof while the other young Chautauquans continued to perform and distract the audience from the lightning. We did have the chant a few years ago in Norfolk, Nebraska, when a tornado warning was sounded during the first day of camp. We were guided from Northeast Community College's many-windowed boardroom to an interior classroom already almost full of administrative staff. As we all agreed that "the stories must be told," the selection of historic figures continued, with the onlookers getting, as one said (as we remember it), "a lot more about our history than I knew existed." A tornado did destroy most of Pilger, the next town east, and on Friday an impending storm inspired the Chautauqua to abandon the tent in favor of the Johnny Carson (yes, that Johnny Carson) High School Auditorium. The absence of one young Chautauquan's family during his performance caused a great deal of distress backstage in the auditorium, but the stories were told.

Now the theme. If one of your goals is to have younger people learning the stories that older people remember, you will want to focus on events that happened in the past, say, 150 years—stories told to our oldest living people by their parents—or maybe even within the memory of those oldest people, so, roughly, 1925 forward. Do you want to emphasize settling and town building, including conflicts between those who were already on the land? Or maybe trails and rails? Or financial booms and busts? Maybe creativity over the years? Or technological changes? You can use a narrow topic and a long time line or, vice versa, a short era and go deeply into that event.

Remember your audiences while deciding on a theme—you want to appeal to as many people as possible. And very likely, you want some stories that involve family members of people who still live here. When our young historians list the elements of a good story, they include such things as people who are like me, adventure, animals, romance, suspense, and various sorts of conflict. Every era has stories with these elements, but some eras are richer sources than others. One of your goals might be to involve older elders in sharing their stories, which would mean that you would want to think about interpreting the 1930s, 1940s, 1950s, or even the 1960s.

Humanities Nebraska has used the themes of "Bright Dreams, Hard Times, America in the Thirties" (shared with the Kansas Humanities Council) and "Visions for America: Notable Nebraska Reformers" for their annual Chautauquas, which have included Youth Chautauqua Camps. We found local applications for both of those in all of the Chautauqua communities. For "Free Land? 1862 and the Shaping of Modern America," we certainly found stories, but we had to depend primarily on written primary sources and artifacts. Interviews were less important to our young scholars because there were few people who had stories that had been told them that were not already in writing. The next Chautauqua for Nebraska is based on World War I with a focus on the home front (theme). Once you have your theme, do not be too hidebound about it—it could be that the young person has a passion for something that takes a stretch and some time traveling to bring them back to the corral, but more on that later.

Sign Up Sponsors

Involve as many partners as you can. You want "buy-in" early on from the organizations and individuals you will need to help you meet your mission, long range as well as immediate. You will also need parental assurance that they can trust their youngsters to be well cared for during your camp, so especially involve those organizations already identified with summer programming for young people. We have had not only libraries and museums but also a Salvation Army day camp and a Girl Scout troop, with the latter two helping with recruitment as well as community goodwill. This project involves both the arts and the humanities. Find out how those organizations can help you with your goals. Put their logos on your publicity and especially on your program that is handed out at the performance.

Site Selection

You need two sites: one for the camp and the other for the performance. Both, of course, need to be wheelchair accessible with readily available bathrooms. A nearby kitchen is handy (but not necessary) for snack and performance-night supper preparation—you can use a cooler and bring cleanup supplies. It is ideal if the sites are close enough to homes or public transportation that young people can get there by themselves or if there are several families in one area who can carpool.

Hold the camp someplace that does not feel like school, ideally a special place associated in young people's minds with adults so that they feel special to be there. You need to convince your young people that you are not tricking them into summer school but rather asking them to make a significant contribution to their community. They need to feel your respect from day one. This is space that they will claim for most of the five days. It will be their base.

Find a museum or library meeting room or a college classroom or meeting room that has tables and chairs, not desks. Desks are not designed for real work. (How many adults, when they go to work, have a surface of only two foot by a foot and a half?) Ideally, the meeting room will be at the same location as most of your history sources. This is usually a historical society's archives or a library's local history collection. Your genealogist will know this. Ideally, you will be the sole users of that space Monday through Thursday, so you will not need to pack up at the end of each day.

Lighting in your space ideally will come from the outside (natural light). This might seem difficult to believe if you have not experienced it, but you know those older fluorescent lights that seemed ubiquitous to institutions, especially schools? Some people, including some with dyslexia, can *see* the many waves of light being emitted, and it is very hard on the eyes and the brain. If you must use a space with fluorescent lights and (heaven forbid) no natural lighting, try for full-spectrum lighting, or at least tell your folks that wearing hats is fine so that they can put a hat brim between their eyes and the lights and/or be patient with the child (or adult) who wants to sit under a table to work.[11] Those are Joyce's observations about light. Ann's are actually auditory. Light fixtures can be extremely noisy, emitting ambient hums and buzzes that create tension. Turn off a fixture that has been howling at you for thirty minutes and notice how you suddenly relax; now imagine spending four hours with that noise. Worst: halogens in gymnasiums. Listen to the light!

TRAIL STORY 5.4

MIX IT UP

Joyce custom-prints exams in her college students' preferred color, if they have one. She knows that some people with dyslexia find that letters are easier to read on pink, gray, or light blue paper. And, of course, other people just might do better on the test because they feel so nurtured by being given a choice. So feel good about mixing up the scratch paper you put out on the table: lined, pastel, or graph paper. Whatever you have will feel friendly to the young historians-to-be.

The meeting space should have one six- to eight-foot table for every two young historians. A blackboard, dry-erase system, or flip chart will be essential, especially on the first day for tasks you will do together, so that visual learners have a chance to follow what you are saying. For example, our camp mantra is "I am a historian, researcher, scriptwriter, actor. I have two responsibilities: accuracy and entertainment." We play with learning styles when we first introduce this mantra. Joyce might start teaching it verbally and then ask Ann to write it on the board because visual learner Ann will want it where other visual learners can see it and learn it. The mantra, of course, also employs rhythm, and, as we say it, we use our bodies. It gives campers something that they have learned by the time they go home even if they are one of the few who do not know for sure who they are going to interpret. You will also need tables for office supplies, snacks, and handouts.

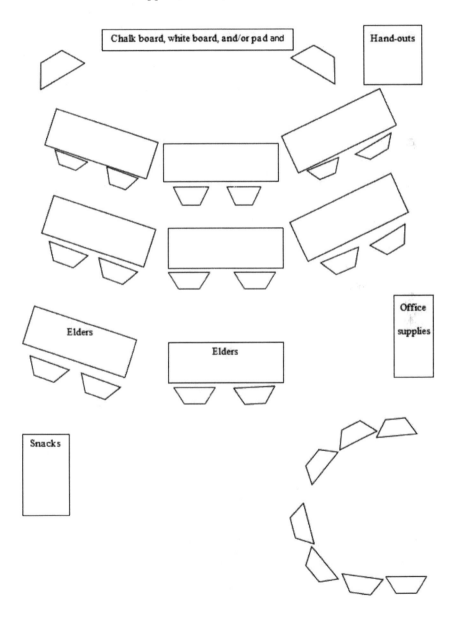

After you have decided where the camp will be held, find a space for the performance. A small theater or auditorium with a stage would be ideal, but a room with chairs and a riser works well also. The performance space should comfortably accommodate everyone you think will come. We estimate that at least five audience members per youngster, plus those involved in with sponsoring organizations and your elders and their families and friends. If your space is large, you can close off the sides and backs of the room, placing chairs strategically to create the degree of intimacy that feels right to you. Chautauquas are usually held under tents with a large portable riser for a stage. Prepare a backup space in case you have threatening weather.

Be aware of lighting in the performance space. In addition to the concerns mentioned earlier in conjunction with the camp workshop space, there are additional challenges with presentation spaces. We have noticed that newer meeting rooms are often set up for audiovisual presentations, not for speaking humans. The former require turning off the lights, and the latter require nice warm lighting. We are not saying, "Don't use that church meeting hall." We are saying that you might need to bring additional lighting so that those small faces can be seen under those really cool hats. Even in the great outdoors, lighting is often needed under a tent.

Where will the historical performers change clothes, and what will you do with what we call their civvies, their street clothes? We travel with a very large horse trailer that we have converted to hold clothes and that has a dressing room in the front, but you will probably want at least one comfortable space as a dressing room. Try not to tie up a bathroom with clothing changes, as most bathrooms do not have enough space to keep clothes off the floor or chairs to sit on to put on shoes and socks. Note the location of bathrooms in both workshop and performance spaces so you can tell everyone else when they first arrive.[12]

Set Your Dates

You have your "where"; now you need your "when." You will probably want five half days for camp, the last one to extend into the evening to make the performance work with most people's workday schedules. While we did several Wednesday-through-Sunday camps to mirror the Chautauqua with which we were working (an adult Chautauquan performed each evening, with adult lectures and children's programming during the mornings and afternoons; our young Chautauquans were on just before the Sunday evening final performance of the Chautauqua), everyone involved agreed that it would be easier on parents and, hence, easier to recruit young people if the camp were Monday through Friday—easy to remember, easy to work into other schedules. The children attend camp five days each week. On four days, they go to the same site. On the fifth day, they go to the performance site if it is different than the camp site.

Time of day: we discovered that young people do not function well in the mornings. Their bodies know that it is vacation time. When necessary, we scheduled to overlap the lunch hour and had peanut butter and crackers on hand for those who forgot to bring a lunch (beware of peanut allergies), but 1:00 to 5:00 works really well. For one thing, parents who work until 5:00 can pick them up as needed. Being consistent with the time makes it easier for families.

One reason you chose the site before setting the dates is that you might be constrained by that site's availability. Libraries, for example, have summer reading programs that have special events that use meeting rooms. Museums might have other camps that they are offering. If you put your bid in early enough, they can incorporate you into their program calendar and provide not only space but also help.

Avoid camp and performace dates that might conflict with large numbers of young people. Check with the recreation commission, the sports leaders, and county extension. When is softball? The 4-H fair? Several Glasco, Kansas, kids missed part of camp to represent their town in a regional pool tournament. For example, do you need to avoid Independence Day or build the performance event into your local Fourth of July celebration because you are *the* place to be every year for the celebration?

Recruiting Young People

You will probably want to work with ten to fifteen young people; set your limit at twenty. Ten to fifteen young historians make a nice program length. If you have, say, twelve young historians and half of them do a performance of about three minutes and half do about five minutes, you have almost an hour ($[6 \times 3 = 18] + [6 \times 5 = 30] = 48$ minutes). Add in your greeting, about two minutes, to the audience. At the end of the performance, when they are all onstage, will be at least another twenty minutes; allow for thirty. For Night at the Museum, you will require each student to give no more than two minutes because you will also have moving time and Vintage Docent time and want to give no more than forty minutes for each tour (the discussion is after all of the tours, with the reception). So you see that more young historians is a good problem to have, but it might still be a problem.

You will do two kinds of marketing: blanket and targeted word of mouth. Where do young families learn about summer opportunities for their youngsters? Is there a special section of the newspaper that publishes such a list? How does the recreation commission advertise? Radio talk shows and local access television are great ways to get the word out. Social media, of course, ranks right up there. Post notices in the senior center. Be sure to say "Free!" on every flyer and Facebook posting and put flyers in the grocery stores and laundromats. Give flyers to social workers, librarians, teachers, and home school cooperatives. Put flyers anywhere these people might see them. You are subtly advertising not only for young historians but also for their audience *and* for young historians (and support) for subsequent years. You are letting everyone know that there is a new community tradition in town! And if we are not looking for the message, we have to see or hear an announcement something like ten times for it to sink in, so get it out there (see the sample flyer in appendix C).

Do not presume that because you think this is the best thing since sliced bread, you will be overwhelmed by applicants and have to have a waiting list. It happened to us once in fifty-seven camps in almost that many communities. That would be a good problem to have but not the one you need to focus on. Focus on getting families committed to giving young people the support they need to do this for one week.

Recruit all students to take part. Find the youngsters who are acting out in class, the kinesthetic learners who learn best when their bodies are involved in the learning. Find the questioners, the "library kids" who make the library their home during the day in the summer. Find the child who welcomes the opportunity to be an expert at anything, who craves knowledge and the opportunity to share it.

Word of mouth includes talking to grandparents. They are more likely to not only make sure their grandkids sign up but also offer their own services because they truly get it that local history is important. Some grandparents will even have their grandchildren who live at a dsitance come in for this opportunity to work together on a meaningful project. Take flyers with you wherever you go and hand them out and/or post them. Talk about this great intergenerational project. Also find out if the person you are talking with has family members who would directly relate to your theme ("Do you know anyone who has dust storm stories?").

Do *not* say, "This will be fun; it's just like school." School is not fun for many young people, and this is *not* school. It is hard work having fun working with colleagues and by oneself. We are "history detectives"! We are doing sneaky history—who knew that history was fun? We are acting and storytelling. Writing is a tool that some of us really, really like, but it is not our writing

---

TRAIL STORY 5.5

BASEBALL STATS AND TRUMPET RIFFS

We get excited about more than obituaries. We also get excited about other stuff in old newspapers. Who is going to browse through 1920s Papillion, Nebraska, newspapers? We are. Especially the one of "we" who is a young baseball aficionado looking for statistics for the team "he" played on. The initially reluctant historian became an ardent researcher when he discovered that his historic figure was known to send a potato instead of a baseball over the plate, just to shake things up a bit. A Depression-era Colby real estate speculator went from hop-hum to hip when a young musician found out that he was known to sit on his porch playing such tunes as "In the Good Old Summertime" on his trumpet as people strolled by. She came onstage playing that song.

that will be on public display but rather our storytelling. It's just that some of us write out a story word for word before we say it, while others listen and construct stories in their heads.

Do not worry if numbers are small the first year—part of the challenge is that this is new, and, until you put on a performance, it is not on anyone's radar. Marketing will need to be *huge*. *You* know it's a great idea, but parents and grandparents need to have the language to be able to sell it to their prospective young historians.

In addition to marketing materials, you will want a registration form. Youth registration forms should include the sponsoring organization(s) and who to contact for more information. The sample registration form in appendix D has a few places for parents or guardians to "opt in" with initials—just to make sure that they have given transportation and photograph permission and that they have thought about the dates, especially that of the performance. You will want to include a space for the following:

- Child's name
- Date of birth
- School attending
- Current grade level
- Parent/guardian(s) name(s)
- Address
- Home phone, mobile phone, work phone
- Email address
- Additional emergency contact name(s) and telephone number(s)
- Physician's name and telephone number
- Food or medicine allergies and/or other medical information of which staff should be aware
- Building/information access concerns
- T-shirt size (indicate if size is child or adult)
- Permit to transport to research sites
- Permit for organization to use child's photograph in media releases, websites, and videos
- Instructions for child to wait or walk after workshop and who will pick up
- Signature and date

- Where to send/take registration form
- Information on days, dates, and times
- How to get more information about the event

Write out the schedule so that as you talk to people, those who are visual learners have a sense of what their young people will be doing at a history camp. Samples are given in appendix E and appendix F.

Recruiting Elders

It is useful to have one adult volunteer/staff member (called "elders") for every four registrants in addition to those conducting the workshop portion of the camp. No one person would have to attend every day. In one community, the local bank donated staff members each day to help with the camp. And it is not fair to count staff who have other duties ("call us when you need us" just does not work).

Young people who give up a week of their summer to help their community keep its stories alive deserve respect. Your goal is to find people who appreciate the gift to be given by these young people, adults who are characterized as follows:

- Are comfortable in a role that is more that of colleague/helper than that of teacher
- Are comfortable being on a reciprocal first-name basis with young people
- Have a sense of humor
- Are flexible
- Are creative in accessing information resources in the community
- Are attentive listeners who encourage rather than judge negatively
- Are available Monday through Wednesday to help identify sources and research (which might include reading to someone who can listen faster than they can read and/or transporting young historians to an interview or other sources) and/or Wednesday through Friday to listen and offer help with finding the good stories in the information and telling those stories; ideally everyone would come Monday to experience the beginning of the process.

Code of Conduct for Youngsters and Elders

Our mission is to share the community's stories with the community.

We share the stories by time traveling so that the past becomes the present.

We are colleagues and indicate our mutual respect by calling each other by our first names.

Elders serve youngsters as research assistants and helpful listeners.

Youngsters serve their audiences by finding, learning, and sharing the stories.

Any writing that young historians do is for their own use—whether notes, storyboards, or fully developed narrative script; spelling and grammar are up to them as scriptwriters/storytellers.

We acknowledge a wide range of learning styles.

We acknowledge that many if not most of us need quiet space to ourselves to do our best work.

We acknowledge that some of us do not know what we think until we have said it out loud.

When we have to go to the bathroom, get a drink, eat, or get supplies such as a new pencil, we can do so—we do not have to ask permission.

When we need to stand up and stretch, we do so.

We are respectful to others around us as well as our colleagues.

Historians have no time to waste, and we will use our time together to work toward our common goal.

The Code of Conduct was inspired by repeatedly having to deal with retired teachers who felt they had to correct written notes to reflect the expectations of their next year's schooling. ("What grade will you be in next year, Dear?" "Well, Mrs. —— will want you to use correct punctuation when you are in her class. Here, let me help you.") Several times we watched a youngster shrink as an elder glowed with a mission we had not given her or him. We share the Code of Conduct, as a handout and verbally, with the elders and youngsters during the first hour we are together. We also advocate sharing the code with elders as you talk with them about volunteering with the camp to make sure it is a good fit. "All relationships have rules," we tell them. "In most relationships, such as those with friends and family, you don't get a list of rules; you find out the rules over time, often by doing something wrong.

In history camp, we don't have much time to figure out each other's rules, so we have written the rules we think will be most useful." Notice that the rules include everything from housekeeping (pencils and bathrooms) to presentation format (we take the audience back in time) and learning styles.

If an adult is likely to be alone with a child and a background check has not been conducted in the past few years, you will probably want to conduct one. The most politic thing to do is to mandate that this be done for all such workers. We have known of volunteers for whom this was a deal breaker, but maybe they could help with other aspects that do not require alone time with a child. Examples where one-on-one alone time might occur include driving a youngster to an interview or other research site and helping a child with clothing. Each state has its own database, which as of this writing will get only one state's records. In Kansas, for example, it will cost you $20 per person to have the Kansas Bureau of Investigation (KBI) run the check. Search "[state name] background check" and look for a website with ".gov" in the address, not a commercial site. We suggest that you receive an individual's permission before running the check, even though this might not be required in your state.

Recruit Historic Figure List Maker/Researchers and Identify Local Sources

The makers of the historic figures list should start with a list of interesting events that happened during your chosen era and theme. Then make a list of individuals who might have been involved in those events or who know about them. This will involve going through local history books, scanning newspapers, and talking to people (see the sample historic figures list in appendix G).

The most frustrating error is when someone makes a long list but there are no sources or not much data or depth of sources. Imagine that you are a child who has chosen to interpret the bank robbery of 1930—your town's one and only bank robbery. The article in the newspaper named the bank teller, the bank president, and the sheriff. You want to be the teller because you want to portray a woman and because something really exciting happened to her. But the article doesn't tell you as much as you want to know about the person you are becoming. What was her personality like? What happened to her afterward? The person who found this story knows the teller's nephew and thought he would be a good interview, but on Tuesday you find out that the teller's nephew went trout fishing for a week and cannot be reached. At least you know from this fact that some of the family stayed in the area, but maybe you should switch historic figures before it is too late.

You will need about half as many interesting events/people as there are young historians (ten young historians = fifteen historic events/people from which they will choose). Write a short sketch of each historic figure to entice a youngster to learn more about that person, such as follows: "Betty Whoop operated the Do Tell Beauty Parlor on Main Street, and anyone who was everyone from 1903 to 1946 had her hair done by Betty. She created elaborate hairstyles and used to tell stories about stage and movie stars who came to her salon. One of her favorite stories was about the time. . . ."

Make a list of print and human resources for each historic figure: resources for Betty Whoop: newspaper (give date(s); Betty's daughter, who is willing to be interviewed; also, her beauty shop is re-created in the museum.

Find out, if you don't know already, what your libraries and local history museum have. Spend time becoming acquainted with them so that you, as the "one in charge," have a sense of how much time is likely to be spent where. Who has old newspapers on microfilm? Can the microfilm reader also print? Will they print a few free for each young historian? And that also goes for copying. We ask that a community provide up to ten copies per historian, and seldom do we need the whole ten, but if someone does go over that amount, it is okay.

Night at the Museum people are selecting artifacts rather than individuals. Our first Night at the Museum sponsor's staff discovered that very few of their artifacts have provenance. Most had been donated with no record made as to their source. That made it very difficult to go after stories. Luckily, they were able to find some artifacts with local connections, and we went with composite characters and knowledge of historical context for some. Museums need the connections to donors that stories provide, and donor families need to know that the gift, as they say, "keeps on giving" through the stories.

Recruiting Audience (Special Invitation)

In addition to publicity that will invite the public to come to the show, you will want to make "special invitations" so that the young actors can help "build the house." At the end of the first day of camp (or definitely by the second day), give each of them a half dozen or so half sheets of brightly colored paper with a simple invitation printed on it. They are to give the invitations to

PHOTO 5.1

"Dr. Bingesser" visiting with her two sons in Cawker City, Kansas. Photo by authors.

TRAIL STORY 5.6

HISTORY IS PERSONAL

Some North Lyon County Historical Performance Troupe members take the opportunity to research family members. In Hunter's first camp, he interpreted Bob Brown, who owned several service stations in Admire, Kansas. In the process, Hunter learned from a family member that his great grandfather had a mechanic shop in Allen, the next town over, where Hunter lives, so the following year he was that great grandfather. He took time off from family when we were interpreting a community a little farther away, but this summer (our fifth) Hunter was the attorney who prosecuted the man convicted of murdering Hunter's great-great grandfather. The young people knew that it happened but said that it is something family members will not talk about directly. They think it might have something to do with the fact that the killer was black and their relatives white. Each of the men Hunter has portrayed over the past four years has been more complex, he said, but all had similarities. He has learned to look deeper when researching and says that he is building his skills as he creates his scripts.

family members to post on their refrigerators and take others to post them in the grocery store or wherever they see a bulletin board or flyers in a business window. One very young girl took hers door-to-door in her neighborhood. She was living with her grandmother, and most of the people were her grandmother's age and had known her since she was a toddler. When she handed them a special invitation, delivered with a smile, no one could tell her to her face that they would rather stay home and watch television. They came (see the sample schedule in appendix E).

Snacks, Troupe Supper, Refreshments

Our philosophy is that if we know that food is available, we (or the youngsters) will not fixate on it. You will have young people for four hours, so it is important that they have a snack—and that the snack bring them out of a low-sugar slump without sending them bouncing off the walls. Accompany the snack with endless water.

Penn State Extension recommends the following snacks:

- Apples
- String cheese and whole-grain crackers
- Prepackaged yogurt tubes
- Trail mix and dried fruit
- Hummus or peanut butter and precut veggies, like carrots, celery, snap peas, and bell peppers
- Whole-grain bread and peanut butter and jam or cheese and lunch meat[13]

We have no control over how long before camp our young colleagues ate or what they had. If they had a lunch without protein but high in sugars at noon, they might be lethargic by 2:00, so be ready to set snacks out when you see the need. If you provide protein like nuts, hummus, or cheese, they will have about four hours before needing more food. Try to avoid processed sugars (cookies and sweet drinks, including juices), which will buy you only two hours—and will cause problems with people with diabetes. Your registration form should ask about allergies. If any of the participants have a nut allergy, neither tree nuts nor peanuts should be allowed in the vicinity unless cleared with the parent of the person with the allergy. Remember to provide hand sanitizer and napkins too.

Why water? We will go for the extended quote here, being humanities scholars and not scientists. We found this cited in a theater training book, so it lends even more credibility to the scientists: "Brain cells need two times more energy than other cells in the body. Water provides this energy more effectively than any other substance. Water is also needed for the brain's production of hormones and neurotransmitters. Nerve transmission requires one-half of all the brain's energy. When your brain is functioning on a full reserve of water, you will be able to think faster, be more focused and experience greater clarity and creativity."[14] We want to know how much of a young person's energy is who they are and how much is what they have recently eaten or drunk.

Costuming

Community and college theater departments are the first source for costumes. The ideal costume, however, is vintage clothing. Put out a call for
white T-shirts and slips, long dark skirts, and tall black socks. People will feel
good about helping out. Then, as you find out who is doing which historic
figure, you can put out the emergency calls: "We need a large white lab coat."

Theater costumes are designed to be seen from a distance, meaning it is
fine to use polyester for someone in the 1890s because the audience can't tell.
Our performers, however, will often (if not usually) be closer to their audiences. You should aim for the quality displayed by competitive reenactors,
who are judged in part by how their buttons are attached and what kind of
underwear they are wearing (or at least when the sleeve of an undershirt is
showing). Sources for information on historic clothing include mail-order
catalogs of the time. The most important thing is that the person wearing
the clothes know the difference between the representational look she or he
is wearing and the "real thing"—and can talk about it. "Thank you for com-
plimenting me on my look. My suit really is from the 1890s, but you can tell
from the soles of my boots that they are more recent because the soles are not
leather." A chart to help you keep track of each person's garments is in the
historian's tool kit at http://www.historicperformance.com. *Telling History*
goes into more detail on creating "the look" for each historic figure.[15]

If you have someone who enjoys styling hair and can look at pictures of the
time to get a sense of what might have been worn, it is fun to have hair styled.
Check with parents first, though, to make sure that certain hair products will
not be a problem—that there are no allergies to them.

Let the actors have privacy while changing (young children have been
taught to be private; at this age, it is likely that they have not yet been exposed
to communal locker rooms or dressing rooms). They are not your children,
even if you think you know them well, so ask permission before touching
them or their clothing. It is about respect—would you expect an adolescent
to tug at your clothing without asking first?

We discovered that in some communities, children are able to grow to
middle school age without having zipped up a zipper or buttoned a shirt. One
boy had not learned to tie his shoes because his mother did it for him and he
usually wore Velcro. Because they have not had the embarrassing clothing
malfunctions that many of us have experienced and/or observed, they will not

PHOTO 5.2
Colleagues helping each other with their look in Baldwin City, Kansas. Photo by authors.

CAUTION: GENDERS CROSSING

A boy who loved music wanted to interpret the local music teacher, Mrs. Wescott. He had the option of portraying her husband, talking about her. But, no, he wanted to portray Mrs. Wescott, not Mr. Wescott. This situation provided the opportunity to talk with the troupe about how unfair is it is when a boy chooses to portray a woman, he gets teased, while it seems fine for a girl to choose to be a man. We used Shakespeare as an example, who wrote for all-male casts—Romeo and Juliet, for example, were both portrayed by men. The young historian/actor was very convincing in dress and wig. Also convincing was a girl in another community who was visiting her cousin. She chose to interpret the surveyor who platted the town. Because of her conservative dress and home schooling, we presumed she would choose to be a woman who knew about the surveyor's work. Guess what? When she strode confidently onto the stage, elegant in the boots, suit, and the top hat that somehow covered all of her long hair, she was very convincing. In fact, it was not until the question-and-answer segment, when the young people took off hats to identify as historians, that her mother finally figured out that that young man was her daughter. We have never had a young historian quite so unwilling to give back her costume as was that adolescent.

   If we think of gender as a continuum (some men seem more feminine than some women and vice versa) instead of as a dichotomy (men are rude and rugged, women are pleasant and gentle), it is easier to let young people try out different roles. In Gering, Nebraska, a girl portrayed a man who was known for dressing and singing as a woman. She felt drawn to his "otherness."

expect colored underwear to show through sheer blouses. You need someone to do costuming who can be respectful of people doing things for the first time.

Gather Materials

Purchase one-inch pocket binders (we get them for two dollars each in bulk at our big-box office supply store) and 1.5- by 2-inch sticky notes. These binders are the ones that you can slip a front and back cover into and really make it your own. There are also pockets inside for items that you don't want to treat to a three-hole punch. Determine which Historian's Toolkit pages (also known as Workshop Workbook—see http://www.historicperformance. com/workshops.htm to use and make copies) you want to use. This is a good time to let us know that you will be using them (for copyright purposes). Everything else is pretty well covered in the list in appendix I.

CAMP BEGINS!

Preparing the Room

Tables should be set up for no more than two people sitting at a six-foot table to give adequate room to spread out. Young historians should be at the front tables and elders to the back. Those who are actually leading the camp will have chairs off to the side at the front of the room. There should also be a sizable chalkboard, whiteboard, and/or easel and pad in front of the room. (See diagram p. 125.)

On each table, stack scrap paper and with it place at least two pencils for every young historian and sticky notes—about one-third of a small or a larger pad. Most archives require researchers to use pencils, not pens. That way, if a stray mark should find its way onto an original document or even a rare book, it can be erased. So pencils become a teaching tool about the cultural practices of historical research and how we are all members of that cultural group. And, of course, sticky notes mark the pages that are most used in the tool kit and the book pages you want to come back to.

One table, off to the side or in the back of the room, should have office supplies so that young historians can readily access scissors, tape, a three-hole punch, an electric pencil sharpener, more paper and pencils, and tissues. Another table at the front of the room should hold handouts such as schedules and the Code of Conduct. Historians' tool kits should be nearby but not readily visible, as should the box of hats for the hat scenario.

For about every seven young historians, there should be one breakout space where chairs can be set up in a semicircle, with a "stage" area on the open side of the circle. If you are short on chairs, you can have your colleagues move their chairs into the space when needed for acting exercises. Breakout spaces can be opposite sides of a large room, in nearby rooms, or in seldom-used hallways. The "audience" can also sit on the floor if need be.

On the first day, there should be a welcoming station just inside the door with the list of registrants and a note if the registration form has not been completed. There should also be a supply of schedules.

Just inside the door, have materials to make name tags. We prefer plastic sleeves with string. We recycle the sleeves and buy new "innards" as necessary. To write the names, we have a large baggie with Sharpies of multiple colors so that people can express themselves in a colorful way—just make sure that the work is done on top of a surface that will not be damaged by bleed-through. Make yourself a name tag with just your first name handwritten on it. Wear it all week. You feel silly wearing a name tag when most people know you? Get over it. It is not about you.

Make sure there are signs posted to help people find the workshop area. One of our least favorite phrases: "But everyone knows. . . ." It is so seldom true.

Welcome!

The timetable in appendix A says to "welcome registrants." Be welcoming. You will want, however, to decide in advance whether you will also welcome an individual or two to camp who has not registered in advance. If it is your first year, you are likely to have room to add a few more students. And, after all, your mission statement does not say, "Teach prospective young historians' parents to register their children in a timely fashion and punish their children if their parents do not do so." In fact, we are certain that you have a statement that reads (although not written), "The more the merrier as long as we have space and stage time." After all, in spite of your best practices, someone will have to drop out at the last minute. And you are building community, so it is about your ongoing relationship with each of these young people.

We also hope that you will welcome parents if they wish to stay for a while. Whether or not the parents want to stay, be sure to give them a copy of the camp's schedule so they can post it at home. We have had parents stay the entire five days and been worthwhile additions, especially when they got into the spirit of being a colleague to all, not just to their offspring.

Your welcome should include a brief introduction, with a handshake, to each young historian as they come in. "Hello, I'm Joyce. And you are. . . . ? It's nice to meet you, ———." Of course, you will modify this if you already know the young people. The important thing is to show them right off the bat that for this week, you are not their teacher but their colleague. Start getting them into the idea of role changes, that they will become experts. Enlist the first to arrive how to show the others how to make a name tag. Show them how to tie a knot to shorten the string so that everyone can see their names when they are seated and/or use a table tent.

If there is anyone who has not yet arrived and it is five minutes after the designated time, get the group involved in something that can be done individually, like using the Sharpies, paper, and other supplies to make a customized cover for the historian's tool kits they will get later. In the meantime, ask someone to call the missing person. Some communities and some families tend to arrive early and some later. Use your judgment but try not to start the "group" stuff until everyone is there. If, however, fifteen minutes have gone by, start introductions and move on through the day's work.

What if you have someone who has to miss a day? The first day is the worst to miss because that is when the group learns about becoming a troupe. It will be important that members of the troupe and elders take late starters under their wings to introduce them to the group culture over the next several days as they participate in group and individual activities.

Occasionally, we let individuals, like the girl whose surgery was scheduled the day of the performance, go through the camp even though we know she won't be there to perform. This especially makes sense when organizers anticipate an ongoing troupe, as they did at the Prairie Museum of Art and History, where museum educator Ann Miner and her volunteers have extended the historical performance season beyond the summer to include cemetery walks and small groups or individuals with expanded scripts entertaining and educating other audiences. The rest of day one is shown in the sample schedules appendix E and appendix F. The hat scenario is spelled out in appendix G.

THE SHOW MUST GO ON—WITH OR WITHOUT ALL OF THE PLAYERS

Janet Reynolds is librarian par excellence in LaCygne, Kansas, who brought us in to do a Night at the Museum camp. One young historian chose to interpret the linotype machine. His grandfather told him that when he was a child, he went to the newspaper office after school to help his father operate a similar machine. Grandfather and grandson researched together, looking at the machine in detail. But the boy's father had custody that weekend and insisted he leave before the performance. Janet calmly filmed the youngster, and when the Night at the Museum tours hit "that certain spot," what seemed like a hologram started talking directly to them from next to the linotype machine, even pointing to parts of the apparatus. At the Prairie Museum of Art and History in Colby, Kansas, one of the historians (portraying a restaurant owner) had to have surgery on the day of her performance. Thanks to Janet, however, we knew exactly what to do: get out the video camera. We even got to try our hand at sound effects because there was a story that involved the breaking of plates in the back room of the restaurant! Both young people enjoyed the extra attention of being on film. And the "restaurant owner" got back just in time for the discussion.

Trust the Process

Almost inevitably on day two of a camp, an elder (or two or three) will be standing back and gazing askance as young people are going hither, thither, and yon to gather information; one young historian is thinking about changing her or his historic figure and do something completely different (after the elder devoted considerable social capital in getting her or him information); two young people are racing up and down the hallway. Only two people are working diligently in the quiet space. That second day is chaos day—always has been and for us probably always will be because somehow it works. Our young colleagues are getting their needs met, including their need to express themselves.

This is one of those moments when elders need to suspend disbelief—it really will all come together in three more days. In fact, even at 1:30 on the day of the performance, some young people will seem hopeless in the eyes of some elders. But with the right attention from the right knowledgeable sources, it all comes together. It is important to have patient elders who are well versed in the details of local history or who know how to find answers. ("Do you know how a telegraph key works? Have you ever seen one? Let's go to the museum. I think they will even let you touch one. Then it will make more sense to you, how you and your husband the sheriff were communicating about rescuing the prisoner from the lynch mob."). That conversation and trip to the museum happened on performance day! Besides, one of the beauties of performance, especially performance where no one needs one of your lines as a cue for their own, is that it can be adjusted even onstage. If the audience is especially responsive, for example, we need to leave more time for them to laugh. It's part of the art that most young people learn only over time.

No matter how much energy is electrifying the space, also provide a quiet area and enforce the quiet policy strictly. One young historian was in tears when he found out, after his performance, that we were leaving. Not only did he have an idea about who he wanted to do next, but he told us that this was the first time that he had had extended time to read quietly. We told him that in five years he would be going to college and reminded him that his new colleague, the theater director for the college, would still be in town. We then gave him a salute (he portrayed a general) and a hug and, when he was out of sight, found our handkerchiefs.

Create a Record

As the young historians get into their look, take photographs of them. We like to do one group photo, but realistically getting everyone into costume early enough to be able to design and print the program is going to happen only if there are, say, half a dozen. So we usually do two group photographs. And even then, someone has to leave early, so we will do a single photo of that person and fit it in where we can.

PHOTO 5.3
All dressed up and ready to interpret at the Santa Fe Trail Center in Larned, Kansas.
Photo by authors.

In Microsoft Office Word 2007, we build our four-page (single sheet of paper folded once) program with a "cover" (page 1) that has a group photo and the who, what, where, and when. The list of who is interpreting whom is on page 3 and very seldom has a photo. The back page usually has the "thanks" list with logos and possibly a picture or two. That leaves page 2 for everything else, including a statement of philosophy. Our is, "Please continue to share with the young historian/researcher/scriptwriter/actors your knowledge of their historic figures and eras. Also, consider asking them to present programs for your events and organizations. It is the intent of this project that they will become a community resource, a speakers bureau that helps explore how decisions have created history. It's not just one event; it's a process!" If you have any trouble, we will be glad to send you an email attachment one of our programs from which you can cut and paste (send your request to ridehist@satelephone.com). We use twenty-four-pound paper with brightness value of at least ninety-six so that the photograph and logo colors do not bleed through.

Do *not* worry about limiting the length of young people's monologues: they have only a few days to prepare, and typically when they are onstage, they will not remember everything they know. We tell them to aim for five minutes. Those few who are very immersed and talk for twenty minutes during rehearsals might need to be cautioned to pick and choose stories so that others have enough time. On the other hand, if you have only, say, six youngsters in your camp, don't even mention a time limit. Typically, even the most verbose young speaker gets a little nervous in front of a large group and forget some of what she or he was going to say. In fact, we assure these speakers that one of the advantages of the Chautauqua-style program is that they are each onstage twice: once for their individual narrative and then for discussion. So if they remember something crucial, they can always work it into the answer to one of the questions they are asked.

Camera-proof the performers by taking lots of pictures during camp and rehearsals. Then you can assure the paparazzi that it will be fine if they record the performance or take stills. And just to make sure, try to have two people recording the entire program.

Prepare the Performance Space

Ask whoever sets up the chairs to keep plenty of room in front and to the side of each chair. Make sure the chairs are sturdy. You will also need space for people using walkers and wheelchairs. Some wheelchairs have high backs, and therefore should be off to the side so they won't block other's views. And speaking of view, if the chairs are in vertical rows away from the stage, audience members will see the back of the person in front of them. Stagger the chairs so everyone can see the stage no matter how tall the people are in front of them. Notice how this is done in theater seating.

If you have helped the young historians to look beyond individual audience members and to look at focus points across the room (left, center, and right), place sticky notes where they can be seen from the stage (or, better yet, have them do it). We also like to say that we have projected our stories onto those sticky notes as well as putting key words on our fingers, so all we have to do is look out across the room to see the cues.

Performance!

As soon as the doors open, someone should be at the entrance handing out the program and answering questions. Almost always, the Chautauqua audience begins to arrive under the tent while dress rehearsal is still in progress. We post several people with programs to assure family members that this is just the dress rehearsal—they are not late. Have some lobby seating if you must hold the audience outside until just before the performance (for final day activities, see appendix K).

Sit front and center if the young people want to see your reassuring face. Do not mouth their lines to them. For one thing, they should be learning stories, not lines, so there are no lines to give them. What if someone freezes? Make like a reporter and go up on the stage and ask her or him questions. Twice when we have worked with people doing very short performances, there have been meltdowns. Both times someone led them offstage keeping them in character, and the audience presumed it was part of the plan. ("As Mr. Smith told you, his wife died recently and he just has not been the same. Hopefully, he can visit with you later, though." "As Mrs. Anderson says, she just does not know how she is going to get everything done, what with having to feed the governor and preparing the rifles and the pheasants for the shoot. We'll let her get on with those tasks and she can talk with us later.") In the case of newspaper editor Smith, by the time everyone else had gone across the stage, he had recovered from his bout with grief, and we almost had to drag her offstage she was on such a roll!

Our favorite part of the camp is after each young historian has performed and they all share the stage, taking questions from the audience, first as historic figures and then as historians. At this point, there is nothing we can do to make a difference. It is all them and all are wonderful. We beam with pride, laugh, and, yes, occasionally grimace and make a note to follow up if a historical error is in danger of being perpetuated. When the entire troupe goes onstage to take questions, first as historic figures and then as historians, you will already have told them that although they are wearing the mantle of authority, they can be glad that that mantle, that cape, has a lining. And that lining is humility. No one can know everything. And if they are asked a ques-

CELEBRATE!

A librarian brought three boys from the library computer room on the first day of a Falls City, Nebraska, to Chautauqua camp. We had just told her that we had only three young people there and needed more. One boy was too young, one just wasn't interested, but the third was bright and eager. He loved to draw, so he chose to be John Falter, known for climbing to the top of the water tower to gain perspective on his hometown, often the subject of *Saturday Evening Post* covers. And the library had an archive of Falter's letters and drawings. We gave a registration form to the young artist to take home to his mother. The next day, the form was not signed. The morning of the third day, he said he had forgotten it, but he broke into his house through a window and awakened his sleeping mother to have her sign it. The camp was Wednesday through Sunday, with performances on Sunday. We and the boy were distraught when we found out on Friday that his family was going camping Friday and he would not be able to perform. We ran into the boy and his father at the convenience store and failed to convince him to commit to be back in time Sunday. The historian said he would pack his tool kit, and maybe, just maybe, it would work. Imagine our delight when he showed up on bicycle, hot and sweaty, less than an hour before the public performance under the tent, but Joyce worked with him, listening and talking through the dressing room door while he got dressed. The library closed early so that all of the staff could attend the Chautauqua. After "John Falter" spoke, the librarians rose to their feet, clapping with gusto. He was so focused on getting off the stage that he did not hear the cheering. Joyce had to turn our young hero around so that he could face his admiration society. The grin on his face was most definitely ear to ear. Against the greatest odds, he had done it. His family was not there, but his librarians and his colleagues were. But where were our handkerchiefs when we needed them?

PHOTO 5.4
Commanding the stage in Colby, Kansas. Photo by authors.

tion to which they do not know the answer, if they are in character, all they have to do is take off their hat or step forward and introduce themselves, "My name is really ———, and I am still researching. Does anyone in the audience know the answer?"—and, if not, offer to work with the questioner to find the answer.

Celebrate, Evaluate, and Start Preparations for More Performances and Next Year's Camp

While you are washing the costumes, enjoy a cup of coffee with committee members and anyone else who wants to join you. Did the event and its process meet your expectations? In what specific ways? It is useful to collect both data and anecdotes that you can use when applying for next year's funding. We have asked audiences to fill out evaluations, which works especially nicely for Night at the Museum tours when there might be an hour or so between the time a person goes on the tour and the time the cast shows up to discuss their process (see the evaluation form in appendix L). The results not only helped with our decision making and that of our museums but also helped them be accountable to their funding organizations, in this case primarily the Kansas Humanities Council.

What changes will you make next year? One very rural historic farm site found that the combination of scarcity of population and the distance parents had to drive to bring youngsters each day meant not only that few signed up but also that if the week became stressful for parents, this was the first thing they dropped. They are considering decreasing the number of days and making each day longer. They could also pick the young people up in town. Ann remembers singing camp songs on the bus to city day camp. Maybe they can write and sing history camp songs during the drive.

Then there is the question of how to make the most of what has been learned—how to share the stories more broadly and continuing to learn. History Day is a competition for young people. The National History Day 2016 theme was "Exploration, Encounter, Exchange in History." Young people in sixth through twelfth grades, usually but not necessarily sponsored by their school, compete on the district, state, and then national levels. They create projects around the theme by asking questions, doing research, and then presenting in one of the following formats: documentary, exhibit, paper, performance, or website. It is one way to use the performances and an excuse to perform for local people as they are preparing for the contest. The official national site is http://www.nhd.org .

Consider Adding Adults

Consider adding adults to an ongoing group. Usually, when a group of people is added to an organization, it is because the mission has changed or, as was the case when girls were added to Future Farmers of America, there are dwindling numbers of the original membership group participating. This was not the case with the North Lyon County Historical Performers Troupe. Adults were added because the young historians did not want to retire after the eighth grade. And it has been a great ride—somewhat literally because we travel as we interpret our communities, all with town populations under 200. Our first "oldsters" signed up in 2013 and included an "army wife" new to the area, a recently retired teacher, and an aspiring professional historical performer (since gone pro). In 2014, three generations of one family attended the camp and performed because we had cared enough to come to their community. In 2015, we had three grandmother/grandchild pairs in addition to other performers.

Ann Miner of the Prairie Museum of Art and History reports about their fourth year of multigenerationality:

> It went wonderfully well! We chose the rich territory of the 1930s for which there are many many local people/stories, artifacts like Depression glass, feed sack dresses, WPA dolls, egg crates, etc that evoke the times, and multiple video and written sources of info from which to draw. We set up a cafe setting on the "stage" where all the historian-actors were seated around three tables, with the scenario being that a reporter from out east was here interviewing folks about their experience in these tough years of the dust bowl. It worked splendidly. We had a standing-room-only crowd, over 100 people! . . . Last fall saw our first "talking tombstone" program . . . , basically a Night [at the Museum] program done at the cemetery, with tombstones as the artifacts. As it was during the school year, we relied more on adults, though Trinity was on board along with one other young woman who plans to be part of this year's summer camp. Definitely will do this again.[16]

Allowing historical performance to be about building the entire community makes the process and the possibilities a great deal more fun. Your historical performers own their community, and the community owns them.

TRAIL STORY 5.10

EVERYONE WHO WANTS TO DO THIS

Several years ago, Joyce found Mallory backstage at the Admire Fall Festival, crying her eyes out. Joyce's initial thought was that the young historian was panicking because she had generously agreed to do *two* first-person narratives to accommodate Clayton relatives who had not seen her do her performance of Robert Clayton the year before. But, no, Mallory was crying not out of fear of failure but out of fear of losing historical performance. Mallory had realized, during her second summer of historical performance, that she was going to "age out," and she was heartbroken. We called a meeting, reminded the young people that this was their troupe, and asked what age would be appropriate. Would, for example, eleventh graders be too intimidating? Mallory very wisely responded—and the others concurred—that "everyone who wants to do this should be able to do it." The next summer, we were delighted to see Mallory's younger brother coaching a retired teacher on how we do things at history camp. And when an older colleague's hat was not sitting right and her shawl was slipping, first-year Courtney did hesitate to help. And because it was all new to the older members, they welcomed the assistance. We were all, as we say, colleagues.

NOTES

1. Ellen Galinsky, *Mind in the Making: The Seven Essential Life Skills Every Child Needs* (New York: William Morrow Paperbacks, 2010).

2. In fact, when Ann took a risk that Joyce thought was uncharacteristic, Joyce would ask, "Is that Ann making that decision, or is it Amelia?" By then, of course, it was always Ann under the influence of Amelia. Joyce's story of overcoming her fear of teachers by meeting them first as Calamity Jane is presented in Joyce Thierer, *Telling History: A Manual for Performers and Presenters of First-Person Narratives* (Lanham, MD: AltaMira Press, 2010), 5, 6.

3. Dorothy Heathcote of University of Newcastle upon Tyne advocated a curriculum in which children took on the role of experts in whatever subject they were studying. "Mantle of the Expert.com: A Dramatic-Inquiry Approach to Teaching and Learning," http://www.mantleoftheexpert.com/about-moe/introduction/what-is-moe (accessed August 17, 2015).

4. Girl Scout staff, volunteers, and consultants provided the means for girls to create the Studio 2B Latina troop in response to Emporia High School staff who wanted girls from diverse Latin American countries to stop fighting. The troop was very successful, even helping girls apply for and enroll in the local college, but it was lost when GSUSA consolidated councils.

5. Some of our favorite local history pundits are Carol Kammen, *On Doing Local History*, rev. ed. (Lanham, MD: AltaMira Press, 2014), as well as her column by the same name in the American Association of State and Local History publication *History News*, and David E. Kyvig and Myron A. Marty, *Nearby History: Exploring the Past Around You*, 3rd ed. (Lanham, MD: AltaMira Press, 2010), which is the text Joyce assigns to her local history class.

6. Thierer, *Telling History*, 38–40.

7. This was a bit difficult for Joyce, who, as you know if you read the first chapter of *Telling History* (pp. 4–6), was working on overcoming her fear of teachers.

8. Heathcote, "Mantle of the Expert.com."

9. As we remember, we were paid for the intersession too.

10. In 2010, the newly elected governor wiped out the Kansas Arts Commission and then began crafting the political downfall of every Republican legislator who had fought to keep it. It was not about the arts but about exercising control and identifying those who would follow him.

11. J. D. Bullough et al., "Effects of Flicker Characteristics from Solid-State Lighting on Detection, Acceptability and Comfort," *Lighting Research and Technology* 43, no. 3 (September 2011): 337–48; *Academic Search Premier*, EBSCO*host* (accessed August 18, 2015); Doris Sikora, "What Great Teachers Do," *Techniques*, October 2013, 39–40.

12. Emporia State University communications major Olivia Finley interned with Ride into History in the summer of 2012. She was paid by the Ride into History Cultural and Educational Project, Inc., to be a participant observer, logging what

we did each camp day. "Find the restrooms," she said, "was second on the first day, after meeting our hosts."

13. Penn State College of Agricultural Sciences Extension, "Take Along Healthy Snacks for Summer Road Trips," July 20, 2015, http://extension.psu.edu/health/news/2015/take-along-healthy-snacks-for-summer-road-trips (accessed August 18, 2015).

14. M. Hearn, "Water and Brain Function: How to Improve Memory and Focus," http://www.waterbenefitshealth.com/water-andbrain.html, cited in Sikora, "What Great Teachers Do," 43.

15. Thierer, *Telling History*, 80–92.

16. Email to authors, July 12, 2015.

6

Using Historical Performance Skills to Enhance Other Traditions of Costumed Interpretation

Back in 1983 Ann purchased a mare for $400 from a Nebraska farmer who had purchased that horse and several others "off the reservation." She was an old-style horse—short and "fleabit gray" (white, with flecks of brown) with Appaloosa characteristics as well as high withers and a sloped butt. Definitely a mustang. She was pregnant and nursing a colt when we brought her home to her new herd. We called her Feathers and soon figured out that she was even younger than we had been told—she must have been bred even before she reached what should have been her full size.

True to her mustang heritage, Feathers was a survivor who paid her respects to humans and appreciated the sight and sound of a bucket but knew that her first allegiance was to her herd. She could find grass under snow and break ice on a pond to get to water. She was "green broke"—that is, she had only recently learned to accept a rider on her back—and we never did think a bridle and bit were something she cared to pay attention to, so eventually we outfitted her with a hackamore (no bit). She approached every ride with someone on her back as a task to get over with as soon as she could. Her walk was as vertical as a trot and almost as fast, and her trot was twice as fast as anyone's but her son's. She insisted on being at the front of any trail ride.

When Feathers was about thirteen years old, we gave riding lessons to some young friends. One of these friends, Sarah, complained that she always had to ride Feathers. She wanted one of the prettier, more compliant horses.

Joyce knew, though, that Sarah and Feathers made a good match, both of them hardheaded. She told Sarah that if she could ride Feathers, she would be able to ride any horse she encountered in years to come. A few years later, Sarah, home from college for the summer, told us that Joyce was right. Sarah had chosen a college with an equestrian program, and she found that, sure enough, because she had learned to negotiate with Feathers, she was confident with all of the horses at her school, even the ones her classmates avoided.

Just in case you missed the point of this story, taking the difficult road makes future roads easy by comparison or at least makes you a more confident traveler. Specifically, historical performance is the Feathers of the costumed interpretation world; historical performance is the most challenging road. Historical performance is also the most rewarding route to sharing history's stories. If you can do a good job with historical performance, you can enjoy just about any type of costumed historical interpretation, whether grounded most firmly in public history traditions or in theater traditions. As we said in the preface, "Learning the process of historical performance for one or more historic figures will enhance all of the other types of costumed work that you do."

YOUR PASSION; YOUR IDENTITY

You probably came to historical performance—or to museum work— through a passion for sharing a particular aspect of history and/or a passion for acting and a desire to earn your living by doing what you love to do. When you began to explore historical performance, you might already have been participating in one of the other traditions of costumed historical interpretation. In this chapter, we want to encourage historical performers and presenting organizations to think about historical performers as able to do all of the forms of interpretation that are represented in Joyce's Venn diagram (see p. 5), slightly revised here from its debut in *Telling History*.[1] To really do historical performance well, you need that passion, *and* you need to be *both* a historian and an artist. You need to be a historian/researcher/scriptwriter/actor. This might require a stretch in your thinking about yourself, but it makes you a very flexible interpreter of history.

Identity is tricky. It comes as much from external messages as from within. If you are a historical performer, it is important that your identities are many: you should identify as someone involved with your subject area, you should identify as a historian, and you should identify as an artist. We have talked about being a historian in chapter 2. Here, we talk about the traditions in costumed historical interpretation in which you might want to participate, peripheral to being a historical performer. We also talk about being an artist. But first, more on that passion for your particular subject matter that brought you to historical performance.

Here is how engineer Doug McGovern describes in third person his conversion to historical performance:

Alive With History is the product of Doug McGovern. He is a photographer, teacher, engineer and historical performer. After retiring from a career in engineering management in 1997, Doug has been able to develop his love of the past initially working on stereo photography. He became interested in stereo vision while developing remotely driven vehicles as an engineer. Stereo television installed in the robotic vehicle allowed the driver to proceed safely around ditches and holes. When Doug had the opportunity to follow the footsteps of his Great Great Grandfather through action in the Civil War (Samuel Cowan, 17th Illinois Volunteer Infantry), he realized that stereo photography, when applied to battlefield scenes, let the viewer "see" the terrain as real. Roads, hills, and trenches stand out. Also, stereo photos of people and action scenes provide a realism that grabs the viewer in a way that regular photos cannot. This inspired Doug to start a company called "Vintage Visuals" to produce and distribute stereo pictures. Of course, the history of these pictures needed to be researched. To understand the times, the techniques, and the talents, Alexander Gardner became a worthy tutor. It was but a short step to then become Alex through developing a historical performance.[2]

Doug's creation of a first-person narrative of Alexander Gardner led him to explore not only nineteenth-century photography but also the Santa Fe Trail, Great Plains railroad history, and the Civil War, all of which were photographed by Gardner. In fact, he discovered that a well-known Gardner photograph of Robert E. Lee was one of two stereophotographs that had been separated. His work has been published in a Civil War photography journal, and he has presented his findings at a regional historians' conference. While his career as an engineer provided him with skills and knowledge, the idea of becoming a historian and an artist took a great deal of imagination and a tremendous leap of faith.

Other members of the Kansas Alliance of Professional Historical Performers are following their passions. Army veteran Anna Smith, who has ancestors who fought in the American Revolution, has created a portrayal of Deborah Samson, the first woman known to have disguised herself as a man to fight in the U.S. Army. Clothing designer Kitty Frank portrays Nell Donnelly, creator of the Nelly Don clothing line, which made her, at age twenty-seven, the second self-made woman millionaire in the United States. (Need we say that Kitty also designs and builds her own clothing for performance?) As an undergraduate, Lynsay Flory refused to believe that missionaries worked to eradicate tribal culture. Being familiar with Ride into History, she decided to become a missionary to the Delaware, having found one close to her own age and unmarried, like her. Lynsay was juried into the Kansas Alliance of Professional Historical Performers, has completed her master's degree in public history, and is working on her doctorate in heritage studies at North Dakota State University. Bonnie Johnson's experience piloting antique airplanes and her desire to encourage girls to follow her into engineering led to Bonnie portraying both pilot Louise Thaden and sister-to-pilots Katharine Wright.

Deborah Divine's passion for art quilts and Belinda and Mike Adams's passion for early trade and trail history let each of them share what were avocational interests with paying audiences. Deborah travels the country sharing Rose Kretsinger's wisdom gained not only from Kretsinger's training at the Chicago Art Institute but also from speaking before groups about her use of natural forms in her award-winning quilts. By presenting to quilting groups and practicing the art form of historical performance, Deborah continues learning about her first art form, quilting.

Continued learning about your subject matter is important to historical performers. For example, Doug McGovern lists on the Alliance website some of his involvement:

> Doug is active in other historical activities including working with local preservation efforts, membership in the Sons of Union Veterans of the Civil War, reenacting with the 8th Kansas Volunteer Infantry (as a civilian photographer), and membership in a Victorian Dance performance group.[3]

Ann portrays Julia Archibald Holmes, the first woman known to have climbed to the summit of Pikes Peak in the Rocky Mountains, which she reached by hiking the Santa Fe Trail in 1858. Ann joined the Santa Fe Trail Association, which not only researches the trail but also preserves it and educates the public as well as Santa Fe Trail Association members. She has written a profile of Holmes for the issue of *Wagon Tracks* that followed Holmes's initiation into the Santa Fe Trail Hall of Fame. Ann has also performed at three national meetings of the organization and is on the national speakers bureau that subsidizes programs for local chapters. Being identified by others with your passion creates a research team for you. At one of her first national Santa Fe Trail conferences, two acquaintances told Ann that Julia's grandson was looking for her. As far-fetched as it seemed, Ted Holmes was the son of Julia's oldest son, who was born in 1859. That son, Ernest Julio, was in his fifties when Ted was born. Ted and Ann continue to share research.

HOW DO HISTORICAL PERFORMERS FIT INTO OTHER PUBLIC HISTORY TRADITIONS?

In chapter 1, we presented a Venn diagram that describes three overlapping circles of "best practice priorities" of various costumed interpretation traditions. The circles are "Accurate Look," "Answers Questions, Knows Historical Context," and "Accurate Script." Inside each circle and inside the overlapping areas of the circles are lists of costumed interpretation traditions. "Historical performance" is in the center of the diagram because it shares characteristics with other traditions of costumed historical interpretation. As we said above, "If you can do a good job with historical performance, you can enjoy just about any type of costumed historical interpretation."

Atmospherics, look-alikes, impersonators, and reenactors desire to re-create something that existed before. They want to be as close to that historic visual picture as possible—short, for example, of being killed on a battlefield (in the case of reenactors). They want to build clothing that is museum quality, that cannot be differentiated from the authentic items.

Atmospherics take historic site visitors back in time visually and usually only visually. They are often captivated with clothing in general, possibly making their own. They might or might not be interested in what people who wore those clothes did other than walk around looking interesting. They might be interested only in the classes of people who wore fancy clothes and then mostly in the clothes, not the people themselves. How do historical performers interact with clothes people? Well, first of all, if they really have knowledge and not just a desire to parade about in upper-class finery, historical performers can often use the sometimes considerable knowledge of costume people, especially if the history (and making) of clothing is not their strongest suit.

Wordplay

Wordplay is one of the joys of historical performance. Members of the audience love it, and the response of those who "get it" is an affirmation for the performer that the audience is engaged. One of Ann's favorite is in her story as Amelia Earhart describing how she first became enamored of flying. It was during (what we now know as) World War I. Earhart was a volunteer nurse aide at Spadina Military Hospital in Toronto, Ontario. She worked "twelve hour days, but in the middle of the afternoon we had a rather lengthy break. My favorite thing to do during that break was to listen to the soldiers tell their stories. And the pilots had the best stories of all. For one thing, they used the English language in a way I had never heard it used before." Almost always, Ann says, as she scans the room while talking, someone's eyes will twinkle, presumably a veteran who thinks back to a soldier's experience with rough language. Ann feigns surprise at catching this: "That's not what I meant . . . [as other adult members of the audience join in on the joke and share a chuckle], although there was some of that. But I was thinking about words like 'dead stick landing, and using 'pancake' as a verb—'we pancaked?!'"

Look-alikes want to look and pose exactly like a historic figure. For example, Lincoln, Kansas, has an annual Abraham Lincoln look-alike contest. Impersonators take it one step further, adding voice to visuals. An impersonator will usually use the actual words of the person being impersonated and mimic her or his voice timber and inflection. If you have not yet been called an impersonator, stick around the field long enough, and you will be. "Impersonator" and "reenactor" are the costumed historical interpretations that are most familiar to our presenting organizations. Often, the error will be in a news release (all the more reason to write your own that is so compelling that they will not want to do it themselves), or it will be in your introduction. In neither case will you have time to correct the presenter. Besides, it sounds churlish and embarrasses the presenter if you say, "I am *not* an impersonator; I am a historical performer." And sometimes we do find ourselves in the role of an impersonator (impersonating an impersonator?): "Would Ann cut a birthday cake on the centennial of Amelia Earhart's birth, with the governor, after the performance in Memorial Hall and before the banquet?" Of course she would, and she would also refer to him as Governor Capper, the governor in 1937.

If the priority of the tradition "reenacting" is an accurate look, living history interpreters prioritize an accurate look *and* having enough knowledge to answer questions, while neither reenactors nor living history interpreters are known for a structured first-person script (the third circle in the diagram).

Joyce met Nolan Sump when he was doing skills demonstration at a small living history event, cutting grass with a handheld scythe. Ride into History workshops and eventual membership in the Kansas Alliance of Professional Historical Performers helped him make the transition to first person and maintain his skills with the support of other performing artists. But just because someone does historical performance does not mean that she or he cannot go "back" to doing skills demonstration—or reenactment. Mike and Belinda Adams (a.k.a. SME Portals of Time) are historical performers, but they came to historical performance via Civil War reenactment and black powder rendezvous. They still enjoy their muzzle-loader buddies and stir those interests into their historical performance offerings. Their website says that they offer a Civil War camp in which they "share their experiences from everyday camp chores to battle fields. A full-day in-depth hands-on program which involves drilling, flag design, rationing, and games." They also know how to make a buffalo hide into a robe and can make just about anything you might want from leather. Norman Joy (NJoy History) is an emotionally engaging Robert E. Lee talking to his family about what it will be like for him *not* to be a soldier for the first time since adulthood. Norman also has two lesser-known characters *and* has recently built in his backyard an entire nineteenth-century, preelectricity workshop. There is not even a lightbulb in that shop, that is how accurate it is.

Reenactors and skill demonstrators are adding to, not subtracting from, their repertoire by becoming historical performers. Likewise, people with no living history or skills demonstration experience can add living history skills from what they learn from historical performance.

"Talking tombstones" is an example in which actors generally focus solely on having (preferably knowing) a script with accurate information, but their clothing may be representative, and the actors are unlikely to know more about local history than what is in their script. Chautauquans, usually scholars, are exacting about historical accuracy in their script and during question-

PHOTO 6.1
Amelia Earhart at an elementary school learning station on map reading. Photo by authors.

and-answer sessions, but the third area, that of their "look," is not always a priority—they are likely to have gotten representational clothing from their college's theater department.

Historical performers emphasize all three. We not only research and craft stories (the script) but also know enough to take questions within historical context—what else was happening at the time described in the stories. And we consider the clothing we wear onstage important because it is the visual component of the message we are presenting to our audience. Therefore, if you can do historical performance—if you can put together a program where you are accurate in your look and what you say, and you can accurately answer questions about the time as well as the person—you should be comfortable with most of the other costumed interpretation traditions in Joyce's diagram. Historical performance is not a form you learn *instead* of another tradition of costumed historical interpretation, rather, it is a form that enhances your participation in the other traditions—with a few exceptions. But we will get to that later. First, let's consider when and how you might want to use the other, not as complex traditions.

PHOTO 6.2
Calamity Jane visits a Texas Panhandle tourism in-service; then Joyce talks about creating local first-person narratives to enhance tourists' experiences. Photo by authors.

If you are a historical performer, your "look" should be good enough that the most ardent "thread Nazi" among the reenactors will not challenge you or that, if you do have an article of clothing that is not historically accurate, you are able to explain what you should be wearing and why you are not wearing it (i.e., too expensive, but after I am paid for this performance, I will be able to afford it).

First person to third person. Ann says that it is still easier for her to meet an audience as someone other than herself, but what doing first-person narratives has finally convinced her is that, with few exceptions, the audience is much more interested in what she has to say than in who she is.

If you have developed a historical performance and have shared it with, say, ten audiences in the past three months, you would probably be comfortable in participating should someone ask you to represent that historic figure in a look-alike contest. You would, that is, unless you absolutely hate the idea of look-alike contests. But you *could* whether or not you *would*. (Pay us enough and we will rationalize a way to enjoy it, such as agreeing to participate in a look-alike contest if we are paid and if someone will hand our card out to audience members.)

As adults, neither of us has been in a play in which another actor depended on us to speak lines that would provide the other actors cues as to what they should say next. We know our ability to learn stories, but we have not tested our ability to memorize lines. Ann wrote what should be categorized as "museum theater," but she wrote it so that the actors needed to learn stories, not memorize lines.

BUT IS IT ART?

There is a rumor that historians cannot act.[4] Pish posh. If your work is not art, it should be. What is art, and why should your historical performance be art? Those of us who are wanting to share our passion via historical performance and have little or no experience in the arts need to embrace the identity of "artist" to do our best for our audiences. We need to accept everything we can get from (other) artists and in turn share what we have learned with others.

Identity is formed as much by what you are *not* as by what you *are*. Ann, for example, has two sisters and a brother who took art in school. She did not take art. She was not "the artist" in the family. Art was drawing and painting and shaping clay. Joyce, who had only one brother with whom to compete, fought hard to take industrial arts in high school, has always taken pleasure in working with her hands to create beautiful objects, and is still a secret artist. But now Ann considers herself an artist even though she still does not draw or dance.

Maybe you played an instrument or loved to dance but never heard those called "art." Never mind any art-squelching messages you received when you were young. Consider the possibility that you have stories that you want to share in an artistic way. You just might find your inner artist, and the inner artist just might become an outer artist. You just might claim that artist identity proudly, as we have.

You might feel comforted to know that the question "What is art?" has long been debated, and the debate continues. Philosophy professor Sally Markowitz discusses the difference between art and craft in the visual arts, noting that "art" has a much higher status than "craft," which makes it important to examine the elitism that is inherent in such a label. The mind/body dichotomy in the cultures in which we suspect that most of our readers have been immersed value mind over body. Therefore, those objects that are used physically (weavings and ceramics) have been classified as different and less than those that exist to be appreciated visually: viewed, appreciated, and contemplated. The first is craft, the second art. And we all know that the mind is to be valued over the body.[5] One who is antielitist might reject the label "art" on the principle of not wanting to be thought of as elitist. So why bother with a definition that might give people the wrong idea about your antielitist goals?

How does this discussion of visual arts fit in with historical performance? In our case, we had to be convinced that we were art. Presenting organizations who used arts funding to bring us in asked why we were not on our state's arts commission roster. "Because we are *humanities scholars*" did not sound like a solid answer. Maybe, "Because we have never studied theater or been in plays?" "Because we did not know that we were art or even that there *was* such a roster" was actually closer to the truth. We were not, of course, averse to marketing ourselves as artists if other people said we were artists and if financial benefits followed. This process of defining and being historical performers has made us nothing if not humble. As we discussed in the previous chapter, if we are going to wear the mantle of authority (and we *should* be authorities on our people and their contexts), we should also line that cape with humility because we will always be learning.

We have since then embraced our arts selves, and we have each been recognized for our accomplishments with arts fellowships. So we are asking those of you with no theater experience or other experience with an arts identity to keep an open mind before you deny that you are and do art. And for those of you who are very comfortable as artists, consider also identifying as "autobiographical performance" as described by Lynn Miller and Jacqueline Taylor, editors of *Voices Made Flesh*. They celebrate the storyteller in historical performance by citing novelist Henry James that "adventures happen only to people who know how to tell them."[6] There is a similar saying about people from particular areas—that, for example, a southerner will suffer any catastrophe just to have a good story to tell. In fact, it often helps one get through a bad time to think about how you can describe the event to others, exaggerating and playing with your own role as well as the roles of others (depending in part on whether those "others" will hear your version of the story).

Why Be Art?

1. Taking your passion as far as you can
2. Status—be art, be respected
3. Roster = seal of approval as entertainment
4. Ongoing training
5. Networking
6. Accessing lists of presenting organizations
7. Funding
8. Striving
9. Professional organizations
10. Science, technology, engineering, and mathematics (STEM)
11. You need "art," *and art needs you*

Why should you claim the title "artist," and why is it likely that you already *are* art or are not far from creating a significant work of art? For at least eleven reasons.

First, true artists are passionate about their art. This passion means that you will create the best possible program for your audience. You will create something magical, something that carries people away from the here and now. If you are not art, you are probably just a lecturer wearing funny clothes. We have seen them. Hopefully, you have not encountered them, but they are far too common, which is one reason we conduct workshops. Don't settle for less than art. Be passionate. Take people back in time instead of telling them about the old days. Show instead of just telling. If you are art, you constantly craft your body and your words to hold the attention of your audience, to help your audience suspend disbelief as you become the person you portray for the benefit of the audience. You are creating, making thoughtful decisions. You are taking risks.

Like a sculptor, you either form your script as you select from the many materials you have gathered (your research), adding stories as a sculptor adds clay, or you pour the words into a mass, not unlike a block of marble, and then you selectively remove stories and words until just the right amount remains to reveal your historic figure. Like a storyteller, you are constantly aware of your audience, adjusting to them, walking closer to those whose attention is straying or who are reaching out to you, adding a story or two when the audience is rapt and you have not been given a certain time to end the performance. Like an actor, you have practiced gestures and phrases that will hold an audience; like a director, you have used timing, rhythm, and cadence to build suspense and provide humor and, yes, to make it easier for you to remember a difficult but powerful phrase. You are in control of the entire process. The art of the historical performer is in the choices of what to add and what to take away. You marry the "look" to the script: What setting shall I use and where and when? Where is my historic figure coming from and going to? What clothing choices will represent audience members' concept of the historic figure? Why might she or he have been wearing this jacket that I like so well?

Like a photographer, you help audiences see the familiar in a new way by highlighting a piece of history or showcasing the unfamiliar in a comfortable setting, one in which audience members are invited to look, listen, and ask questions (although if you ask Calamity Jane as portrayed by Joyce about the father of her child, you are likely to be reminded that she has not asked you about your personal life!). Unlike most visual art, your work changes. Each time you perform it, you are different, your audience is different, and the venue has likely changed. Your art, your artwork, evolves.

Second, you should want to be art because art demands status and respect. It is a positive label for what you do, and, let's face it, you need all of the positive labels you can get while developing the "brand" for your historical performances. The more really great labels you use, the more likely that one of those descriptors will connect with a potential presenting organization. Claim historian; claim artist. The label "art" indicates that you have training and skills that other historical interpreters might not have. You are not only "education" but also "entertainment."

Third, being on an arts commission–juried roster of performers assures presenting organizations that you have met the criteria for that roster. You are art. Remember the Good Housekeeping Seal of Approval? Like the vacuum cleaner or toaster that received the seal, by being on the theater roster you have earned the stamp of approval from a governmental or not-for-profit agency that says that in their book you are not only art but also really great art. Our marketing material says that we have been on the Kansas Arts Commission (KAC) roster even though the KAC has not existed for years. What this does is tell people that we are really, really worth bringing to their community, their venue. Not only do we know history (we are, after all, scholars with doctorates), but we are also entertaining.

Ride into History did not get onto the KAC Touring Program roster the first time we applied. We had worked very hard on our application—we had driven fifty miles to get to the office in Topeka, delivering a videotape plus ten copies and one "original" of a two-inch-thick application, including marketing material; a list of everywhere we had performed in the past few years; publicity we had received; our plans for Ride into History; and an artist statement an hour before the application deadline. We had received so much encouragement that we really thought we might be accepted. But no. So after we received the letter of denial, we swallowed our pride and called the KAC office. We asked how we might do better next year. The staff member was very friendly (she actually remembered our application and was not trying to avoid us—that was a good sign). She pulled our file. The process was public. People in attendance at the juror's deliberations knew what was said about us, and just because we were unable to be there does not mean we do not get to "hear" what was said. She listed specific concerns, including that our video was overproduced, and encouraged us to apply again because if a couple of the jurors had ranked us just a point or two higher, we would have made the roster. She advised us to take advantage of nearby university theater professors for some tips. After we had done so, we felt very "theater" because the seasoned theater folks were quite complimentary and we learned from them. Being juried a second time and receiving the hearty congratulations that followed increased our confidence immensely. What at first was a frustration actually made us stronger. In fact, it became one of Henry James's "adventure[s]." A few years later (after we had been successful), KAC asked us to give a workshop on how to get on the KAC roster. Our failure became an adventure story (overcoming adversity) that we put to good use.

The fourth reason to aspire to art status is that artists have special career/craft development opportunities. Be open to everything, especially if the cost is minimal. For example, Ann was selected to attend the Kennedy Center for the Performing Arts Artists as Educators series of workshops, which helped her encourage history and language arts teachers to incorporate the arts in their teaching. Arts organizations offer business workshops or classes for artists: marketing, photographing your art, handling your income taxes, and copyright and trademark issues. Arts (and humanities) organizations offer grant-writing workshops. They are aimed at presenting organizations, not at performing artists, but go—and take your calendar. You want to learn how to write a grant so that you can assist presenting organizations who have never written a grant but need the funds to bring you in (e.g., a school that does not know to send someone to the grant-writing workshop). But there is another reason: at the workshop, you will have a chance to meet people who might want to bring you in. At the beginning of each workshop, chances are that the workshop leader will have the attendees briefly introduce themselves. Chances are that *you* will be the only artist there, so when you introduce yourself and explain what you do, *you* will be the one who catches the attention of the presenters: they will want to book you. They will think that if they can get you tentatively booked during the workshop's break, they will have a good start on filling in their season. They will have met two goals: learning to write a grant and knowing what they are going to do with the money.

Another source of continuing education is arts organization conferences. They can be expensive, but putting yourself out there will call attention to you in a way that just staying at home and being on a roster cannot. It conveys the message, "We are confident that we are the best thing since sliced bread, and we will not be satisfied to just let the home folks know it." We felt our credentials leap by metes and bounds when KAC staffers and area arts presenters not only saw us at the Arts Midwest/Mid-American Arts Conference in Milwaukee but also saw that we had invested in exhibit space. We had rented only half a booth, but we were there, and we were different—in a good way. There were few artists with booths. Most exhibitors were agents who represented performing artists, or they were large organizations. Think orchestras. Think dance troupes.

Fifth is networking. At arts events, we have met and become friends with storytellers, musicians, dancers, dramatists, and visual artists who have sparked our creativity and inspired cooperative projects. We have also met staff members of presenting organizations who are very interested in a troupe with which they are not familiar. And if we can take a slightly intrigued arts organization staff member by the elbow and introduce her or him to someone who is familiar with our work and will spontaneously give us a rave review, we are as good as booked! We also meet legislators. At one reception, Ann was standing in a semicircle with a mix of people she both knew and did not know. Suddenly, a legislator turned to her and said, "I just figured out who you are! You're Amelia Earhart. I didn't recognize you without your hat." Ann did not tell the legislator that she does not wear a hat, especially as Amelia. What Ann realized was that the legislator did not recognize Ann without Joyce, who is seldom without a hat. Bottom line: having a recognizable brand (like Joyce's Western hat) is a must, but that brand must also be where the people are, and people who are important to making what we do possible attend arts events.

Sixth, arts agencies have lists of people and organizations who bring artists onto their stages. These are the organizations, the schools, and the communities that are looking for something new—*you*! The Mid-America Arts Alliance, for example, makes available to their artists lists of organizations that have received grants from them. Doesn't it make sense to send your marketing material to those people who have already shown their ability to write a grant, who will be looking for something new, and who know where to go to get the money to get you to their venue?

It is exciting to work with individuals and organizations that have never before presented anything other than lectures, and your ability to guide them to the funding agencies with which you are allied increases your status a hundredfold. We once thought that a very dynamic historical society was doing a lot of programming because we drove six hours twice a year to perform or lecture or present a workshop. It was several years before we found out that we were the whole of their dynamic programming.

Seventh, arts rosters open funding doors. Often, presenting organizations can apply to bring an artist to their venue, but the process is somewhat arduous. When Kansas had an arts commission and we were on the Kansas arts roster, the presenter did not have to convince the commission that we were worthy of funding.[7] It was a very simple process for the presenting organization—fill in a few blanks and send the application for half of our fee (including travel) to the commission, knowing that if there was still money in the traveling roster fund, they would receive their request. They did not have to justify our worth because the commission knew that we were worthy. Once we were selected for the roster the first time, we still had to reapply every three years. We were challenged to stay on top of our work, an arduous process but a worthy one.

However, let's make that strenuous process the eighth reason to claim status as an artist. It made us better at marketing our art. For example, one year the KAC staff told us that we needed a new photograph to go in their catalog. We whined, but they were right. And now we should have another new one but without the commission—everyone likes the photo with Amelia Earhart crouched on the wing of the plane explaining with a globe her plan to fly around the world to a skeptical Calamity Jane, whose horse was at hand. When we first applied, they required a videotape from artists. The requirement changed as technology changed until we were posting on YouTube. One of the things we really appreciate about the arts roster, as opposed to the humanities speakers bureau roster, for instance, where scholars' pay is an honorarium that presumes a full-time academic job, is that arts people are respectful of artists as entrepreneurs. They do not want artists to be the stereotypical "starving artist." We set our own fees and have a great deal of latitude about our product—as long as it is "art"!

Nine: As an artist you can join professional arts organizations that make the world a better place *and* help you network. Women in the Arts & Media Coalition, for example, and the Kansas Alliance for the Arts in Education. Then there are the informal potluck-dinner-based groups that gather to share strategies and sources for sharing the good news about your art.

Reason #10 to be involved with the arts today: STEAM power! School curricula are emphasizing science, technology, engineering, and mathematics (STEM) in hopes of graduating more young people who can make contributions in those fields. But knowing that all of the STEM in the world will flail hopelessly on the ground without the creative power expressed in the arts, there is a widespread movement to also encourage more art in schools (STEAM). Margaret Weisbrod Morris, director of Lawrence Arts, hires artists to work with young people in carefully structured after-school STEAM programs:

> Based on the idea that critical thinking, problem solving, and the ability to innovate are essential skills, the goal of ARTspace is to create a learning environment where young people exercise thinking skills through creative practice. A central function of the program is to provide the space and time outside of school for students to play with ideas.
>
> Yes, but just what kinds of things are the young people doing?
>
> Students in "Space Ninja Training Camp" cement their understanding of aerodynamics as they design, build and launch handmade bottle rockets. They also *develop characters and story for the context of their launch* [emphasis added]. Within this scenario, they study factors that affect their rocket's launch and trajectory to develop a practical understanding of the relationship between purpose, function, and design.[8]

Does this not sound familiar? Does it not sound like something historical performers do, developing characters and stories that fit historical context?

Playing the Narrative

Ann was under contract to research the "more comfortable" family (that of newspaper editors and publishers William Allen White and Sallie Lynsay White)[1] that lived across the street from Verna Lawton and her adopted mother at the turn of the nineteenth century. After the project was completed, the stories in Verna Lawton Morrison's memoir haunted Ann.[2] The Whites' home is now a state historic site: the four-room house in which Verna grew up has been replaced by William Allen White Elementary School. Ann had never written a play, and the idea of doing dialogue was not enticing. But these stories begged to be told. Ann heard the voice in Verna Lawton's memoir changing to that of Verna's adopted mother. So she began by researching the neighborhood and the stories behind the stories: How did the Whites' neighbors earn their livings? How racially integrated was the neighborhood? Where did people buy groceries? Where did paupers live? Her findings began to live in her mind as the play that, thanks to a local foundation, she wrote, directed, and produced on two "stages" simultaneously. One of those stages was the living room of Red Rocks, the home of the Whites; the other was on the front lawn of William Allen White School, where the home of Verna and her adopted mother had been, and a scrim took the audience to "my grandmother's porch"—two first-person narratives on two separate stages simultaneously, with two audiences moving from one to the other. Ann portrayed neither. Instead, she was playwright, producer, and director, all things she had done before but only when she was also the actor. It was scary, but she obviously loved the adrenaline. Joyce portrayed the butler, who moved the two audiences from one stage to the other while also providing comic relief. A member of Joyce and Ann's North Lyon County Historical Performance Troupe portrayed Verna at age fourteen in 1912 running from Red Rocks to her Mama Lina's gathering on the lawn to tell the story about the "good Kansas fried chicken" that President Theodore Roosevelt had requested for Sunday dinner, which just slid off the warming oven to the floor. Sallie White was portrayed by social sciences teacher Barbara Fowler, who had created a first-person narrative for her master's degree project. Special education teacher Ann Fritz, no experience but always ready for anything, agreed to try on Mama Lina—definitely a reaching out from the other side.

1. The *Autobiography of William Allen White* (New York: Macmillan, 1946) is still the most readable source about the journalist William Allen White.

2. "The Little Girl across the Street" is in the Laverne Lawton Morrison Collection at the Emporia State University Library and Archives as a typescript with notes.

PHOTO 6.3
Joyce (George) tells Barbara Fowler (Sallie) to pretend George is one of her middle school students. Photo by authors.

Finally, reason number 11 why we should all embrace our identity as artists is because "art" needs us. When legislation is introduced that threatens the arts (hard to believe, perhaps, but in Kansas we are suffering from the results of the zeroing out of the arts budget), artists hear what is happening and are able to participate in attempts to curtail the damage and then, should the worst happen, are part of a community of artists and arts organizations who are there for each other.

BUT WHAT KIND OF ARTIST ARE YOU?

Yes, the passionate kind of artist, but when you have to check a box, just what is your art? Go for theater, but remember that you are also a scriptwriter and

PHOTO 6.4
Verna tells Mama Lina about Colonel Roosevelt's chicken hitting the floor. Mama Lina's ring and nail polish were removed, but Verna's braces stayed. Photo by authors.

that you direct your own performance. You want to be where people expect art to be, but you want also to be the value added. Twice recently, presenters from out of state have said almost the same thing to Ann: "There are a lot of Amelia Earharts out there, but you are different. You are *more than just an actress.*" (Ann says, "Definitely not another pretty face!") You *should* consider yourself "art" and work at that art if you are a historical performer. And you should be able to explain how you are "art."

Historical Performers Are All Ginger Rogers

Though many consider [Fred] Astaire the single greatest dancing talent in film history, a punch line from the Bob Thaves' [1982] comic strip "Frank and Ernest" has become a much-quoted appeal for equal credit and equal rights: "Sure he was great, but don't forget that Ginger Rogers did everything he did . . . backwards and in high heels."[9]

Ginger Rogers has been quoted as saying, "The only way to enjoy anything in this life is to earn it first."[10] Historical performers can ride the most challenging horse and dance backward in high heels. I know that is what audience members think of us when we keep them entranced with a forty-five-minute monologue, take questions in character, and then take questions as scholars, even going smoothly back and forth between character and scholar as needed without confusing our audience—we obviously can do anything *and* do it gracefully. But sometimes what looks like the most difficult art is actually easier than what looks simple.

The most difficult request for some introverts to fill is to schmooze (make small talk) in character. First of all, there is the matter of pride—where is the art? It is too close to impersonation. Second, you have not had the opportunity to wow them first with your monologue, the thing over which you have the most control.

Ann was in her teens and was very active in her church (then Congregational). She has no conscious memory of helping with summer Bible school, but she must have done so because what she does remember is the advice that the youth pastor gave her about working with children: before you respond to a request from a child by saying "no," think first, "why not?" He was encouraging her to deny a request only if there was a really good reason that an action should not be taken. Ann has come to apply that philosophy to her historical performance work: if someone is willing to pay her fee to do something that she has not done before and that lets her apply in a new way her knowledge and skills, her ability to "be" the icon that is Amelia Earhart, or to introduce other historic figures, she will give it a try. Thus, in addition to giving somewhat traditional Chautauqua-style historical performances across the United States from two Smithsonian museums in the east to the Northern Mariana Islands (specifically Saipan, Tinian, and Rota) in the west, Ann has been paid to do the following:

- Cut a birthday cake for Amelia as Amelia, cut a birthday cake for Kansas as Amelia, and schmooze in character at a grain association vendor exhibit social (at least the first two followed actual performances).
- Open the state legislative session with an abbreviated joint house performance in the House of Representatives chamber.
- Speak as Amelia at the governor's mansion "for only three minutes" to inspire and applaud the Amelia Earhart Centennial Committee (without, of course, mentioning that she was 100 years old; it's always 1937 in Ann's Amelia-land).
- Judge an Amelia Earhart look-alike contest (twelve and under and over twelve).
- Judge an antique car contest (the Amelia Earhart Award).
- Tell stories in character on the porch of the Amelia Earhart Birthplace Museum as visitors arrive.
- Be featured on the Foods page of the *Kansas City Star*.
- Plan and implement a two-day Girl Scout Senior Event around Amelia Earhart (actually, Ann volunteered her services; she was not paid for this one).
- Recruit library summer reading club members at an airport open house and fly-in.
- Be interviewed as Amelia Earhart on radio and television to promote a performance or other event.
- Schmooze in character at an art gallery to open an exhibit of jet photographs.
- Substitute for the last living Amelia Earhart colleague when *she* could not travel to Atchison.
- Open a mall (we tried to outprice their budget with four nineteenth-century performers but failed, so the money *was good*; we did sidewalk historical performances, but now know we should have switched to atmospherics and/or living history).
- Opened the new (second) Amelia Earhart bridge as Amelia speaking metaphorically about bridges because the first Atchison bridge named after her was not built until after she disappeared (while avoiding the governor, who had killed the Arts Commission—his approval record in 2016 was 29 percent, making him officially the least liked governor in the nation).
- Be a station for Kansas Day celebrations in schools and libraries.
- Be a station at a fly-in.

- School district Kansas Day live-streamed program.
- Write a first-person script for a museum to give to a young actor.
- Be interviewed by the Kansas City, Missouri, library director as Amelia, seated, in front of a live audience for an hour-plus-long question-and-answer session while being recorded for a series for public television—without launching into any stories.
- Tell stories as Amelia to a busload of tour operators traveling about thirty miles while occasionally looking back over her shoulder to determine how many more stories she could tell before the bus arrived: "The best part of the tour," several said.
- Reenact in a cockpit Amelia's last-known radio transmission for a film consultant.
- Film a selfie, quick-and-dirty "emergency" ad for Amelia's hometown (whoops, another freebie!).

Is it art? Most of it not, but it does pay the bills. We used to say we never turn down a gig, but that has changed. We do learn. But you don't know until you try. Sophistication comes with experience. As Rachel Carson said about untested pesticides, just because you *can* do something doesn't mean you *should*. Experience taught us, for example, that just because we *can* do 4-H fairs does not mean we *should*. We have learned to communicate what it is that we do best but also how we can adjust that best to create a (positively) memorable experience for a group of people and continue to make our living doing what we love to do. We also know how to refer gigs to others. Ride into History is theater. Wild Women of the West is pageantry. For most fair arenas and for parades, you want them, not us.

Joyce is known for her signature performance as Calamity Jane, but she is also her own icon, as her recent induction into the Kansas Cowboy Hall of Fame testifies. In 2016, Joyce was among the four "cowgirls" who broke the glass ceiling in the "Year of the Cowgirl" at Dodge City's Kansas Cowboy Hall of Fame. In future years, any person can be nominated for one of four categories of "cowboy." Joyce was the 2016 Cowboy Historian, and our friend Jane Koger was the Cattle"man"/Rancher. Both thought that the struggles with gendered language were a hoot. Joyce's academic credentials and her experience as a university professor who has also worked with exceptional children have influenced her historical performance experience, which she has stretched to include the following:

- Helping preschool children explore Calamity Jane's saddle, bridle, spurs, and boots
- Riding horseback in parades, in character
- Riding through city streets in a horse-drawn white coach lined in red velvet, followed closely by a herd of longhorn cattle
- Consulting on historical performance for the Pew Center for Arts and Humanities and the Pennsylvania Humanities Council, Philadelphia (live-cast across Pennsylvania)
- Planning an interpretive plan for the Laura Ingalls Wilder Home and Farm as part of a consulting team
- Consulting on costumed interpretation for the Wyoming Territorial Prison, Laramie
- Rewriting her Kansas settler script to fit Wyoming settlement and statehood
- Opening for the Dixie Chicks for the inauguration activities of the National Cowgirl Hall of Fame back when it was in Hereford, Texas, and we listened to the group on audiocassettes
- Teaching children of all ages to rope from a saddle
- Involving audience members in building a travois
- Giving hands-on demonstrations of trade goods after performances of Grower, an earth lodge woman in 1803
- Following each of the horse-enhanced twenty-two school performances with horse hugs and biology lessons (Why is manure green? Why do Pepper and Spirit urinate differently? Why are their hooves different colors?)

And then there are the honors—not only the formal honors but also occasional spontaneous ones, sometimes when a situation seems especially grim. For example, an event organizer told Joyce when she arrived at the venue early for a promised supper that in order to be fed, she was to change clothes and come back dressed as Calamity Jane and hang out with the Wild West impersonators. A cowgirl poet ran up against a similar problem: she was told that she was not dressed like a cowgirl poet. He expected both of the women to be in skirts. Poet Theone Woker's response was to write a poem ("Dress Is Optional"), dedicate it to Joyce, and read it at the event.

Together, we have expanded not only gender roles but also "historical performance" to include the following:

- A local Studio 2B Latina Girl Scout oral history project
- A workshop on youth programming for a Chautauqua troupe
- Short historical performance workshops for historic site consortia
- Consulting on historic site programming
- Consulting on incorporating first-person narratives into a heritage curriculum
- Conducting historical performance workshops for adults
- Coaching adult historical performers
- Participating in school residencies, including one performance by us and culminating with students' performances
- Conducting summer local history camps, culminating in youth performances
- Conducting weeklong Night at the Museum events
- A two-act play with two direct-address, first-person narratives, one on each of two stages with the audience switching stages between acts

Few of the above activities are in the list of costumed historical interpretation forms. They do, however, keep us challenged and employed. Whether the idea comes from a presenting organization or is an idea of our own for which we must either find a presenting organization or become one, we have learned to stretch our boundaries. We ask ourselves what the benefits might be *before* we say "no," and because we have ridden that mustang, we know we can handle those many other possibilities for applying historical performance.

NOTES

1. Joyce Thierer, *Telling History: A Manual for Performers and Presenters of First-Person Narratives* (Lanham, MD: AltaMira Press, 2010), 7.

2. Kansas Alliance of Professional Historical Performers, "Alive with History," http://www.historicperformance.com (accessed December 27, 2016).

3. Ibid.

4. This stereotype was told to us as fact by someone responsible for programming at an Indianapolis organization. It is in our notes, but we do not want to embarrass the individual who obviously had neither seen our credentials nor seen us act—us and many, many others. The point is that if one person thinks this, others do, especially those influenced by this person.

5. Sally J. Markowitz, "The Distinction between Art and Craft," *Journal of Aesthetic Education* 28, no. 1 (1994): 67–68), http://www.jstor.org/stable/3333159.

6. Lynn C. Miller, Jacqueline Taylor, and M. Heather Carver, eds., *Voices Made Flesh: Performing Women's Autobiography* (Madison: University of Wisconsin Press, 2003), 4.

7. As of this writing, there is once again a Kansas roster, and we are still (again?) on it. The grant application process has become more complex under the more limited funds of the Department of Commerce Kansas Creative Arts Industries Commission, but hope has returned.

8. Margaret Weisbrod Morris, "Catching STEAM," December 7, 2016, http://blog.americansforthearts.org/2016/12/07/catching-steam?utm_source=MagnetMail&utm_medium=email&utm_term=ridehist@satelephone.com&utm_content=creativity%5Fconnection%5F12%5F19%5F16&utm_campaign=Creativity%20Connection%3A%20December%2019.

9. American Film Institute, "High Heels: Ginger Rogers Centennial Retrospective Series," http://www.afi.com/silver/new/nowplaying/2011/v8i1/rogers.aspx (accessed December 27, 2016).

10. Official Ginger Rogers website, http://www.gingerrogers.com/about/quotes.html (accessed December 27, 2016).

7

Dreams and Plans

Thus far, we have discussed how to put historical performance into practice: how to overcome our human foibles to ask the best questions of available research material and how to make the answers interesting to various audiences. In this chapter, we look at the possibilities for the future of historical performance—the future of the past as it were. How can we not only make better performances but also strengthen performances with a better pool of performers who have increased opportunities to perform to a greater diversity of audiences? That we are asking these questions illustrates our belief in the power, love, and responsibility we claimed in the preface: if we who have the power to move people with history's stories do not accept the responsibility to perpetuate excellent historical performance, who will?

How can historical performance make the world a better place? By encouraging people to understand the decisions of historic figures and, hence, those each of us makes. Director of the Cambridge Historical Society Marieke Van Damme says of her house museum/local historical society that was recently programmatically rejuvenated, "Our goal is to talk about contemporary issues affecting the city today and offer the historical perspective. We don't think that history equals nostalgia. It's about how history is still affecting our lives today, and that's how we hope to educate people." Each year since Van Damme became director, the historical society has focused on a single theme for their few events. The first year, it was the question "Are we home?," which included housing issues. The second year it was "What does Cambridge make?," which included the things Cambridge has manufactured as well as labor and wage history. "We [the Cambridge Historical Society] think like historians, and we think critically. We think about *the reasons people make decisions*, and we're always talking about empathy. . . . We got here because people made decisions, so let's talk about that because we are now at a point where we have to make new decisions." History for Van Damme is about past, present, *and* future. She knows that her Gen-X contemporaries are sympathetic to an approach to history that emphasizes people more than things.[1] Such an approach emphasizing change over time is ideal for American studies scholars like Charles Pace.

Future generations can benefit from learning about and experiencing the difficult decisions made by past generations. But how will they know about those decisions if the stories are not shared and if they are not told well so that people listen to the sharing of these stories. How do we make better performances? By each of us monitoring our own work and by critiquing each other—which requires a willingness to accept (or at least listen to) critique. The most important thing we bring to a performance is our preparation, especially asking the important questions. Not "What happened to Amelia Earhart?" but "Why is Earhart still remembered? What was it about the decisions she made that still speaks to people today?"

Students of humanities, including historical performers, know that our most important task is to figure out what are the most important questions and then seek the answers. In addition to the content questions we discussed in chapter 2, historical performers also have process questions: How will this interpretation work for this audience? How can I make even better interpretations? And we share our discoveries with each other.

Probably the best way to work toward better performances is to improve the work of those who perform. Ride into History has been giving workshops for adults for more than fifteen years for those who want to try historical performance. Some people want to learn to honor an ancestor by sharing their story with friends and family. Others identify with one particular era or lifestyle, such as French fur trading and black powder shooting.

One thing we can do to bring the field along is to look not only for people who want to do a historical performance but also for those who want to *become* historical performers. For the latter, it is about identity. These are the people who want to run away and join our circus. They have no particular historic figure in mind; they just want to do what we do, which delights us. A historical performer is one who researches, writes, and performs historical performances *and* who commits to ethical relationships with audiences and with presenting organizations—performances that are both accurate and entertaining, not reenactments but interpretations. We are finding fear, but we are also finding excitement and passion. Loren Pennington, Professor Emeritus of History at Emporia State University, has received a great many accolades for his fifty-plus years of academic contributions, but he says that what he wants on his gravestone is "He was Father of the Kansas Chautauqua." He is looking forward to "one more" Chautauqua performance.

Heidi Vaughn's costumed historical interpretation students at the University of Central Oklahoma are just discovering historical performance. We asked them to evaluate Joyce's book *Telling History*,[2] which they had read as one of their textbooks. One of the students hoped for a career at a living history museum at which she could give first-person narratives for "older children and people who like history." She twice expressed a lack of confidence in

PHOTO 7.1
Recent attendees at a Preserving the Past through Performance workshop. Photo by authors.

her own abilities, saying, "I do not think I have what it takes to start my own business" and "The one thought that keeps occurring to me is this all seems so overwhelming." She thought that the process would be too "scary" without "a mentor who can provide help." Solo work is daunting, but perhaps it is not so much a mentor that is needed as it is a colleague or two or three—or could this book be that mentor? Certainly, we say that if you have read one of our books or attended a workshop, feel free to follow up with a phone call (620-528-3580) or email (ridehist@satelephone.com). We will be honest if we need to schedule the call at another time. Right now, for example, to finish this book we are taking no telephone calls. In fact, Ann's sister is here for a week cooking for us and answering the phone. Email is checked only at the very end of the day when we are too brain-dead to do anything else.

Are we "looking for love in all the wrong places"?[3] We believe that those operating from a conviction that historians cannot act and that young people cannot do history are, indeed, looking in the wrong places. Experience tells us otherwise. People can learn to act—some better than others. Historians should be encouraged to seek those skills.

We must help people move beyond stereotypes. Historians *can* act, and actors *can* research and interpret history. Of course, not all historians want to act, nor do all actors want to research and write their own scripts. But universities are where we might discover the crossovers—actors who love historical research and historians who secretly want to let their passion for history play before an audience. These are people who did not know they could make a living doing either acting or history, much less be allowed to spend their lives doing (thrill of thrills) both theater and history. We think we need to "grow our own Chautauquans," finding historical performers among college students.

Right now we are working with Allison DeMeyer, who recently completed her BS in history at Emporia State University and will soon also have her BFA in theater. A masters degree in theatre history is her next academic goal. During an internship with the Museum of World Treasures in Wichita, Kansas, she researched, developed signage for, and led tours of the Creating the Crown exhibit. In addition to being a costumer, she was dramaturg for five plays at Emporia State, researching the historical context and the scriptwriter/author. She worked with the actors to help them bring to life characters who moved, behaved, and spoke appropriately for the time and their various social standings, and provided publicity color, which just might have been why all shows were sold out. She researched, wrote, and performed a local nineteenth-century first-person narrative for a Preserving the Past through Performance class taught by Joyce, and she has consulted for us on the prospects of diversifying Chautauqua audiences.

Also coming right along is an athlete who is a social science education major. Amanda Simon discovered Babe Didrikson Zaharias, Associated Press "Female Athlete of the Year" for six years in track, basketball, and golf. Simon has also discovered the importance of Title IX to subsequent generations of athletes and wants to tell the stories of those who excelled without equality and how change over time has led to an explosion of athletic women like her. She will pursue a master's degree in history. In 2016, Simon traveled with us to Nebraska to interview six professional Chautauquans about their work, their background, and their aspirations for their and Chautauqua's futures. Executive director of the Humanities Nebraska, Chris Sommerich described Chautauqua for Simon as a learning environment that brings a community together. She shared her findings at the Kansas Association of History conference and Emporia State's Research and Creativity Day, both in 2017,[4] and is now working on her masters degree.

We are going even further into the future. We are inviting selected young historians of the fourth through eighth grades with great energy and intellect, with whom we work in weeklong summer Humanities Nebraska Chautauqua camps to help us with future summer camps in other communities. A Red Cloud performer inspired us. She met us three summers ago. That first summer she threw herself into learning Red Cloud's story and gave a powerful performance. The next year, she appeared on the final day of camp in a neighboring town, offering to coach performances. This year, she worked with us for several days, and her spur-of-the-moment reprise of her first-person narrative as Red Cloud was perfect for the youngsters rehearsing their performances on the final day. She did not hesitate to arouse great empathy from her audience, and because she was closer to their age, it was easier for them to identify with her than with Ann's lengthier performance of Amelia Earhart earlier in the week. The Ride into History Cultural and Educational Project, Inc., a not-for-profit with which we are affiliated, is providing money for lodging and travel for young people, especially the college students.

We have a model of historical performance now that says it is done by college professors during their summers off, and it should be older people doing it because historic figures are old! Fewer and fewer scholars are doing Chautauqua. It is sad to have someone perform who is not a true scholar of that person and/or era. Too often the organization sponsoring a Chautauqua determines a theme before finding out if there are Chautauquans who are already interpreting their historic figure. As a result, we occasionally have someone "filling in," someone "willing" to "pitch in" to make it happen. Occasionally, we have the fortunate happenstance of an actor discovering her or his true passion and plunging into it wholeheartedly, but usually the last-minute recruit is holding space, taking the role for the real scholar/performer who never appears. We talk about the responsibility of wearing the mantle of authority that is lined, always, with humility, but perhaps we should add another possibility: the performer who considers herself or himself a scholar of anything and everything but wears only suspenders. She or he knows what she or he has to know to teach her or his college students but little else. This is in part because she or he is not passionate about a topic and does not plan to perform as this historic figure elsewhere. She or he is doing the performance as a favor. Instead of identifying with the historic figure, finding "the role within," as Susan Dunhaupt says, the casual Chautauquan merely "puts on a role."[5] She or he never loses herself or himself in the historic figure, never getting close to the actor's goal of "living truthfully under imaginary circumstances,"[6] but instead is always the college professor. Everyone is short-changed. Most of us have memorized the Gettysburg Address, and we enjoy the opportunity to repeat the portions we remember under our breath while someone recites it in its brief entirety. But what will hold us, what will keep us in our seats, will be President Lincoln talking about what *led* to the Gettysburg Address. Why that speech at that time? Stories, yes. Speeches, no. This examination of Lincoln's decision making is what true historical performers spend time researching. They go beyond the public speeches to the decision maker's circumstances, her or his historical context. A few years back, Joyce described in one of her college classes how President Lincoln wrote the Gettysburg Address on the train to Gettysburg, telling why he included in it what he did and, yes, why it was so brief. One of her students protested vociferously that he could not have written it because that's what speechwriters do.

While we often think about how our interpretation of a historic figure influences our audiences' experience of that person, we sometimes neglect the fact that our portrayal changes our own lives. Everyone is changed: the audience, the historic figure, and, yes, us. Carmine Gallo, in writing about inspirational speaker Tony Robbins, says, "Change your story change your life, because whatever your story is will become the shaper of your life."[7] If you tell a story about an event in your life as an account of your failure, you shape yourself as a failure. If, however, you tell the story about that event describing yourself as a learner and a survivor, even someone who can laugh at your own mistakes, that is what you will be—it is what you will be in your own eyes as well as in the eyes of everyone around you. Historical performers learn to do for themselves what they do for their historic figures—both the stories and the telling enhance their own lives. Fourth grader Courtney felt small and scared her first summer with the North Lyon County Historical Performers. She said that when she walked out to meet the flatbed wagon that had just brought her audience to her historic figure's lumberyard, she just "looked at the tires and began." The applause that followed made her feel big and brave. A schedule conflict kept her from participating the following year, but the year after that she was off and running on day one, taking such historical questions to her research on her grandfather's military service as, "Why did he go to war? What did he do? What was it like?" We are working on a better, larger, more engaged pool of historical performers. But where and for whom will they perform?

We have heard concern about age demographics. The largest audience for Chautauquas is people over sixty. And this makes sense. You are creating an experience that is just not young-child friendly. Let's face it. And the group with the most leisure time is those over sixty, especially retired people. However, what if you stirred in some activities that would be of interest to young people? What about *horses* (and other important things for those a little older, like family and courtship). In chapter 2, we listed some topics in which our audiences might be interested. We need to think about those subjects when we frame our stories and market performances. Ride into History's name came from an exhibit that Tom Van Sant and Joyce created as graduate students to entice undergraduate undecided majors into history. Joyce displayed her antique saddle collection, and they wrote "Ride into History" in white on a red barn board. When it came time to name their historical performance troupe, which did all performances on horseback in those days, that board was still around to remind Joyce what a nifty name it was. And the logo featuring a horse reinforced the link between time travelers and their means of transportation. People who thought they did not like history (all dates and names when they were in school) or theater (you have to dress up and sit still) loved the idea of watching horses under trees in a park (who doesn't like horses?).

A horse and carriage brought the professional Chautauquans to the outdoor Humanities Nebraska Chautauqua kickoff event at Peru State College in June 2017. The Chautauquans were in costume, and while they had to share audience attention with the horse, it most definitely made an impression. Ironically, this was also the first year that the Humanities Nebraska Chautauqua (World War I: The Forgotten War) was held on stages indoors instead of under a tent. There is something about vintage transportation that can bring people back in time. In Hastings, Nebraska, owners of antique cars parked them in Chautauqua Park near the Chautauqua Pavilion, creating a visual attraction that extended the appeal of the Chautauqua.

Indoors or outdoors? Heat and humidity make outdoor events a challenge. And the traditional striped Chautauqua tent that seats hundreds is expensive. So you move the annual event into the high school auditorium or theater. Seats are comfortable, temperature is controlled, and there is a lighting and sound booth and, hopefully, a tech to operate the equipment within. But what about those people who find it physically or psychologically difficult to go into a school building, especially if they are not sure they want to "do this," never having been to a Chautauqua or experienced historical performance? They are willing to put their big toe into the water, but don't ask them to go wading. For them, the outdoor venue is better. They can wear their "usual" clothes, slip into a seat at the back, and make an easy escape if they want to. (And, of course, they do not escape because they have been seduced by the stories of historical performers.)

This leads to the caveat that those who *do* leave in the middle of a performance might be doing so from necessity. They might be choosing to come in spite of other commitments that conflict. Could you possibly provide on-site child care for your event? And if it is an outdoor event, could you assure parents of young children that it will be just fine if their child plays in the grass at their feet? Or flies a kite? Or wanders in and out a bit? Wouldn't it be nice to build fond memories of attendance at historical performance? "Do you remember when we met Will Rogers and he showed us a rope trick?"

Answer: Golf carts! (and the question is . . .). While organizations worry that younger adults are not attending arts and humanities events, they might add another worry: older adults who want to attend are losing the ability to access events. Uneven ground makes it difficult, even with a walker or cane, to feel confident in walking from a sidewalk to a tent. Even getting from handicapped parking can be daunting if you have to use a walker for a long distance. A small remuda of golf carts and drivers ready to taxi audience members from curbside to tent seating or even from parking to the front door of an auditorium would be a simple fix. A report by the RAND Corporation tenders a reminder that even people who *want* to participate in arts events can be discouraged to the point of staying home when faced with "practical barriers, such as a lack of money, time, or transportation." Finding a way to make it possible for them to participate would not necessarily give you a different demographic, but it would add to the people you serve.[8]

And people need to know about your events. Reach out to them through social media as well as newspapers. Take advantage of social media—how can people's texts describing your splendid interpretation draw a larger audience if there is only one performance of each historic figure. Book smaller venues and multiple performances. Bring in three scholar/performers, have each do two performances in three days, and do it in a theater seating, say, 150 people. The energy in a full house will create an engaged, enthusiastic audience that will help sell the next performance.

Do not use a scholar/emcee. Use a local emcee who will help set the stage for time travel, introducing the historic figure as though the audience were in that other time—or whatever the historical performer wants (it might be that the playbill will describe the setting and the performer will come onto stage describing where and when they are). Let historical performers take their own questions (remember—smaller house, perhaps even a house where they can get down into the audience), repeating those questions.

If we are passionate about what we do, if we are passionate about the stories that have the power to share love, then we have the responsibility to do our best and to help others do their best. After all, "the secret of joy in work is contained in one word—excellence. To know how to do something well is to enjoy it."[9] That should be motive enough, but most of us want more than our own pleasure: we want to extend that pleasure to others.

NOTES

1. Heidi Legg, "Interviews with Visionaries Around Us: Marieke Van Damme, GenX" http://www.theeditorial.com/essay/2017/6/22/marieke-van-damme-genx (accessed July 27, 2017).

2. Joyce Thierer, *Telling History: A Manual for Performers and Presenters of First-Person Narratives* (Lanham, MD: AltaMira Press, 2010).

3. The song "Looking for Love" by Wanda Mallette, Bob Morrison, and Patti Ryan was on the *Urban Cowboy* soundtrack.

4. Amanda Simon, "The Future of the Past: What the History of Chautauqua Can Suggest about Its Future to Public History Practitioners, Academics, and Students," Kansas Association of Historians Conference, Overland Park, Kansas, 2017.

5. Susan Dunhaupt, conversation with the authors.

6. Sanford Meisner, quoted on the Sanford Meisner Center website, 2015, http://www.themeisnercenter.com/history.html.

7. Carmine Gallo, *The Storyteller's Secret: From TED Speakers to Business Legends, Why Some Ideas Catch On and Others Don't* (New York: St. Martin's Press, 2016), 36.

8. Bob Harlow, "Determining What Kinds of Barriers to Audience Engagement Need to Be Removed," from Kevin P. McCarthy and Kimberly Jinnett, *A New Framework for Building Participation in the Arts* (Santa Monica, CA: RAND Corporation), in the American Alliance of Museums weekly email newsletter, January 20, 2015.

9. Pearl Buck, *The Joy of Children* (New York: John Day, 1964), in "The Quotations Page," http://www.quotationspage.com/quote/1780.html (accessed July 28, 2017).

Appendix A

Historical Performance Camp Preparation Timetable

When	Activity	Who
	Create your committee	
	Determine your theme	
	Identify mission, structure, and goals—Why are you doing this and how? How will you know if you are successful?	
	Identify main sponsors—organizations like the library and/or museum that are already known by parents as providing safe learning environments for their children	
	Identify site for the camp and for the performance	
	Determine dates and write out schedule	
	Design and begin to implement publicity campaign	
	Design and print registration form, flyers, special invitations	
	Keep a list of everyone who has made a significant contribution of time or money (for the printed program)	
	Recruit young people and recruiters	
	Recruit elders—colleagues during the camp and who know local history	
	Recruit historic figure or artifact list makers	
	Identify local history sources, especially archives and newspaper indexes	
	Arrange for photocopying of sources	
	Recruit providers of snacks	
	Recruit provider of performance-evening pizza	
	Recruit costumers and hairstylist (optional)	
	Arrange for sound system if needed (two wireless lapel microphones) and technician to be there during much of rehearsal as well as the performance	
	Conduct background checks on those who might be alone with a child	
	Purchase one-inch pocket binders (we get them for $2 each in bulk at our big-box office supply store)	
	Determine which tool kit pages to use and identify	
	Identify sources of clothing for "the look" of each historic figure	
	Give yourself a day off	
	Welcome registrants; days 1 to 5 of the camp (see schedule and activities lists)	
	Recruit audience (hand out special invitations)	
	Find missing costume pieces	
	Take photographs and prepare a program	
	Set up performance space	
	The performances, including question-and-answer sessions and refreshments	
	Evaluate, celebrate, and start preparations for next year	
	Launder and return costumes	

Appendix B

Daily Responsibilities of Local Arrangements Chair during Historical Performance Camp

Day One

- By noon, have location open and well marked
- Provide three feet of table space and one chair for every young historian and elder
- Provide 6-foot registration/name tag table near entrance
- Provide 6-foot table near outlet in back or side of room for office supplies
- Provide two chairs and podium in front of room
- Greet young historians and elders as they come in
- Make sure each young person has provided a registration form
- At 1:15 attempt to contact registrants who have not appeared
- Participate in historic character selection, "selling" historic figures
- Participate in acting exercises
- Document activities with digital camera/video
- Set out snacks at about 2:00 (graham crackers, apples, peanut butter, popcorn, water)
- 4:00-ish: put away snacks after a "last call"
- 5:00: stay with youngsters until departure arrangements are accomplished; special invites to go

Tuesday through Thursday

- Have location open by 12:45
- Greet young historians and elders as they come in
- At 1:15 attempt to contact registrants who have not appeared
- Document activities with digital camera/video
- Help young historians find resources they need to be successful, take them to those resources as needed, or find someone else to do so
- Set snacks out at about 2:00
- Wednesday and Thursday: listen to stories, one-on-one
- 4:00-ish: put away snacks after a "last call"
- Find sources for costume needs
- 5:00: make sure youngsters are picked up by guardians or whatever the arrangements are

Thursday

- Take photos for program and proof the program, except for photos
- 5:00: remind young Chautauquans that tomorrow you will meet at the performance site at 1:00

Friday

- Post a reminder by 12:30 at the usual site that you are at the performance site (or, better yet, post a volunteer with a vehicle there until 1:15 in case anyone shows)
- Make sure there is plenty of water for everyone (trash can for cups and/or recycling)
- Have ice and cloths if it is hot and/or very humid—a little on the back of the neck works wonders
- If sound is not there, track down technician
- Set out snacks early—at 1:30
- Listen to youngsters as they practice individually
- 3:45: get/send for pizza and more water (and caffeine as needed by elders)
- 4:00: eat pizza

- 4:15–6:00: greet visitors; tell them that they are welcome, but this IS ONLY THE DRESS REHEARSAL
- Distribute programs
- Who will welcome the audience and introduce the program?
- Listen and applaud! Help corral costumes and make sure historians leave *with* their tool kits

Appendix C

Sample Flyer

Real History! *Real Fun.* RIDE INTO HISTORY

YOUTH CHAUTAUQUA CAMP

Chautauquan n: a person taking on the persona of someone from the past to tell their story and stories of their place and time

FREE!!

[Date]
[Location]
4th-8th graders
Sponsor
[contact:]

Become a historian/
researcher/scriptwriter/actor
while having fun working as a
team with other
"Young Chautauquans"!

WANTED:
History detectives, actors, storytellers,
and playwrights!
No experience necessary; we'll share ours!
Ride into History's Ann Birney and Joyce
Thierer (Amelia Earhart and Calamity Jane)
have together been scholar/performers for over
30 years.

Kansas-Nebraska
Chautauqua
*Bright Dreams, Hard Times:
America in the Thirties*

Appendix D

Sample Application and Registration Form

Historical Performance Camp

Name: _____ Date of Birth: _____

School Attending: _____

Circle Current Grade in School: 4th, 5th, 6th, 7th, 8th

Parent/Guardian/s Name/s: _____

Address: _____

Home phone #: (___) ___-____ Cell phone #: (___) ___-____

Parent's work #: (___) ___-____ E-mail address: _____

Emergency Contact Name: _____ Phone #: (___) ___-____

Physician: _____ Phone #: (___) ___-____

Food and medical allergies and/or other medical information of which camp staff should be aware:

_____

Participants are to be picked up from camp at 5 p.m. daily except later the last day. Please indicate if student will be picked up by anyone other than the person/s listed above or if she or he may be allowed to walk or ride home:

_____

Please initial by the following requirements:

_____ My child is available **1:00–5:00 Mon.–Thurs.** [dates] *and* **1:00–7:30 Friday [date]**.

_____ I give permission for staff to transport my child to research sources, such as to interview an elder in the presence of one of the staff members or to visit the Santa Fe Trail site on Highway 99.

_____ I give permission for my child's photograph to be used by sponsors in media releases, websites, promotional videos, and publications.

_____   _____

Parent or Guardian Signature   Date

Make a copy of this form for your own records and give or mail it to [local name and address]

The first 20 young people to apply will be chosen. Applicants will be notified immediately as to their selection status.

Young people coming out of grades 4 through 8 will investigate, create, and perform as a local historic figure. Campers will meet at [location] Monday through Thursday [date] and perform on Friday [date]. Camp leaders are [ ]

NOTE: THIS CAMP IS FREE and is brought to our community by [ ] and [ ] with support from [ ], [ ], and some really fine volunteers. If you would like to help out, contact [ ].

Appendix E

Sample Schedule

Historical Performance Camp

Monday (1:00–5:00 each day, additional coaching as desired)

- Introductions, including resource people
- From now on we are . . . H/R/S/A
- What is a first-person narrative?
- Hat scenario
- Ann as Amelia Earhart
- Joyce leads pre- and postdiscussion
- Mission: *Local* history
- Choosing a character
- Historians' tool kits
- Page by page through the tool kit
- One-day first-person narrative
- Research/TWO RESPONSIBILITIES/Definition of HISTORY

Ann & Joyce cells:

620-344-0314; 620-344-0896

Staying at _____

HISTORY is

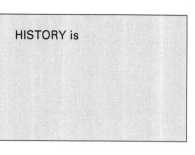

Tuesday

My TWO RESPONSIBILITIES:

1)

2)

- Cacophony
- More research (finding sources)
- Historical clothing
- Acting exercise
- Decisions, conflicts—look for them as you research
- Audience (This is not about you; it's about the audience!)
- What is a good story?

Wednesday

- Telling the stories and tying them together
- Acting and focusing
- [in the evening lay out and print a draft of the program]

Thursday

- Photo day! And proof the program—make sure your name is right
- Acting
- Answering questions in the first person
- Moving in and out of character
- What more can you do with your historic performance?
- Rehearsal ————————————————→
- [in the evening &/or next morning print the programs]

Friday

- 1:00 Rehearse on-site
- 4:00 Eat, dress in costume
- 4:30 Dress rehearsal
- 6:00 What we've all been working toward: THE PERFORMANCES!!
- 7:30 Celebrate!!! (with dignity, of *course*). Change clothes

Rehearsal:

1. Backstage: Do relaxing exercise; think about focus; get into character
2. Enter in character
3. Tell one story in character
4. Morph into scholar (change your appearance, give your name)
5. Tell why you chose your character—what you admire about that character
6. Tell why you chose that one story to tell
7. Become character again
8. Exit

Sample Schedule

Night at Your Museum Camp!

Monday 1:00–5:00

- Introductions
- Our mission: make artifacts come alive, learn to do museum research, learn and tell the stories behind the artifacts, encourage the public to wonder about the stories behind all artifacts
- Historian/researcher/scriptwriter/actor
- First-person interpretation—a play with the audience onstage with you
- Hat scenario
- Historians' tool kits
- Two responsibilities
- Tour the museum, including places the public just does not get to go and including a surprise
- Choose an artifact
- Begin to research your artifact

HISTORY is

Tuesday 1:00–5:00

- Historian/researcher/scriptwriter/actor
- Page by page through the tool kit
- Research historical context and more about your artifact
- Tell us something about your artifact
- Who should interpret your artifact? (interpretation)
- Cacophony (first person)
- Build the "house": take flyers, encourage audience

Wednesday 1:00–5:00

- Historian/researcher/scriptwriter/actor
- What makes a good story
- Audience (it's not about you; it's about the audience!)
- Write script
- More research
- Costumes
- Practice script in dyads

I have two responsibilities:

1)

2)

Thursday 1:00–5:00

- Historian/researcher/scriptwriter/actor
- Rehearse in order
- Revise scripts
- Rehearse individually in place
- Dress rehearsal
- Critique, discuss changes for public tours
- Revise
- Rehearse individually

Friday 1:00–8:00

- Partial costume
- Rehearse individually in place
- Full costume/dress rehearsal
- Rehearse in order
- 3:00 public performances begin; tours also at 3:30, 5:30, 6:00, 6:30 (45 minutes each—scheduling depends on layout of museum and number of young docents; they will have supper following the 3:30 tour)
- Tours end at 7:15; discuss process with audience, answer questions, and have refreshments

Appendix G

Sample Historic Figures List

Name	Significance	Other	Resources
Gertie Troyer (Roupp)	Assistant cashier April 17, 1930, when Hesston bank was robbed of $688; 4 months later, she married Paul E. Roupp	If related to Milford and Willard Roupp, or even if not, she could interpret them, too, or vice versa	Hesston history p. 78 Obituary [printed from *Gospel Herald* online] Family?
Ray Hackenberg	Grew up in Hesston so would have been youngster during 1930s; Naval Reserve in WWII served in Pacific on antisubmarine and convoy duty; Hesston superintendent of utilities, retired 1987	Includes a short essay on "the performance of military duty." Was there conflict in the community about fighting? Was he of Mennonite heritage?	*Memories of War Years*
Esther Weston Sadowski	Grew up in Newton, enlisted in Coast Guard; back to Newton, married, 5 children, eventually to Washington state	Great detail, including that she was earning $37 working six days (48 hrs) at Woolworths (Hesston faculty making that a *month* ten years earlier!); SPARS director was Dorothy Stratton, who was Purdue dean when Amelia Earhart was there counseling	*Memories of War Years* Obituary Thelma Weston? (sister, Newton at time of Esther's death)
Lloyd Nickl	In 1929, petroleum company he worked for closed, so moved to Hesston and bought gas station, tried to make profit by selling soft drinks, then was first to sell beer in Hesston; also tried adding a station	Also story of Bill Hoffman's truck catching fire at station could be told by daughter, Jean Ford; good example contradictions between/within a source: p. 78 says 1946 sold station to Jackson, p. 200 says 1936	Hesston history City directories, census
John Deschner	Poultry breeding; 1936 World Champion broadbreasted turkey tom; insurance agent First wife died after 2 yrs. Loved baseball, hunting, fishing 2 sons d. 1955	Could interpret his second wife Gladys, a nurse	Hesston history bios. p. 153; Son Mervin's family? On the same page in the book Hesston history bios. census
Mabel Kauffman	Dairy farm one mile south 1912–1936 when husband, James, died; took in roomers and laundry	Did she have children at home when her husband died? Could interpret dairying, then talk about decision to move to town	

Appendix H

Special Invitation

Appendix I

Office Tools and Supplies for Historical Performance Camp

- ☐ Binders for youth and elders
- ☐ Historian's tool kit pages
- ☐ Schedules (one each for young historians, parents, elders)—we print on canary
- ☐ "Code of Conduct"—we print it on gold
- ☐ Color printer, extra cartridges, and 24-pound bright white paper for programs
- ☐ Special invitation paper (bright color)
- ☐ Scratch paper and/or lined notebook paper
- ☐ Computer
- ☐ Files on thumb drive
- ☐ Camera, memory card, batteries, connector cord
- ☐ Blue workshop box with office supplies including pencil sharpener
- ☐ Name tags (we prefer the ones with strings that can be used every day—change from first name only to historic figure's name)
- ☐ Sharpie markers for name tags and tool kit covers
- ☐ Three-hole punch
- ☐ Scissors
- ☐ Tape
- ☐ Glue stick
- ☐ Measuring tape

- ☐ Magnifying glass
- ☐ Pencil sharpener
- ☐ Tissues
- ☐ Hand sanitizer
- ☐ Sewing kit
- ☐ Costume for your sample performance
- ☐ Pencils—at least four for each participant
- ☐ Flip chart(s), easel(s), and markers (or, if whiteboard, erasable markers or, if blackboard, chalk)
- ☐ Basic first-aid kit
- ☐ Clipboard or special folder or binder to keep your own notes
- ☐ Hat scenarios and a box of hats and handkerchiefs and vests

Appendix J

Hat Scenario Exercise

Estimated time: 25 minutes

Goal: students will successfully complete in an abbreviated form all the steps of being a historian/researcher/scriptwriter/actor.

Outcome: Each student will have thought about an historical issue, asked questions about the context, created a script, and performed as a historical persona. This success will empower them for the longer assignment.

Materials:

each group (see step 4) will need a kit, which includes:

- a slip of paper for each student, each of which has one role written on it (a copy of the roles is attached)
- a hat appropriate for the scenario's era
- a large dish towel, bandana, or piece of cloth
- a vest
- a copy of the scenario
- a copy of this page

Steps:

1) Before the event, decide whether to use the following or another scenario; print and cut apart the roles.
2) Give this sheet and a kit (see "Materials" above) to each teacher/group leader.
3) Greet the students as historian/researcher/scriptwriter/actors.
4) Introduce one of Ride into History's scenarios or another scenario to the group as a whole, saying something like:

> You have already traveled back in time once today (if they saw a performance earlier). Now we are going to travel again. But this time, you get to do what (Joyce or Ann or . . .) did—you get to become someone historical and make a presentation. There are some differences, however. For one thing, you won't have very much time to prepare—just a few minutes. And, you will perform for a very small group, only about [six] of your fellow historian/researcher/scriptwriter/actors. Here's the first of what you need to know to carry out your assignment. [Modify if you will do a scenario other than "Moving West."] Everyone is going to pretend to go back in time to the 1870s, just after the Civil War. We are all living in a small town in Missouri. Each of you is going to draw from a hat a character you are going to portray. Whoever you draw, that is who you are going to be, just for these 15 or 20 minutes. You may draw a man even though you a are a girl, or your character may be from Germany when your own ancestors are from Mexico. This is part of the challenge—to get into the head of someone from another time and other circumstances and think about what they might have thought. Here is the scenario, the story into which you will step:
>
> Some of your neighbors are talking about packing up and moving to Kansas, to the former Indian Territory. They want you to go with them. They are convinced that they will have a better life in Kansas. What do you think? Do you want to go? Should you go? Do you think you would have a better life in Kansas? Why or why not? You will have five minutes to ask the group leader questions to help you make up an answer to those questions. You will talk to the audience as though they are your neighbors, who are trying to convince you to go with them.

5) To prepare them to be respectful audiences for each other, ask what they as performers want from an audience: attention, respect, applause.

6) Divide the class into as many groups as there are teachers (usually four) and go to separate rooms (preferably) or separate corners of an auditorium or gym.

7) Once the groups are in the breakout rooms or areas and the young historians have drawn roles from the hat, leaders should stress that there is no wrong answer for any role. The important thing is for the characters to tell why they believe as they do. If a student feels uncomfortable portraying someone who they feel is very different than they are, remind them that a scriptwriter, like a novelist or a historian, has to be able to imagine being every one of his or her characters (including a pig or a spider—E. B. White).

8) Spoon-feed as necessary. This is not a test over knowledge of the era but an opportunity to experience success. Feel free to help the young historians understand historical context and individual motivations.

9) Have each student get up, choose an article of costume if they want one, present, receive applause, and sit down.

10) Afterward as time permits: Ask them what the most difficult thing was for them (talking about something when they really did not know much about it, getting in front and performing). Tell them how well they did and remind them how much easier it will be when they can choose their character and have more time to research and write their script.

"Moving West" Scenario

It is in the 1870s, after the Civil War. You live in a small town in Missouri. Some of your neighbors are talking about packing up and moving to Kansas to the former Indian Territory. They want you to go with them. They are convinced that they will have a better life in Kansas. What do you think? Do you want to go? Should you go? Do you think you would have a better life in Kansas? Why or why not? Talk to the audience as though they are your neighbors who want you to go with them. [Cut the roles into strips.]

ESTHER BROWN, CLOTHING STORE OWNER
Tell people who you are, whether or not you want to go west and why or why not.

JED SMITH, LIVERY STABLE OWNER (he keeps other people's horses for them)
Tell people who you are, whether or not you want to go west, and why or why not.

A WOMAN WHO OWNS A BOARDING HOUSE IS A WIDOW AND HAS SEVEN CHILDREN
Tell people who you are, whether or not you want to go west, and why or why not.

AN EIGHTEEN-YEAR-OLD WOMAN SCHOOLTEACHER
Tell people who you are, whether or not you want to go west, and why or why not.

A YOUNG PREACHER WITH TWO YOUNG CHILDREN
Tell people who you are, whether or not you want to go west, and why or why not.

A FORMERLY ENSLAVED MAN WHO IS AN EXPERT CARPENTER
Tell people who you are, whether or not you want to go west, and why or why not.

A FORMERLY ENSLAVED WOMAN WHOSE SPECIALTY IS PLOWING
Tell people who you are, whether or not you want to go west, and why or why not.

A FIFTY-YEAR-OLD IMMIGRANT FROM GERMANY WHOSE FAMILY SAYS THEY DO NOT WANT TO MOVE AGAIN
Tell people who you are, whether or not you want to go west, and why or why not.

CIVIL WAR VETERAN (former soldier)
Tell people who you are, whether or not you want to go west, and why or why not.

COWHAND WHO WANTS TO BECOME A RANCH OWNER
Tell people who you are, whether or not you want to go west, and why or why not.

Appendix K

Sample Historical Performance Camp

Final Day Activities

Beginning at 1:00 AT THE PERFORMANCE SITE

- Sign each other's programs and programs for sponsors
- Establish special seating in program order
- Practice individually; also rehearse with microphone as a group
- "Round Robin," going around to each elder with your story
- Eat pizza [at about 3:30 an elder goes for the pizza unless it is being delivered]
- Wash up and bathroom
- Costumes in performance order
- Dress rehearsal as soon as costumed

Evening, about 5:45

- As audience arrives, volunteers/elders hand out programs
- Historians are in their seats, getting into character
- Elders help public/family keep their distance from the transitioning historians

6:00 Program begins

- Ann (or emcee) takes stage: welcomes, thanks, gives overview of program
- Joyce gives the first historic figure a microphone while Ann talks about the process and what will happen after the individual performances; first two historians face away from the stage, practicing first lines
- Each historic figure presents, then returns to Joyce, who will have them pause until applause dies down; Joyce touches shoulder of each when it is time to go on and moves microphone to next historic figure
- After all have presented, Joyce gives the first and last person in line each a microphone

ENTIRE TROUPE ONTO STAGE

- Wait for the applause to end (unless it goes on too long; the audience might not remember that there is more to the program and this is not the bow at the end of the play)
- Hold microphones forward a bit so all in the audience can hear the entire group
- Center person leads with count of 1-2-3 and deep breath and says at a good clip, "I am . . . !" "I have . . ."
- Wait for the applause to end, then, before audience can pick up and leave, the historic figure with the microphone on stage left, asks, "Do you have any questions for us as historic figures?"
- Point, identify, repeat question so all can hear; pass the nearest microphone for the response
- Ask, "What other questions do you have?"
- When there are no more hands up, "Are there any more questions for us as historic figures?"
- When there are no more questions, one of the individuals with the microphone says, "Seeing no more questions, we will make a transition and become the historians, [step forward two steps, taking off your head covering or jacket]; "Do you have any questions for us as historians?"
- Then, if no more questions, "Seeing no more hands, we want to thank you for being a very generous audience" [look to the center so all is timed and do the practiced bow and smile]
- Audience will applaud; exit the stage

POSTPERFORMANCE

- Greet friends and family in the audience [with dignity and composure as young historians would]
- Historians return historic figure's clothing to green room
- Historians pick up historian's tool kits and anything else left at chair
- Have sweet dreams about becoming humanities scholar/performers some day

Appendix L

Night at the Museum Evaluation

Please check all that apply to you:

1) How did you learn about the tours?

  ____ a) from a relative or friend who was participating
  ____ b) someone who had been on a tour
  ____ c) newspaper or radio
  ____ d) other _____

2) Did you learn something about how historians do research?

  ____ a) I learned how artifacts can help tell a story
  ____ b) I learned that researchers use accession records
  ____ c) I learned that researchers use books
  ____ d) I learned that researchers use oral interviews
  ____ e) I did not learn anything
  ____ f) I already knew everything about historical methods

3) Please mention briefly one thing that you learned about an artifact or event or person.

4) Would you take another such tour here or elsewhere?

  ____ a) most definitely
  ____ b) probably not

5) About when were you last in this museum?

  ____ a) never
  ____ b) ten or more years ago
  ____ c) more recently than ten years ago

6) What else should we know?

Bibliography

BOOKS AND ARTICLES

Balgooy, Max van. *Interpreting African American History and Culture at Museums and Historic Sites.* Lanham, MD: Rowman & Littlefield, 2015.

Bedford, Leslie. "Storytelling: The Real Work of Museums." *Curator: The Museum Journal* 44 no. 1 (January 2001).

Bench, Raney. *Interpreting Native American History and Culture at Museums and Historic Sites.* Lanham, MD: Rowman & Littlefield, 2015.

Bhattacharjee, Yudhijit. "Why We Lie." *National Geographic* 231, no. 62 (June 2017).

Bridal, Tessa. *Effective Exhibit Interpretation and Design.* Lanham, MD: AltaMira Press, 2013.

Bryan, Charles F., Jr. *Imperfect Past: History in a New Light.* Manakin-Sabot, VA: Dementi Milestone Publishing, 2015. Quoted by Bob Beatty in "From the Editor," *History News: The Magazine of the American Association for State and Local History* 71, no. 4 (2016): 2.

Buck, Pearl. *The Joy of Children.* New York: John Day, 1964.

Croston, Glenn. *The Real Story of Risk: Adventures in a Hazardous World.* Amherst, NY: Prometheus Books, 2012.

Dudzick, Tom. *Miracle on South Division Street.* Playscripts Inc., 2013.

Earhart, Amelia. "Miss Earhart's Adventure on the Floor of the Sea." *Hearst's International-Cosmopolitan*, November 1929, 102.

Ferentinos, Susan. *Interpreting LGBT History at Museums and Historic Sites.* Lanham, MD: Rowman & Littlefield, 2015.

Freeman, Martha, ed. *Always, Rachel: The Letters of Rachel Carson and Dorothy Freeman, 1952–1964.* Boston: Beacon Press, 1995.

Galinsky, Ellen. *Mind in the Making: The Seven Essential Life Skills Every Child Needs.* New York: William Morrow Paperbacks, 2010.

Gallas, Kristin L., and James DeWolf Perry. *Interpreting Slavery at Museums and Historic Sites.* Lanham, MD: Rowman & Littlefield, 2015.

Gallo, Carmine. *The Storyteller's Secret: From TED Speakers to Business Legends, Why Some Ideas Catch on and Others Don't.* New York: St. Martin's Press, 2016.

George, Susanne K. *The Adventures of the Woman Homesteader: The Life and Letters of Elinore Pruitt Stewart.* Lincoln: University of Nebraska Press, 1992.

Kerber, Linda K., et al., eds. *Women's America: Refocusing the Past.* 8th ed. New York: Oxford University Press, 2016.

Kyvig, David E., and Myron A. Marty. *Nearby History: Exploring the Past Around You.* 3rd ed. Lanham, MD: AltaMira Press, 2010.

Lantzer, Jason D. *Interpreting the Prohibition Era at Museums and Historic Sites.* Lanham, MD: Rowman & Littlefield, 2015.

LaPage, Will. "The Ethical Interpreter." *Legacy: The Magazine of the National Association for Interpretation*, March–April 2016.

Lepore, Jill. *The Whites of Their Eyes: The Tea Party's Revolution and the Battle over American History.* Princeton, NJ: Princeton University Press, 2010.

Lewis, Michael, et al. *Handbook of Emotions.* 3rd ed. New York: Guilford Press, 2008.

MacGregor, Jeff. "The Maestro." *Smithsonian* 46, no. 8 (December 2015).

Markowitz, Sally J. "The Distinction between Art and Craft." *Journal of Aesthetic Education* 28, no. 1 (1994): 67–68.

McDonald, Tamar Jeffers. "Carrying Concealed Weapons: Gendered Makeover in Calamity Jane." *Journal of Popular Film and Television*, Winter 2007.

McKee, Robert. *Story: Substance, Structure, Style, and the Principles of Screenwriting.* New York: HarperCollins, 1997.

Miller, Lynn C., Jacqueline Taylor, and M. Heather Carver, eds. *Voices Made Flesh: Performing Women's Autobiography.* Madison: University of Wisconsin Press, 2003.

Mitchell, Theresa. *Movement from Person to Actor to Character.* Lanham, MD: Scarecrow Press, 1998.

Morrison, Toni. *Beloved.* New York: Knopf, 1987.

National Geographic Magazine. "In Search of Lake Woebegon." December 2000.

Roosevelt, Eleanor. *You Learn by Living.* Philadelphia: Westminster Press, 1960, 25. Also in Susan Daniels and Michael M. Piechowski, *Living with Intensity: Understanding the Sensitivity, Excitability, and Emotional Development of Gifted Children, Adolescents, and Adults* (Scottsdale, AZ: Great Potential Press, 2009), 24.

Rose, Julia. *Interpreting Difficult History at Museums and Historic Sites.* Lanham, MD: Rowman & Littlefield, 2016.

Shapera, Ann-Elizabeth. *Easy Street: A Guide for Players in Improvised Interactive Environmental Performance, Walkaround Entertainment, and First-Person Historical Interpretation.* Phoole Skoole Press, 2012. Available at http://www.lulu.com/spotlight/phoole.

Sikora, Doris. "What Great Teachers Do." *Techniques,* October 2013, 39–40.

Spolin, Viola. *Theater Games for the Lone Actor.* Evanston, IL: Northwestern University Press, 2001.

Stanislavski, Konstantin. *Creating a Role.* New York: Routledge, 1961.

Stanislavski, Konstantin. *An Actor's Work: A Student's Diary.* New York: Routledge, 2008.

Stewart, Elinore Pruitt. *Letters of a Woman Homesteader.* Boston: Houghton Mifflin, 1913.

Thierer, Joyce. *Telling History: A Manual for Performers and Presenters of First-Person Narratives.* Lanham, MD: AltaMira Press, 2010.

Ware, Susan. *American Women's History: A Very Short Introduction.* New York: Oxford University Press, 2015.

White, William Allen. *Autobiography of William Allen White.* New York: Macmillan, 1946.

WEBSITES

American Film Institute. "High Heels: Ginger Rogers Centennial Retrospective series." http://www.afi.com/silver/new/nowplaying/2011/v8i1/rogers.aspx. Accessed December 27, 2016.

"'Atomic Blonde' Director Brings Stuntman Skills to His 'Punk Rock Spy Thriller.'" *NPR Weekend Edition,* July 30, 2017. http://www.npr.org/programs/weekend-ed ition-sunday/2017/07/30/540359324/weekend-edition-sunday-for-july-30-2017.

Becker, Carl L. "Everyman His Own Historian." American Historical Association Review Presidential Address. *American Historical Review* 37, no. 2 (January 1932): 221–36. https://www.historians.org/about-aha-and-membership/aha-history-and -archives/presidential-addresses/carl-l-becker. Accessed July 31, 2017.

Bellis, Mary. "History of Kleenex Tissue." https://www.thoughtco.com/history-of -kleenex-tissue-1992033. Accessed July 18, 2017.

Bullough, J. D., et al. "Effects of Flicker Characteristics from Solid-State Lighting on Detection, Acceptability and Comfort." *Lighting Research and Technology* 43, no. 3 (September 2011): 337–48. *Academic Search Premier,* EBSCO*host.* Accessed August 18, 2015.

Crane, Susan A. "Historical Subjectivity: A Review Essay." *Journal of Modern History* 78, no. 2 (June 2006). https://doi.org/10.1086/505803. Accessed July 23, 2017.

Croston, Glenn. "The Thing We Fear More Than Death: Why Predators Are Responsible for Our Fear of Public Speaking," November 29, 2012. https://www .psychologytoday.com/blog/the-real-story-risk/201211/the-thing-we-fear-more -death.

"Florence Pugh on Her Role in 'Lady Macbeth.'" *Weekend Edition,* July 16, 2017. http://www.npr.org/2017/07/16/537509464/florence-pugh-on-her-role-in-lady -macbeth.

Graff, Everett D. *Hard Knocks: A Life Story of the Vanishing West.* 1915. Accessed through the Newberry Library's American West database, July 30, 2017. http:// www.americanwest.amdigital.co.uk.emporiastate.idm.oclc.org/Documents/ Images/Graff_4789/97#Chapters.

Hajek, Danny. "Hollywood Jet Gives Fearful Fliers the Courage to Soar." *NPR Morning Edition*, May 17, 2016. http://www.npr.org/2016/05/17/478234178/hollywood-jet-gives-fearful-fliers-the-courage-to-soar.

Hearn, M. "Water and Brain Function: How to Improve Memory and Focus." http://www.waterbenefitshealth.com/water-andbrain.html.

"History Relevance Campaign." https://www.historyrelevance.com/value-history-statement. Accessed July 31, 2017.

Honig, Tom. "KLONG—A Word for Modern Life." *Santa Cruz Observer*, May 16, 2011. http://www.tomhonig.com/santa_cruz_observed/2011/05/klong.html. Accessed September 12, 2017.

Jenkins, Rob. "The 4 Properties of Powerful Teachers." *Chronicle of Higher Education*, March 16, 2015. http://chronicle.com/article/The-4-Properties-of-Powerful/228483.

Kansas Alliance of Professional Historical Performers. http://www.historicperformance.com.

King, Martin Luther, Jr. "Where Do We Go from Here?" Speech delivered at the 11th Annual Southern Christian Leadership Conference Convention, Atlanta, GA, August 16, 1967. http://kinginstitute.stanford.edu/king-papers/documents/where-do-we-go-here-delivered-11th-annual-sclc-convention.

Legg, Heidi. "Interviews with Visionaries around Us: Marieke Van Damme, GenX." http://www.theeditorial.com/essay/2017/6/22/marieke-van-damme-genx. Accessed July 27, 2017.

Manly, Carla Marie. *The Fear Handbook*. http://www.drcarlamanly.com/fearHandbook.php. Accessed July 25, 2017.

"Mantle of the Expert.com: A Dramatic-Inquiry Approach to Teaching and Learning." http://www.mantleoftheexpert.com/about-moe/introduction/what-is-moe. Accessed August 17, 2015.

"MBTI Basics." http://www.myersbriggs.org.

Morris, Margaret Weisbrod. "Catching STEAM." *Americans for the Arts* blog, December 7, 2016. http://blog.americansforthearts.org/2016/12/07/catching-steam?utm_source=MagnetMail&utm_medium=email&utm_term=ridehist@satelephone.com&utm_content=creativity%5Fconnection%5F12%5F19%5F16&utm_campaign=Creativity%20Connection%3A%20December%2019.

Nadworny, Elissa. "Through Performance, Mississippi Students Honor Long-Forgotten Locals," May 25, 2015. http://www.npr.org/sections/ed/2015/04/17/400363343/through-performance-mississippi-students-honor-long-forgotten-locals.

Official Ginger Rogers website. http://www.gingerrogers.com/about/quotes.html. Accessed December 27, 2016.

"Oxytocin Affects Bonding between Dogs and Humans." http://www.smithsonianmag.com/science-nature/dog-gazes-hijack-brains-maternal-bonding-system-180955019.

Quotes—The Official Licensing Website of Amelia Earhart. http://www.ameliaearhart.com/about/quotes.html. Accessed March 16, 2016.

"Samuel Taylor Coleridge: *Biographia Literaria* (1817)." Chapter 14. http://www.english.upenn.edu/~mgamer/Etexts/biographia.html. Accessed December 23, 2015.

Sanford Meisner Center. 2015. http://www.themeisnercenter.com/history.html.

Sisson, Natalie. "Five Reasons Why the Fear of Public Speaking Is Great for You." *ForbesWoman*, October 9, 2012. http://www.forbes.com/sites/work-in-progress/2012/10/09/five-reasons-why-the-fear-of-public-speaking-is-great-for-you/#2ede0ad1168f.

"Take Along Healthy Snacks for Summer Road Trips." Penn State College of Agricultural Sciences Extension, July 20, 2015. http://extension.psu.edu/health/news/2015/take-along-healthy-snacks-for-summer-road-trips. Accessed August 18, 2015.

Weissman, Jerry. "Another Humorous View on the Fear of Public Speaking." *Forbes*, June 17, 2014. http://www.forbes.com/sites/jerryweissman/2014/06/17/another-humorous-view-on-the-fear-of-public-speaking/#3f10eaa67729.

Zhang, Yubing. "Life Begins at the End of Your Comfort Zone." Tedxstanford. Tedx Talks June 18, 2015, https://www.youtube.com/watch?v=cmN4xOGkxGo. Accessed January 7, 2018.

OTHER MEDIA

Birney, Ann, and Joyce Thierer. "Survey of Costumed Historic Interpretation Students at University of Central Oklahoma." August 2015.

Dunhaupt, Susan. Conversation with the authors, July 29, 2016, and July 26, 2017; notes with authors.

Harlow, Bob. "Determining What Kinds of Barriers to Audience Engagement Need to Be Removed." In Kevin P. McCarthy and Kimberly Jinnett, *A New Framework for Building Participation in the Arts* (RAND Corporation), in American Alliance of Museums weekly email newsletter, January 20, 2015.

Morris, Laverne Lawton. "The Little Girl across the Street." Memoir typescript, Emporia State University Library and Archive.

Sharp, Pauline. Note to the authors, June 30, 2017.

Simon, Amanda. "The Future of the Past: What the History of Chautauqua Can Suggest about Its Future to Public History Practitioners, Academics, and Students." Kansas Association of Historians Conference, Overland Park, 2017.

Summey, Terri. Conversation with the authors, July 29, 2017; notes with authors.

———. "Emotional Intelligence as a Framework for Reference and Information Competencies." Poster session, Emporia State University Research and Creativity Day, April 27, 2017.

Index

Page references for figures are italicized

About the Authors

Ann E. Birney is the managing partner of Ride into History and executive director of Ride into History Cultural and Educational Project, Inc., which makes history accessible through the arts, and the Kansas Alliance of Professional Historical Performers. Her signature performance is as Amelia Earhart. Like Joyce Thierer, she has been on arts and humanities commission rosters as well as receiving the Kansas Arts Commission mid-career award. She has completed the Lied Center/Kennedy Center for the Performing Arts' Artists as Educators seminars. She has a doctorate in American Studies from the University of Kansas. She considers hers "the best job in the world" and also brings to life Santa Fe Trail traveler Julia Archibald Holmes, author/environmentalist Rachel Carson, and composite 1894 teacher/suffragist Elizabeth Hampstead.

Joyce M. Thierer is the founding member of Ride into History, a historical performance touring troupe. Her signature performance is Calamity Jane. She is also a professor at Emporia State University, where she teaches women's history, the history of the West, Kansas history, agricultural history, and historical performance. Her PhD is from Kansas State University. She grew up the fifth generation on a diversified Flint Hills farm that included a living history museum. She is author of *Telling History: A Manual for Performers and Presenters of First-Person Narratives*. In 2016, she was among the first women inducted into the Kansas Cowboy Hall of Fame.

Together or individually, the authors have performed from Saipan to Maine and from Texas to Minnesota, averaging four programs a week each in their busiest year. Now they spend much of their time conducting workshops and camps.